THE COMMON WRITER

THE COMMON WRITER

Life in Nineteenth-Century Grub Street

NIGEL CROSS

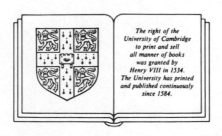

The right of the
University of Cambridge
to print and sell
all manner of books
was granted by
Henry VIII in 1534.
The University has printed
and published continuously
since 1584.

CAMBRIDGE UNIVERSITY PRESS

Cambridge

London   New York   New Rochelle

Melbourne   Sydney

Published by the Press Syndicate of the University of Cambridge
The Pitt Building, Trumpington Street, Cambridge CB2 1RP
32 East 57th Street, New York, NY 10022, USA
10 Stamford Road, Oakleigh, Melbourne 3166, Australia

First published 1985

Printed in Great Britain at
the University Press, Cambridge

Library of Congress catalogue card number: 84–29247

British Library cataloguing in publication data
Cross, Nigel
The common writer: life in nineteenth century
Grub Street.
1. Authors – Salaries, pensions, etc. – Great
Britain   2. Authors, English – 19th century
I. Title
808'.025'0941   PN165
ISBN 0 521 24564 8

CONTENTS

ACKNOWLEDGMENTS

I must first thank the Committee of the Royal Literary Fund for employing me to catalogue the Fund's archive and for generously allowing me to make full use of it for this book. I owe especial thanks to the Fund's former secretary, Victor Bonham-Carter, whose encouragement has been invaluable, and to Janet Adam Smith, former president, for her close and constructive attention to the project.

Particular thanks to Caroline Dakers and John Sutherland for reading the manuscript and offering helpful advice, also to Andrew Brown who is that rare thing, an editor who understands my subject.

My thanks to Sibylla Flower for material on the Guild of Literature and Art; to Ann Palmer for giving me her extensive notes on Civil List pensions, and to Peter Evans of the Newspaper Press Fund, Air Commodore Saunders of the National Benevolent Institution, and the governors of the Charterhouse for allowing me access to their respective records.

Others who have kindly supplied me with references, clues and advice are: James Dybikowski, Simon Eliot, K.J. Fielding, Peter France, Elizabeth Gotch, N. John Hall, Julia Harding, Elizabeth James, Whitney R.D. Jones, Leanne Langley, Robin Myers, Thomas Pinney, R.L. Purdy, Charles E. Robinson, Michael Sheldon, Anthony Mackenzie Smith, Graham Storey and Robert H. Super.

For the past four years I have fitted the writing and much of the research for this book into the schedule of an itinerant journalist. As so much of *The Common Writer* pries into the finances of literary production, it would be cheating not to reveal my own accounts. To the Leverhulme Trust I am immensely grateful for the award of a Fellowship worth £2,500. To my publishers I am grateful for the promise (made in 1980) of £250 on receipt of typescript and £250 on publication; I understand that this – for an academic press – is a noble gesture.

INTRODUCTION: THE COMMON WRITER

TITLES that remain in print long after the deaths of their authors are at the top of the hierarchy of books. Not only do they influence our thought, they continue to earn money for publishers, academics and film producers. It is these extant books that we are accustomed to think of as literature. But at the time of the first edition, no one knows for sure which books will survive, and few care.

There is an illusion that these literary survivors have been carefully screened; first by the original reviewers and readers, and then by successive generations of readers and critics. This is to ignore the pressures of publishing economics and the often random business of literary criticism. Of course the best work of Dickens, Thackeray, Eliot, Tennyson, Browning and Hardy has passed the litmus test of public and academic approval. But their worst work remains in print, while the best work of their forgotten contemporaries was pulped for waste paper long ago. One or two obscure reputations flicker in reprint series, but too often reprints are subject to the same pressures that excluded such writers from the received version of English literature in the first place. Trollope's many out-of-print novels have recently been reissued but not his friend Robert Bell's powerful *Ladder of Gold*. Libraries will buy Trollope because they have heard of him, Bell is unknown. G.H. Lewes's tedious and pretentious novel *Ranthorpe* has been reprinted, presumably because Lewes was the partner of George Eliot. Robert Brough's enjoyable and informative *Marston Lynch* is forgotten.

Literary studies, which exert a decisive influence on the re-publication of dead authors, have stuck to the comforting idea of a great tradition, a world of literary giants that somehow stands apart from the mass of ordinary writers. A glance at the annual list of literary thesis titles confirms that there is scant interest in more than a handful of nineteenth-century writers. Such a narrow focus betrays a fairly thorough ignorance of the social and economic conditions of authorship and publishing. As Robert Darnton has observed, 'despite the proliferation of biographies of great writers, the basic conditions of authorship remain obscure for most periods of history'.[1]

In *The Unknown Mayhew*, E.P. Thompson complains about the lack of information about the writer and journalist Henry Mayhew – 'there is something like a conspiracy of silence about him in some of the reminiscences and biographies of his contemporaries'. Thompson detects a 'delicate evasion' which he attributes to embarrassment at Mayhew's imprisonment for debt and financial incompetence.[2] It is more likely that Mayhew suffered the fate of all minor writers who did not write autobiographies; he was not a big enough name, even in his own time, to rate an index entry.

Publishers aim to sell books, and books teeming with accounts of unknown or forgotten writers are unlikely to be profitable. The chances of a minor writer being able to place a volume of memoirs depends almost entirely on the inclusion of a substantial number of new anecdotes about more famous writers. The insignificant George Hodder, for example, was able to publish his memoirs because of his connection with Douglas Jerrold (who was just big enough), Dickens and Thackeray. The public and the publisher wanted intimate glimpses of great writers not an account of George Hodder's friendships with Mayhew's unknown brother Gus or someone called Robert Baxter Postans. This emphasis on a few famous writers consolidates their fame and reduces the rest of the literary corps to the ranks of the unknown. It leads to a simplistic view of literary culture, for without the common writer there would be no literature at all.

Writers are people mentally and physically engaged in writing for publication. They expect to be paid for their literary labour in cash or honour – preferably both. There are, of course, many part-time writers, and many writers who only write one book. On the other hand, outside the ranks of journalists, there are only a few people who can claim to be full-time writers. Most have to work in non-literary jobs where the business of earning a living can squeeze out authorship altogether.

This study focuses on those nineteenth-century book writers who attempted to sustain their literary activity over a number of years. Though many were part-time writers – doubling as clergymen, politicians, ladies-in-waiting – they would not have regarded themselves as amateurs. They can best be described as persistent writers. This emphasis on book writers excludes most writers of street literature – broadsheets and chapbooks – but includes writers of book-issued fiction, however dreadful. In practice, the writing, production and reading of books was a middle-class monopoly.

Assuming that the number of writers increases roughly in proportion to the number of titles, then book production figures suggest that the population of writers rose fifteenfold during the nineteenth century. Presumably this increase applies equally to persistent writers and to the authors of only one book. Persistent writers were more likely than others to identify themselves as 'authors' to the census takers. There were three decades from the 1860s when the census consistently listed authors, editors and journalists under the same heading: 2,443 in 1871, 3,434 in 1881 and 5,771 in 1891. This is about as accurate a set of figures as we can hope for; by 1871 there would have been far less reluctance to admit to authorship than earlier in the century.

By comparing the census figures with the number of new book titles we find that in any one year self-confessed writers outnumber new titles by about three to two.[3] So there might have been some 550 persistent writers in 1800 when there were some 370 new titles, and 9,000 writers by 1900, when there were over 6,000 new titles. Allowing for five generations of writers – most writers who completed census forms were aged between twenty-five and forty-five – it seems that there were about 20,000 persistent nineteenth-century writers. Such a figure is imaginative rather than literal, but it marks a useful reference point for placing individual writing careers in perspective.

Much of the evidence presented in this book is drawn from the archive of the Royal Literary Fund. Some 3,000 people applied to the Fund between 1790 and 1918, of whom 2,500 were awarded one or more grants. This is a much larger sample, providing much more biographical detail, than has previously been studied. Raymond Williams, when examining the social background of authors in *The Long Revolution*, discussed 163 writers from 1780 to 1930. R.D. Altick in his 'Sociology of Authorship' investigates the backgrounds of 737 nineteenth-century authors.[4] Both Williams and Altick confine their studies to élite authors listed in the Oxford and Cambridge reference books, using the *Dictionary of National Biography* (*DNB*) as their main biographical source. Altick acknowledges that 'when the audience for the printed word has a broader base, as it has had in the past century and a half, the study of the people who produced its reading matter must be similarly broadened'. His survey aims to include 'all but the very lowest stratum of hacks', but as he relied on the *Cambridge Bibliography of English Literature* (*CBEL*) which listed only 849 writers from a potential constituency of at least 20,000, he has overstated the case. There are, for example, over 400 applicants to the Royal Literary Fund with entries in the *DNB* who are not listed in the *CBEL*, and they are clearly not the 'lowest stratum of hacks'.

Though the Royal Literary Fund sample is large, it might be considered unrepresentative; focusing on failed writers in contrast to the *CBEL*'s claim to list all writers of relative success. Of the applicants to the Fund 194 are listed among the 1,200 or so writers in the new edition of the *CBEL*. In terms of the total number of applicants to the Fund this represents a more or less average proportion of élite writers. Behind the figures are the names. Peacock, Coleridge and George MacDonald, for instance, applied to the Fund as young, unestablished writers. W.H.G. Kingston, James Grant and Ouida were all popular novelists who applied towards the end of declining careers. There were few writers without private incomes who did not experience periods of financial hardship; though, as it happens, the Fund also received several applications from the erstwhile rich – Sir Samuel Egerton Brydges and Mary Russell Mitford for example, whose authorship was not responsible for their vanishing fortunes. Finally, the picture of authorship that emerges from the Fund's archive is corroborated by other manuscript sources and contemporary letters, diaries, biographies, memoirs and novels – fiction often gives the more complete and honest account of literary life.

The principal and limited aim of this book is to provide detailed information about representative authorship and the publishing climate. But as John Gross warns, 'any picture of the literary world which concentrated exclusively on minor figures would be as unnatural as one which left the minor figures completely out of account'. Dickens exercised an unrivalled influence on the workings of the Victorian literary world, and he is, if not exactly the hero, a central and crucial figure. Other writers who are given due prominence are Byron, Hunt, Coleridge, Southey, Lytton, Thackeray, Trollope, Gissing and Henry James. This emphasis on the author as novelist is a reflection of the dominance of fiction in nineteenth-century literary production. If the great women novelists receive only a passing mention, it is because, through force of circumstance, they kept aloof from a male-dominated literary society and, with the notable exception of Harriet Martineau, played hardly any part in the politics of authorship.

There is little point in discussing the work of writers solely on the grounds that no one else has done so. I have, however, thought it useful to examine the careers of unfamiliar writers in some detail, in order to extend the study of authorship beyond the famous and sometimes misleading examples. For the most part I have selected writers who were relatively well known at the time and whose work is above the run of the mill. This means, of course, that they are not quite common writers, in the sense of absolutely average, but they are common enough by the standards of orthodox literary history. Their careers demonstrate, as the careers of the exceptional Dickens and Eliot cannot, that the prerequisites for literary success are education, social status, and monied leisure.

The chapters which follow are arranged by theme and in a rough chronological order. It is possible to identify three overlapping periods which map out the changing economic conditions of authorship. The period up to 1840 was a time of rapid advances in technology, commercial confusion, and literary insecurity. The years 1840 to 1880 saw the book and newspaper trade settling down into general profitability, except for some bumpy patches in the transitional 1840s. The majority of writers were able to make ends meet as they and their middle-class publishers produced just about the right quantity of reading matter to satisfy the middle-class reader. After 1880 publishers began to look beyond the middle classes towards a mass audience, leaving their middle-class writers to sink or swim.

I have not thought it necessary to rehearse the history of literary legislation – the various copyright acts and international treaties – because they made very little difference to the lives of ordinary writers. The extension of the copyright period under the Acts of 1814 and 1842 for example, had no effect on the majority of writers because they rarely owned the copyright of their books. Publishers, however, did benefit; they were given more time in which to exhaust the copyrights they had bought from their authors. James Grant sold the copyrights of his popular historical novels to Routledge for between £100 and £250 a time. Between 1856 and 1882 Routledge sold 100,000 copies of Grant's *Romance of War*: no wonder Grant described authorship as 'a hopeless treadmill'.

Chapter 1 describes the place of the Royal Literary Fund in the literary history and literary politics of the period. Founded in 1790, the Fund was the most successful and resilient nineteenth-century authors' organisation. But its reluctance to provide leadership, and to represent authors as a professional body, led to a succession of attempts to establish a writers' union. The Fund stuck to the easier business of charity – cure rather than prevention – and evolved into an impregnable Victorian institution quite capable of withstanding a barrage of criticism from Dickens.

The records of the Fund make it clear that the calamities of authors are the natural consequence of writing for a living. Few activities other than gambling are so risky. Throughout the century, as the book trade set its sights on the mass market, more and more writers were called into existence. But as literature does not pay, a web of institutions was needed to support literary activity (Chapter 2). Without this informal welfare state for writers, the whole business of literature would have collapsed. As major writers are one in a thousand, 999 people had to find ways and means of surviving as writers to enable a Dickens or a George Eliot to emerge from their ranks.

To combat this lemming-like literary progress, writers adopted a Bohemian character which matched failure with insouciance. However, failure became less inevitable with the commercial growth of Fleet Street in mid-century (Chapter 3). Journalism provided writers with a literary income even when they were not writing books. By the 1850s there was a paying trade of letters. It was however very much the territory of the lower middle class. To succeed at writing the kind of books that would be discussed and reviewed, a university education and a private income were indispensable. For this reason working-class writers who aimed to supply middle-class culture failed miserably (Chapter 4). Few working-class writers had the time or the knowledge to write convincing middle-class novels. Most turned to poetry in a vain attempt to compete with their aristocratic idols: Byron, Shelley, Tennyson. They remained the one group of writers to attract old-fashioned patronage; but this was because they were curiosities – models of self-help – it was not a tribute to their literary merit. Those that dosed their poetry with politics or their blood with alcohol quickly lost their patrons.

Less than one in thirty writers published by the middle-class publishing firms could claim working-class credentials. Women, too, were a literary minority (Chapter 5). About one in five nineteenth-century writers were women. And as working-class writers found the economics of authorship turned them into versifiers, so women discovered that their informal educations and limited employment opportunities channelled them into writing fiction. Over 80 per cent of women writers wrote fiction for adults or children. Yet, despite male fears (and sneers), male novelists outnumbered women novelists by three to one. There is no evidence that women were paid less for their novels than men. There were, however, so few openings in journalism for women writers, or in any half-way respectable employment other than teaching, that many were dependent on pot-boiling for a living.

My final chapter examines the literary world as described by George Gissing in *New Grub Street*. By the mid-1880s the Victorian literary giants were dead or dying, and there was – among fastidious readers – a feeling of pessimism and a fear of democracy. The rolling forward of the mass market under the guidance of men like George Newnes, W.F. Tillotson and W.T. Stead, gave most writers far more commercial opportunities. But, according to Gissing and Henry James, it also led to a lamentable decline in literary standards. And although the facile writer, who could tailor copy to suit all markets, was richer than ever before, those writers who could not command a large readership were poorer than at any time since the beginning of the nineteenth century. The age of New Grub Street culminates in the applications of Joseph Conrad, James Joyce, Edward Thomas and D.H. Lawrence to the Royal Literary Fund.

I

LITERATURE AND CHARITY: THE ROYAL LITERARY FUND FROM DAVID WILLIAMS TO CHARLES DICKENS

In 1773 Benjamin Franklin, in England as the agent of the American colonies, asked to meet the author of a heterodox pamphlet which he particularly admired. The pamphlet, *Essays on Public Worship, Patriotism and Projects of Reformation*, had been published anonymously, but Colonel Dawson, the Lieutenant Governor of the Isle of Man, was able to introduce Franklin to its author – David Williams, a Dissenting minister of radical views. Franklin and Williams were so impressed with each other's abilities that they decided to form a debating club which would meet convivially 'over a neck of veal and potatoes at the Old Slaughter Coffee House'.[1] As well as Franklin, Williams and Dawson, the club included Josiah Wedgwood and his éminence grise Thomas Bentley; the painter and architect James Stuart; the philosopher-clockmaker John Whitehurst; Daniel Solander, Keeper of the Natural History Department at the British Museum; Thomas Morris, a song-writing army captain; and Thomas Day, the eccentric educationalist and writer of children's books.

The Club of Thirteen, so called because of the limit on its membership, may have been less famous than the Literary Club of Reynolds, Johnson, Burke and Goldsmith, but as an example of the abundant intellectual activity of the period, it was no less impressive. Several of its members, Whitehurst, Wedgwood, Bentley and Day, were also members of the Lunar Society – Erasmus Darwin's name for the group of progressive scientists and writers who met once a month at each other's Midlands homes to discuss pottery, steam or literature. Williams's club lasted little more than a year, breaking up when Franklin fled England to escape arrest in 1774. But at least two topics discussed at its monthly meetings led on to greater things: one was a proposal to revolutionise the church service and the other was a proposal by Williams for the founding of a literary fund.

Williams did not believe in leaving authors 'to the discretion and patronage of the government, nobility, and opulent gentry'.[2] His own experience had taught him something of the pitfalls of authorship: 'in the annual estimate of the fruits of my labour, I generally thought myself fortunate if I received half the sums due to me by verbal agreements – of promises of patronage I never took any notice'.[3] He called for the protection of literary property and the establishment of a fund to assist authors in distress, arguing that of all members of society, authors, through the influence of their writings, were among the most productive. Although the idea of a literary fund was favourably received by the club, it was decided that a new church liturgy was a more pressing necessity, and Williams, as a professional theologian, was commissioned to write it. After the decision to proceed with the liturgy, Williams had a private conversation with Franklin which made him more determined than ever to establish a fund for authors: 'as I quitted the room, he pronounced these words which have a thousand times, rung in my ears: "I see you will not give up a noble idea. I do not say you will not succeed but it must be by much anxiety and trouble, and I hope the anvil will not wear out the hammer"'.[4] It was to take Williams another sixteen years to forge his noble idea into an actual literary fund.

DAVID WILLIAMS was born at Waenwaelod, Caerphilly in 1738. His father, an eager Calvinist, ran a small mining provision store which earned just enough to send Williams to the local grammar school and then on to the Dissenting Academy at Carmarthen. Once ordained Williams went successively to Frome, Exeter and Highgate as a Dissenting minister. It appears from his autobiography that he was anything but a dedicated churchman – 'I spent nineteen parts in twenty of my time among women'.[5] He was also an ardent playgoer and it was the theatrical world that inspired one of his first literary works – an open letter to Garrick, published in 1772. An actor in Garrick's company, Henry Mossop, had been imprisoned for a small debt, and Williams blamed Garrick. He wrote accusing Garrick of avarice and vanity, comparing his talents unfavourably with Mrs Cibber, for whom he had a passionate admiration. He was also extremely critical of Garrick's controlling interest in the London press. The letter is most interesting in that it is Williams's first public statement about the arts and the plight of unfortunate artists.

In 1772 he married and established a small school at Lawrence Street, Chelsea to which he admitted boarders at the high annual fee of £100. He combined the relaxed educational philosophies of Jan Amos

9

Comenius and Rousseau with his own; his progressive ideas meeting with 'far less obstruction from the indocility on the part of children, than from the obstinacy and prejudice of their parents'.[6] On the death of his wife in 1774 he was obliged to give up the school, but as a result of the experiment he published *A Treatise on Education* (1774) and *Lectures on Education* (1789).

Meanwhile he had published his *Essays on Public Worship* in 1773 which earned him the sobriquet 'the Priest of Nature'. In 1776 there appeared the club's commissioned *Liturgy on the Universal Principles of Religion and Morality*. More than any of his other works, this seems to have established his reputation as an original and influential thinker as well as an infidel – a deist rather than a Christian. Thomas Bentley took a copy to Rousseau in Paris who said 'Tell Williams it is a consolation to my heart that he has realised one of my highest wishes, and that I am one of his most devoted disciples.'[7] And Voltaire wrote acknowledging a copy: 'It is a great comfort to me, at the age of eighty two years, to see toleration openly taught and asserted in your own country, and the God of all mankind no longer pent up in a narrow tract of land. That noble truth was worthy of your pen and your tongue. I am, with all my heart, one of your followers, and of your admirers.'[8] Others who thought highly of *Liturgy* included Rudolph 'Munchausen' Raspe and Frederick the Great, and it appears to have had some influence on the French Revolution for 'it inspired, at least in part, the worship of Reason and of the Supreme Being in 1793 and 1794, and was adopted almost in its entirety by the theophilanthropists under the Directory'.[9]

After the death of his wife and a brief spell of preaching in the Margaret Street Chapel, Westminster, where his attempts to practise his own liturgy proved unpopular, Williams seems to have made his living by coaching private pupils and by authorship. He did not confine himself to religious and educational subjects; he translated Voltaire, wrote political philosophy and historical works, and was commissioned by Robert Bowyer to complete Hume's *History of England* to rival Smollett's version. This last contract was broken by Bowyer as a result of Williams's political activities: 'he had been branded . . . a Democrat; and he was informed that his engagement respecting the History of England could not be carried into effect, in consequence . . . of an intimation having been given that the privilege of dedication to the Crown would be withdrawn if he continued the work'.[10]

His major political work, *Letters on Political Liberty* (1782), influenced several British radicals, among them Thomas Holcroft, and led to the imprisonment in the Bastille of its French translator, Jean-Pierre Brissot. In it Williams had 'strikingly represented . . . the absurdity of petitioning an offending body to reform itself'.[11] This was followed by *Lectures on Political Principles* in 1789 which was translated by John Bridel and later presented to the republican Convention. Thomas Morris, commenting on the lectures in his biographical sketch of Williams, remarked 'I admired first Montesquieu, then Rousseau, but when I had read David Williams I considered those authors as writers of Romance'.[12] His standing in France was so high that in 1792, together with Sir James Mackintosh, Thomas Paine and Joseph Priestley, he was nominated a citizen of the new republic. Unlike Paine however, he refused to allow himself to be elected a member of the Convention on the grounds that he was inexpert in French affairs.

In December 1792 he was invited to Paris by Brissot, who had become the leader of the ruling Girondist party, to help with the drafting of the new constitution. His restraining influence had little effect on the French legislators, though he impressed Madame Roland who called him a 'profound thinker'[13] and rated his abilities higher than Paine's. Williams was still in Paris when Louis XVI was executed and the Pitt administration expelled Chauvelin, the French ambassador. The Convention declared war on England, but on the same day Le Brun, the Minister for Foreign Affairs, wrote a letter to Lord Grenville, his English counterpart, suing for peace. Williams was asked by Brissot and Le Brun to deliver the letter to Grenville, together with an unwritten elaboration of the French proposals. He thus found himself in the unique position of acting as the French diplomatic representative to his own country. However, on his arrival in London, Grenville refused to see him and Williams let the whole affair drop: 'he appreciated that the British government was bent upon war. Moreover, he avoided communicating Le Brun's proposals in writing, for the contents of his letter might have reached France, and in that case would have sent the Girondist government instantly to the guillotine'.[14]

AFTER THE DISSOLUTION of the Club of Thirteen in 1774, Williams was busy with education, religion and politics; he did not pursue his plan for a Literary Fund until the mid 1780s. During that period his own experiences of authorship probably confirmed him in his self-appointed mission. His plan, for all its long gestation, was timely. It amounted to a considered response to the comparatively rapid expansion of the book trade in the last quarter of the eighteenth century. Before 1756 there were fewer than 100 new titles registered annually. By 1792 the annual total of new books had risen to over 370. During the same period the annual sale of newspaper stamps rose from 7.5 million to 17 million. The propaganda campaign of organised Dissent as well as that of the British government, contributed to this steady increase in reading matter. It was also a time of innovative publishing. John Newbery discovered a prosperous young market when he began publishing children's books in 1744. John Bell (later one of the Fund's first committee members) pioneered the publication of cheap pocket books with his British poets series launched in 1777. And in 1790 William Lane founded the Minerva Press which provided a steady stream of romantic and Gothic fiction for avid novel readers. Perhaps the most important development was the spread of the circulating library which enabled readers to borrow books as well as buy them. By the 1770s there were circulating libraries in almost every important provincial town.

With the establishment of authorship as a profession, or at least a recognised commercial activity, the fate of individual authors began to interest readers. Samuel Johnson published what was probably the first modern study of the vicissitudes of an author, his *Life of Mr Richard Savage* (1744). Richard Savage had died in debtors' prison in 1743, more as a result of profligacy than through lack of literary success. However, his life became synonymous with the extremities of authorship. Other writers, particularly Smollett in his novels, drew a vivid picture of the author as a starving Grub Street hack exploited by unscrupulous booksellers. The image of author as victim was indelibly established with the suicide of Chatterton in 1770.

It was against this background of growing professionalism and competition undermined by considerable misery that Williams began to contemplate a literary fund, though the concept owed as much to the emancipation of political thought as to commercial change. The growth of radicalism favoured fraternal, rather than paternal, effort; and Williams was an admirer of Voltaire and Rousseau. But as far as a literary fund was concerned he was also practical and recognised the value of ruling-class support.

He first broached the subject with Adam Smith, whom he described as 'one of the harbingers of the reign of knowledge'. Although Smith had written in *The Wealth of Nations* that authors were unproductive members of society he found Williams's contrary argument sufficiently persuasive to say 'it seems to be a political proposition of great importance', and to recommend him to interest Pitt in the project. This must have been in 1784 or 1785. Pitt, no friend to literature, was polite but dismissive, so Williams took his proposals to the leader of the opposition. He found Fox, a late riser, in the middle of 'the offices of a slovenly toilet . . . . It was with difficulty I could induce him to say or hear anything serious on the subject of authors. He perused the paper I gave him, and said: "Burke is the proper person to be consulted; his head is as full of metaphysics as your own".' It was unlikely that Burke, the grand conservative, even though he had been a friend of Franklin, would have had much time for the radical 'Priest of Nature'. Certainly Williams's interview with him was not a success:

at the appointed hour he entered his drawing room, into which I had been shown, like a maniac; and uttering execrations on authors and scribblers, he approached me with such gesticulations as a Welsh constitution interpreted into hostile signals, and I prepared for battle. But the gesticulations were oratorical, and he looked fiercely in my face and said: 'Authors, writers, scribblers are the pests of the country, and I will not be troubled with them.'

After one last unhelpful interview with Joseph Banks, President of the Royal Society, Williams was temporarily worsted by the anvil – 'I then relinquished all thoughts of the undertaking, as I could not engage in it any man of eminent and popular reputation'.[15]

Although Pitt, Fox, Adam Smith, Burke and Joseph Banks (only Reynolds seems missing from the list) were uncooperative, Williams was soon able to enlist more constructive support from less well-known men. For some time he had been in the habit of meeting with friends for a monthly dinner at the Prince of Wales Coffee House; it was a second best Club of Thirteen. In 1788, Floyer Sydenham, Greek scholar, Platonist and the 'beloved friend of several of those members', died in a debtors' prison where he had been incarcerated for non-payment of a victualler's bill. Williams, with a flair for publicity, persuaded the club to start a subscription 'to expiate the grief and shame of the event, by a MONUMENT TO HIS MEMORY, in the institution of a Literary Fund'.[16] Of the eight original subscribers, none were 'men of eminent and popular reputation'. Hugh Downman was a country doctor and minor dramatist who had collaborated with Williams in the translation of Voltaire's works; Thomas Dale and Alexander Johnson were both busy London doctors, and Dale was also a classical scholar and linguist; J.F. Rigaud was a portraitist elected to the Royal Academy; Robert Mitchell was an architect; James Martin was MP for Tewkesbury and the dedicatee of Williams's *Letters on Political Liberty*; Isaac Swainson was the promoter of a vegetable syrup supposed to cure venereal disease, and Alexander

Blair was probably the business partner of Lunar Society member and chemist James Keir.

In addition to a public advertisement soliciting subscriptions, Williams drew up a 'Constitution for a Society to Support Men of Genius and Learning in Distress' (1788), published by John Nichols. It was written with vigour: 'Princes are influenced; ministers propose measures; and magistrates are instructed; by the industry of literature: while the authors of hints, suggestions, and disquisitions, may be languishing in obscurity; or dying in distress.' An account was opened at Coutts and subscriptions trickled in. On 10 May 1790 Alexander Johnson took the chair at the first recorded meeting of 'the friends of the Literary Fund, held at the Prince of Wales Coffee House, Conduit Street'.

The priority of the first meeting of the Fund was to elect a committee of management and draw up a constitution. But as only eight out of thirty or so subscribers attended, another meeting was arranged for Tuesday 18 May. To this meeting ten subscribers turned up, and five sent apologies for their absence; all fifteen were then elected to the committee: Johnson was confirmed as chairman, Thomas Dale and Lockyer Davis, bookseller to the Royal Society, were appointed registrars, and Edward Topham, editor of *The World*, and Edward Brooke, a bookseller, were appointed treasurers. It was decided to meet monthly at the Prince of Wales Coffee House, and, as a first step towards distributing the meagre funds, to place advertisements in five London papers. A month later, as no claims had been received, further advertisements were taken out in thirteen newspapers. At last, on 6 July, the Literary Fund met to consider their first application. A Lieutenant Samuel Stanton, the author of a work on duelling 'written from humane motives to stop the practice' appealed to the committee for aid to discharge his debts. The application was rejected, and after two more unsuccessful appeals, Lieutenant Stanton was committed to Newgate as a debtor. The Fund had decided early on in its history that it did 'not wish by any means, to excite or encourage those to commence or continue as Authors, who may happen to fancy that they possess the necessary qualifications'.[17]

In December 1790 the Fund relieved its first author. Dr Edward Harwood was a Dissenting minister and the author of *Cheerful Thoughts on the Happiness of a Religious Life* among other religious works, and some indifferent classical translations. His contributions to biblical scholarship were said to be learned and he was the friend and champion of

Joseph Priestley. He had been paralysed and bedridden for eight years and had no private resources. 'I should at this time in my life', he wrote, 'have been a rich Rector but the Athanasian Creed was a bitter pill I could never swallow. . . . If I had a little assistance in my deplorable condition it would enable me to purchase a little wine, which would chear my spirit.' He was granted 10 guineas and subsequent sums amounting to 25 guineas up to his death in 1794. The annual report for 1802 noted: 'In the infancy of this Institution, and when its funds amounted to little more than was required for the expenses of printing and advertisements, this deserving object [Dr Harwood] repeatedly received assistance, which, if it did not place him in affluence, rescued him from misery and despair.' It must have pleased David Williams that the first successful applicant was a Dissenter and friend to radicals.

Having established itself to the extent of relieving a distressed author, the most pressing object of the committee was to increase the funds of the society, so that no applicant need be turned down through lack of money. At first the treasurers were empowered to receive and bank subscriptions, but as the office was honorary and its holders were busy men, it was decided to appoint a collector who would receive a commission or 'poundage' on all annual and life subscriptions. This had the immediate effect of increasing the number of subscribers from around 50 to 150. However, in comparison with other charities whose operations were more appealing to the benevolent, the Literary Fund had few subscribers. As Franklin had told Williams in 1773, 'an Institution for the relief of misery which is so far from being intrusive or obvious – so far from pressing on the senses that it withdraws from observation – is an Institution whose object will ever be lost to the common classes of subscribers to public charities'.[18] The Literary Fund then, by respecting the delicacy of its clients' feelings and ensuring their anonymity, lost the valuable publicity that would have attracted as many subscribers as it would have deterred applicants.

But if applicants to the Fund were anonymous, subscribers were not, and there was valuable publicity to be gained from aristocratic patronage, especially as the nobility could afford to subscribe much larger amounts than the gentry. From the beginning, and in spite of Williams's republicanism, it was considered vital to have as many peers in the printed lists of subscribers as possible. The best way of achieving this was to invite an illustrious peer to become president.

There were, among late eighteenth-century aristocrats, many who still possessed the Augustan virtues of refined taste in art and literature combined with military or political skill. The committee saw nothing incongruous about offering the presidency to Lord Rawdon, later the Earl of Moira and a Commander-in-Chief of the Army. He was a generous subscriber to literature as well as a popular hero and a close friend of the Prince of Wales. Rawdon, however, declined the honour on the grounds that he was too busy to do it justice; instead, he donated 20 guineas as a token of his goodwill. The presidency was then offered to the Duke of Leeds, who had been Foreign Secretary; to the Duke of Portland, a former Prime Minister; and to the Marquess of Lansdowne, the former Secretary for the American Colonies and afterwards Prime Minister. All three were Whigs and Lansdowne was known to have radical sympathies, but they all pleaded overwork or ill health.

In 1799 the Marquess of Bute sent an unsolicited annual subscription of 10 guineas and he was immediately pressed to accept the presidency, as the committee wished 'to express their highest sense of the importance of the Patronage and Encouragement of a Nobleman of his Rank and Talents to the several objects of the Institution'. Bute's rank was less spectacular than it might have been. He was neither a cabinet minister nor a general, but he was at least the son of a Prime Minister. He was not very enthusiastic about his appointment, accepting it 'provided it is not a troublesome affair'. By 1801 he had obviously found it troublesome for he resigned, although he continued his subscription. This time the committee chose more wisely and the eleventh Duke of Somerset became president until his death in 1837. Somerset was a distinctly literary lord, his academic interests were legion; he was a Fellow of the Royal Society and the Society of Antiquaries and at different times president of the Royal Institution and the Linnean Society.

In later years Somerset was to blame Williams for the allegedly slow progress of the Fund. He told Sir Henry Ellis that Williams's 'tenets both as regarded religion and politics were for a long-time a draw-back to the Society's success'.[19] Certainly in the 1790s the Fund had strong links with radical and reformist politics. John Nichols, the Deputy of the Farringdon ward and close friend of John Wilkes, was appointed registrar and printer; for thirty years he was the Fund's most active, generous and revered officer. Other committee members included James Martin, MP and President of the Society for Constitutional Information; Thomas Christie, who with David Williams had been invited by the French assembly to help with the drafting of the revised constitution; and the poets Edward Topham, Edward Jerningham,

Robert Merry and Miles Peter Andrews, members of the Della Cruscan school (named after the Academia della Crusca in Florence), who wrote under female pseudonyms, and who were pilloried by the Tory satirist William Gifford for their fervent revolutionary views. Among the well-known radical subscribers were John Wilkes, Sir Francis Burdett, Gilbert Wakefield, Capel Lofft, and the American Joel Barlow.

However, also on the committee were several loyal monarchists and Tories, notably the versifier W.T. Fitzgerald, a Homer to the House of Hanover; H.J. Pye, appointed Poet Laureate by Pitt for his services as MP for Berkshire; Sir James Bland Burges, barrister and Under Secretary at the Foreign Office; and John Reeves, King's Printer and Chairman of the Association for preserving Liberty and Property against Levellers and Republicans. The Fund was certainly trying hard to avoid taking sides.

Within a comparatively short space of time the Fund acquired an apolitical character with a firm emphasis on blameless philanthropy. The office of vice president was instituted in 1791 to add lustre and lucre to the Fund and to establish it as a major organ of patronage. In the first ten years the vice presidents included a cluster of lords, including Moira; Earl Spencer, Nelson's First Sea Lord, Home Secretary and 'owner of the finest private Library in Europe'; and the Earl of Chichester, another Home Secretary and, to the great benefit of the Fund, intimate with the Prince of Wales. The lords were supplemented by baronets and knights, including the elder Sir Robert Peel, Sir John Sinclair and Sir George Staunton, and an admixture of MPs and aldermen. This rapid progress into respectability was something Williams had to bear for the sake of his fellow authors: 'He was a great stickler for reform, both in respect to government and religion . . . the society he had founded was liberally supported by many gentlemen who held offices under government; so we often beheld him in his latter days connected both with the eminent divines of the established church and respectable placemen, who were alike eager to promote his humane views.'[20]

Williams always hoped that the Literary Fund would develop into a wider, more progressive institution than a simple charity. He wanted it to incorporate a college for the sons of authors and 'decayed and superannuated Genius', with a library and archive for the use of its members. He expected it to play an active rôle in the encouragement of literature and science.[21] As a club, fund and college it would be a Royal Society of Authors. But by first establishing a fund with its charitable apparatus, he effected his first priority at the expense of all others. As Dickens was to discover, to attempt to graft the larger aims onto the specific minor function was impossible.

So instead of evolving into an organisation for reform, a society of authors for the protection and advancement of authors' rights, the Literary Fund became a charitable organisation modelled, it would seem, on Parliament itself. The subscribers to the Fund were the equivalent of Householders, men whose standing and wealth gave them the right to elect the committee. The committee, a kind of House of Commons, had the management of the Fund and selected their cabinet of chairman, registrars and treasurers. There was a council consisting of ex-committee members and all the vice presidents, which acted as an upper chamber, with the right to suspend the committee's activities 'if any irregularities or abuses appear'. The president was both head of the council and of the committee. The applicants to the Fund, like the unenfranchised population at large, accepted whatever was doled out to them, except during the summer recess from the end of May to the middle of October, when they had to fend for themselves. This basic structure continued throughout the nineteenth century. The only real change was in the rôle of the one non-elected and salaried officer, the clerk, who began as a mere functionary but after a change of title to secretary in 1837 exerted more power and influence than any other member of the Fund – the power of the senior civil servant.

The bulk of the Literary Fund's income came from private sub-scribers and the occasional legacy. There were also fund-raising activities ranging from amateur theatricals to public dinners. The anniversary dinner became the chief occasion in the Fund's calendar, serving the dual function of attracting extra subscriptions and drawing public attention to its charitable work. Celebrated authors and public men, anyone who was rich and likely to be sympathetic to literature, were invited to become stewards. The guests would be urged, in post-prandial speeches, to subscribe to the Fund, or to increase their subscriptions if they were already members. In this way, with around 200 guests, the profit from the dinners was reckoned in hundreds of pounds. The first anniversary dinner was held in 1793 at the Crown and Anchor Tavern in the Strand. Sir Joseph Andrews, vice president, took the chair and 50 invitations were accepted at 7s. 6d. each. The more distinguished the chairman the more invitations were accepted and the greater were the profits. The Prince of Wales, and the King of the

Belgians, for example, earned the Fund three times the average profit from three times as many guests.

The form of the dinners was remorseless. Courses were punctuated by songs, glees and poetic recitations. Nearly everyone made a speech, ending in a toast. Most of the guests still managed to enjoy themselves. Ladies watched the proceedings from the gallery; they were allowed light refreshments, including lemonade. In 1800 there were 314 male guests who, whatever they ate, managed to drink 294 bottles of port, 69 bottles of sherry and quantities of strong beer, porter and punch. The 1800 anniversary was an occasion of great patriotism when literature took second place to such loyal toasts as 'One Mind, one Heart, one Voice from the Cottage to the Throne', 'May the Trident of Neptune be always wielded by the Genius of Britain', 'The Hero of the Nile' and so on. One toast in particular – 'The Constitution of England, untampered and unimpaired by French Quakery' – must have rankled with David Williams. At the same dinner Henry James Pye delivered an anniversary address in his best worst form, urging the diners to subscribe to Nelson's reputation:

> Fostered by you, the hallow'd Muse shall give,
> The Hero's fame in deathless verse to live.

The annual dinner, if it was the most striking event in the Literary Fund's calendar, was not the only method of attracting publicity and extra revenue. In 1791 Thomas Morris was commissioned to produce a play for the benefit of the Fund. The proposal at first met with a major obstacle, 'no other Gentleman besides Capt. Thomas Morris being willing to take part', but finally *Richard III* and an unnamed farce were staged on 16 April at the Haymarket 'at Opera prices'. The theatre was lent by the management, and the actors and actresses performed without payment. It is not known how much the plays produced but the Fund later paid back £15 in grants to three unemployed actresses who had played Lady Ann, Prince Edward and another part.

Additional sources of income included a gift from Lord Mountmorres of the unsold copies of his *History of the Irish Parliament* – he shot himself a few months later – and donations from the millionaire W.J. Denison, and a group of Englishmen living in Hyderabad. These one-off donations and legacies were put together to form a 'permanent fund'. Proposed by William Boscawen in 1797, the idea of the permanent fund was to invest 'all future subscriptions for life, casual benefactions, legacies, and all profits arising from plays, concerts, books etc., to the purchase of stock in some of the national funds; the interest only of which . . . to be employed for the purposes of the Institution'.

The only failure among all the fund-raising and publicity activities was the committee's complete inability to persuade a cleric to preach a sermon for the benefit of the Fund. A subcommittee had been formed in 1793 with the brief to secure the services of a bishop. The Bishop of London 'politely declined'; the Bishop of Norwich promised to think about it; the Bishop of St David's gave 'a downright refusal'. In desperation the committee extended its frame of reference to include 'any Bishop or Clergyman' and eventually, in 1802, Dr Samuel Parr, 'the Whig Johnson', agreed to preach at St Brides. However, Parr procrastinated and in the end his sermon was never given. The committee did not give up hope that it would receive some official episcopal blessing. It even formally established an Ecclesiastical Committee to consider the applications of poor clergymen separately from authors, but this subtle form of bribery failed and the committee was dissolved. It may be that the presence of such unorthodox clergymen as Williams and Charles Symmons on the committee frightened the established Church from patronising the Fund. The Fund however was the unceasing patron of the more humble class of literary clergymen.

Although summaries of the Fund's accounts were published at the back of the annual reports, it was not until October 1801, when a separate analysis of the first ten years was published, that it was possible to get a clear idea of income and expenditure. Of a total of £3,898 subscribed to the Fund, £650 was spent on administration, £1,658 was reserved for the permanent fund and a total of £1,590 had been granted on 194 occasions to 103 applicants. The average value of a grant was a little over £8, and no applicant was permitted to apply more than once a year. The range of grants, however, was wide. A persistent applicant or one whose authorship was negligible might receive as little as one guinea, while a major author might receive as much as 20 guineas – the kind of sum an employed labourer might hope to earn in a year.

Literary Fund grants were necessarily limited and could achieve little more than rescuing authors from temporary, if acute, difficulties. On the other hand, as Pye and Fitzgerald constantly reminded their audience, the fate of Chatterton, Savage or Otway was a thing of the past. Among those who received grants in the Fund's first decade, were the constitutional historian John Louis De Lolme, actor and dramatist Charles Macklin, transvestite diplomat Chevalier D'Eon, novelist

Charlotte Lennox, Welsh bard Edward Williams, philosopher Thomas Taylor, Coleridge, Chateaubriand, and Jean, widow of Robert Burns. To mark this achievement J.F. Rigaud RA was commissioned to design an engraving for the Literary Fund to preface a celebratory quarto edition of poems together with the regulations of the Fund and list of subscribers. It was doubtful whether a collection of poems by Pye and Fitzgerald would have attracted anything other than ridicule, but fortunately it was decided to preface the volume with a history of the Fund by David Williams.

Claims of Literature, as the work was eventually called, was published by William Miller in January 1802. It was Williams's last important work and the only one, as he writes, that 'was ever carefully corrected by me . . . [as] I was under the inspection of a committee'.[22] 160 pages long, it was less a history of the Fund than an analysis of the conditions of authorship and a manifesto of authors' rights, written with his usual impatient lucidity. Copies were delivered to the Prince Regent and Thomas Jefferson, President of the United States. Jefferson replied:

[I] have read with satisfaction the very judicious reflections it contains on the condition of the respectable class of literary men. The efforts for their relief made by a society of private citizens are truly laudable, but they are, as you justly observe, but a palliation of an evil, the cure of which calls for all the wisdom and the means of the nation [14 November 1803].

However, the politics of the work did not please everyone and were the cause of the first major dispute in the Fund's history.

Although Williams, Nichols and their liberal friends outnumbered the conservatives on the committee, whatever political rivalry there may have been was always friendly. A dining club had been formed open to all members of the Fund, at which both radicals and reactionaries would meet and congratulate each other on their latest literary production. But on the publication of *Claims of Literature* the two political extremes publicly clashed in the persons of Williams and Sir James Bland Burges. Burges accused Williams of writing a radical polemic to the injury of the Fund. Williams proceeded to defend himself from the accusation:

Sir James, from the first moment of his entrance into the Society, had endeavoured to pervert it by mingling religion and political enquiries with the cases of the unfortunate claimants. . . . All the pretentions of such bigotry were always nobly resisted by Mr W. Boscawen and Mr Fitzgerald, the more nobly as their general political and religious principles were those of Sir James. . . . Is it to be supposed, that I would tamely have suffered a liberal and independent institution to be converted into a gloomy and suspicious court of inquisition?[23]

Burges's proposal to condemn *Claims* was defeated and he resigned from the Fund and withdrew his subscription.

By 1806 the quarrel was forgotten and the Literary Fund's institutional status was assured. The Earl of Chichester had persuaded the Prince Regent to become patron of the Fund and part with 200 guineas a year for rent and maintenance of premises. The Literary Fund moved into its first headquarters at 36 Gerrard Street, once the home of Edmund Burke, and David Williams, in ill health and without an income himself, was installed as 'Resident Visitor'. The Fund had become, in fifteen years, a major charity with 200 annual subscribers including 20 peers and the Duchess of Devonshire; many baronets and knights; London's most eminent publishers: Longman, Cadell and Murray; John Walter, the proprietor of *The Times*; and John Penn, the proprietor of Pennsylvania.

The Fund's most generous benefactor was Thomas Newton, an eighty-five year old bachelor with literary tastes. In 1805, inspired by the Prince's example, he decided to make a will in favour of the Fund: 'This is the Institution for the Representative of NEWTON',[24] he is alleged to have remarked, alluding to his supposed descent from Isaac. He died in 1806 leaving property worth over £8,000 to the Fund with the proviso that it should secure incorporation by royal charter. Unfortunately for the committee, the Attorney-General, Sir Vicary Gibbs, was a virulent opponent of the press who associated the Fund with the likes of Cobbett: 'there is much danger of its becoming a debating society, and taking something of a democratic tincture'.[25] Thanks, however, to the persistent efforts of the Fund's chairman, Sir Benjamin Hobhouse, the charter was eventually approved in 1818, two years after the death of David Williams.

THE SMALL AMOUNT of aid distributed to the needy author, coupled with the almost total absence of notable men of letters from the ranks of the subscribers, led to increasing criticism of the management of the Literary Fund. In 1812 the only authors of any eminence in the subscription lists were George Crabbe, Monk Lewis and Isaac D'Israeli. In contrast to their publishers, the great authors of the day – Scott, Lamb, Wordsworth, Byron, Southey, Campbell, Shelley – did not choose to be associated with the Fund, although they were active in helping fellow authors. In 1812 Southey wrote to John Murray to propose an attack on the Fund in the *Quarterly Review*: 'I should like to say something about the absurd purposes of the Literary Fund with its

despicable ostentation of patronage'.[26] The article, a review of D'Israeli's *Calamities of Authors*, duly appeared and became the forerunner in
a series of published attacks on the Fund that were to last well into the
century:

We have, it is true, a literary fund for the relief of distressed authors, the members of
which dole out their alms in sums of five, ten, and twenty pounds (never, we believe,
exceeding the latter sum), dine together in public once a year, write verses in praise
of their own benevolence, and recite them themselves. Nothing can be more evident,
than that such liberality is as useless to literature as it is pitiful in itself. The
wretched author who applies to these literary overseers, receives about as much
from the bounty of the General Committee as the law would have entitled him to, in
the course of twelve months, if he had applied to the parish to support him and his
family as paupers.

. . . He who, from his own means, relieves a case of individual distress, does good
at the same time to his own heart; and that which is wisely and bountifully given
blesses him that takes as well as him that gives. But in this joint-stock-patronage
company, a donation is paid and received like a poor-rate – save only that there is
rather more humiliation on the part of the receiver, who, in this case, solicits, as a
charity, what, in the other, he would have claimed as a right [September 1812].

Southey's principal objection to the Literary Fund was that it
distributed a pittance which was almost useless, and did so with
patronising ostentation. Nowhere was this ostentation more evident
than at the annual dinners when Pye and Fitzgerald recited their
appalling verses. At the 1812 anniversary, several months before
Southey's attack, Fitzgerald praised the founding of the Literary Fund
in these terms:

> Thus did Reflection's eye forsee that plan,
> Which dawn'd in wisdom would enlighten Man.
> When Learning's patient victims should no more
> Their Fate unpitied by the world deplore!
> Nor slighted Genius hide his pensive head,
> To write, degraded, for precarious bread.

Southey disliked the Literary Fund because it was run by poetasters
like Fitzgerald rather than by men of letters. It had been founded by
doctors, lawyers and clergymen, and from the start the literary pretensions of the committee were very slight. On the first committee, the only
writers of imaginative works were the Della Cruscan poets Edward
Topham, Edward Jerningham, Robert Merry and Miles Peter
Andrews. Typical of their verse was Jerningham's 'Il Latte', a laudable
if ludicrous homily in favour of breast feeding. It was the kind of subject
that won for its author the epithet of 'snivelling Jerningham'. The Della

Cruscans were publicly ridiculed, and had their literary careers completely destroyed in 1791, when William Gifford published *The Baviad*, a
well merited attack on their pretensions and dullness.

W.T. Fitzgerald and H.J. Pye inspired a similar contempt. Fitzgerald
was distinguished by featuring in the opening lines of Byron's 'English
Bards and Scotch Reviewers':

> Still must I hear? – shall hoarse Fitzgerald bawl
> His creaking couplets in a tavern hall.

The attack was kept up by Horace and James Smith who included
Fitzgerald among their parodies in *Rejected Addresses*. Fitzgerald seemed
flattered rather than chastened by such attention. James Smith met him
at the anniversary of 1822 and described the following conversation:

Fitzgerald (with good humour): Mr Smith. I mean to recite after dinner.
Mr Smith: Do you?
Fitzgerald: Yes: you'll have more of 'God bless the Regent and the Duke of York'.[27]

If it was bad enough having to listen to Fitzgerald and Pye recite their
'vainglorious vauntings'[28] at the annual dinners, it was worse still that
their poems should be printed as a preface to every annual report. With
the exception of Isaac D'Israeli, no author of any general reputation
consented to serve on the committee until Edward Bulwer Lytton
accepted nomination in 1832, only to lose his place for non-attendance
two years later. There were, however, distinguished specialists on the
committee such as the antiquarian writer John Britton and the classicist
and translator William Sotheby, but they did not write anniversary
poems. The Fund was popularly associated with Fitzgerald, Pye and
the illustrious and corpulent heroes of their verses, the sons of George
III.

Ostentation, particularly at the annual dinners, antagonised potential subscribers. In May 1819 the *Journal of Belles Lettres* commented on
the poor receipts of the Literary Fund dinner compared with the Artists'
Fund and the Theatrical Fund: 'At this period of the year London is full
of men the most renowned in the annals of literature: why were none of
these at the dinner?' Perhaps because the Duke of Kent had turned
down the chair: 'owing . . . to the very advanced state of the Duchess's
pregnancy, I have been under the necessity of declining all . . . until
the awful moment [the birth of Victoria] is over'. Poor Sir Benjamin
Hobhouse, chairman of the committee, had to take the Duke's place.
Fitzgerald wrote gloomily 'I really fear we shall make but a bad figure
without a Royal Chairman. . . . the Lying in Hospital found means to

put in their chair the greatest of all Great Guns! The Duke of Wellington – most heartily do I wish we could do the same.'

It would have made little difference. The Literary Fund never found it easy to persuade eminent writers to attend the dinners as stewards or honorary guests. Scott, in writing to decline an invitation to the 1820 dinner, echoed Southey:

both by circumstances and inclination I am in the habit of devoting such sums as I can afford to the relief of persons less fortunate in literature than I have been myself and whose merits and necessities I have some opportunity to judge – which will, I hope, be admitted as an apology for declining to subscribe to the general fund [22 April 1820].

Other authors expressed similar views. Landor wrote trenchantly in 1847, 'I carefully avoid both public dinners and public men, and have done so all my life'. Mill wrote in 1849, 'to take part in a public demonstration of this nature is so foreign to my pursuits and tastes that I am compelled to decline'. Wordsworth wrote in the same vein in the same year, 'I am obliged to decline, having never been in the habit of attending public meetings'. Not all authors were so antisocial. Theodore Hook, Bulwer Lytton, W.H. Ainsworth, Thomas Moore, Charles Dickens, Robert Browning and J.G. Lockhart all accepted the office of steward. One celebrated author was particularly sorry not to be able to attend the – by then – famous dinners. In May 1850, Charlotte Brontë was nursing her sick father at Haworth and had to postpone a visit to London:

I do regret one great treat, which I shall now miss. Next Wednesday is the anniversary dinner of the Royal Literary Fund Society, held in Freemasons' Hall. Octavian Blewitt, the secretary, offered me a ticket for the ladies' gallery. I should have seen all the great literati and artists gathered in the hall below, and heard them speak; Thackeray and Dickens are always present among the rest. This cannot now be. I don't think all London can afford another sight to me so interesting.[29]

Most authors, like Southey and Scott, appeared reluctant to contribute a trifling annual sum for the benefit of an anonymous recipient, when by direct assistance to a friend in need there was an immediate and apparent beneficial effect. Samuel Rogers, who contributed £36 15s. to the Literary Fund over the period 1821 to 1855, gave Thomas Miller 300 guineas in 1841 to set up as a bookseller. Nearly all the wealthier authors of the period were similarly generous to their less well-off colleagues, and when their private gifts are compared with the charity of the Literary Fund, Southey's criticisms strike home. When the Literary Fund gave Coleridge £30 in February 1816 out of their annual income of about £2,000 and stocks worth nearly £17,000, Byron sent him £100 'being at a time – when I could not command 150 – in the world'.[30] Shelley gave Peacock £100 a year for seven years and made an outright gift to Leigh Hunt of £1,400; the Literary Fund gave Peacock three grants totalling £61 and Hunt two grants totalling £100. In 1815 Scott and Byron sent C.R. Maturin, author of *Melmoth the Wanderer*, 50 guineas each; in 1822 the Literary Fund voted him £25. In most cases private, friendly assistance far exceeded the sums granted by the Literary Fund.

Nevertheless, though the grants were small, they were useful and sometimes vital. When Peacock applied in 1812, aged twenty-seven, as the author of two volumes of poems, the comparatively large grant of £30 was reckoned by his friend and publisher Edward Hookham to have saved his life. Peacock was in the middle of writing a long poem *The Philosophy of Melancholy* (1812), the theme of which seems to have driven him to contemplate suicide. Hookham wrote: 'I have but too just reason to read that the fate of Chatterton might be that of Peacock'. A year later Edward's brother Thomas wrote to ask for another grant for Peacock who was still 'in a state of such mental dejection, that the most distressing consequences are apprehended'. A further £10 was awarded. It is possible then, that timely Literary Fund aid (before Shelley came to the rescue) may have secured Peacock's future.

A less dramatic, but typical example of the Literary Fund's usefulness was when the ageing Robert Bloomfield was granted a total of £90. Bloomfield had been the most patronised poet of his time. A ploughman poet discovered by Capel Lofft, in 1804 he was paid the enormous sum of £4,000 by Vernor and Hood for a new stereotyped edition of his book *The Farmer's Boy* (1800). In 1818 the rage for Bloomfield had evaporated, and he was left, destitute and half-blind, to apply to the Literary Fund. He was given a £40 grant. The great disadvantage of private patronage was its fickleness, as John Clare, another Literary Fund beneficiary, was also to discover.

Very few authors were so talented or fashionable that they could count Shelley, Scott and Rogers among their friends, and literary dukes and duchesses among their patrons. For most authors whose work had contemporary merit the Literary Fund was a discreet and uncapricious source of aid in times of illness and debt. The critics often overlooked this fact. When R.H. Horne attacked the Fund in 1833, he asked two questions: 'Has its bounty ever enabled man to bring forth a fine tragedy, epic, history, novel or work of science? How many men of genius has it relieved from distress?'[31] The answer to the first question was that it was never the object of the Fund to sponsor a literary work, though it did so on several occasions. The answer to the second charge was that by 1833 the Literary Fund had given grants to some 20 men and women of enduring reputation and at least 600 other authors. And it was to recognise Horne's own literary merit by granting him a total of £430 in his declining years.

Nearly twenty years after Southey's attack the Fund found a champion in J.G. Lockhart who had become a subscriber in 1830 following the Fund's grant of £20 to Thomas Richards, a literary surgeon whom he had warmly recommended. In January 1831, as editor of the *Quarterly Review*, Lockhart included a flattering reference to the Fund, ironically in a review of Southey's *Lives of the Uneducated Poets*:

We hope to be pardoned for taking this opportunity of bearing witness to the wise and generous method in which the Managers of the London Literary Fund conduct that admirable Charity. It may not be known in many parts of the Empire that such an Institution exists at all, and even this casual notice may be serviceable to its revenues. We have had occasion to observe the equal promptitude and delicacy with which its Committee are ever ready to administer to the necessities of the unfortunate Scholar, who can satisfy them that his misery is not the just punishment of immoral habits. Some of the brightest names of contemporary literature have been beholden to the bounty of this Institution, and in numerous instances its interference has shielded friendless merit from utter ruin.

IN JANUARY 1836 Joseph Snow retired as clerk and collector of the Literary Fund. Among the applicants for his job, converted to that of secretary, was the twenty-five year old Octavian Blewitt who gave John Elliotson and Mary Russell Mitford as his referees. The post was given to C.P. Roney, later knighted for his services as Secretary of the Great Industrial Exhibition of 1853. Roney resigned in March 1837 to take up a more lucrative job and Blewitt renewed his candidature against stiff competition. Francis Mahony, the 'Father Prout' of *Fraser's Magazine*, wrote from Paris to the registrar, Thomas Crofton Croker, to offer his gratuitous services in return for free lodging: 'I should prefer a residence in London where I could turn my time to better account and enjoy the pleasure of your Society and that of some other valued friends.' The committee preferred to make a more orthodox appointment and chose the Rev. W.H. Landon who had been strongly backed by committee member William Jerdan. Landon was the brother of Letitia Landon, 'L.E.L.', whose album verses Jerdan had first published in the *Literary Gazette*, and in whom he had a sentimental interest. Landon's appointment was a disaster; he was lax in his duties and careless in his accounts. He was forced to resign in January 1839 and Blewitt applied for a third time. The only other short-listed candidate was Jerdan's son, William Freeling Jerdan. On 13 March 1839 Blewitt was chosen as secretary by 31 votes to 14. At the same meeting Charles Dickens was elected to the committee.

A few months later, the day after the committee meeting of 13 November 1839, the twenty-seven year old Dickens wrote a friendly note to the twenty-nine year old Blewitt:

Mr Dickens may perhaps take this opportunity of congratulating Mr Blewitt on his accession to his present office, and of venturing to thank him individually for the zeal and earnestness he evinced yesterday in the performance of its duties. Mr Dickens is sensible that he needs an excuse for obtruding such an expression of opinion upon Mr Blewitt, but he would rather require it in such a case than do violence (by a formal silence), to his very warm and sincere feeling.

It was a promising start in a new era of the Literary Fund that was to end twenty years later in recrimination and lost opportunities.

Blewitt, the son of a prosperous London merchant, studied medicine but never qualified. In 1833 he became assistant to Sir James Clark, the physician, and taught classics to his son. Later he travelled abroad, particularly in Italy, on which country he wrote two popular guide-books for John Murray. He had begun his literary career with a successful topographical work on Torquay dedicated to Bulwer Lytton, and this was followed with a work which gives a clue to his orthodoxy, *Treatise on the Happiness Arising from the Exercise of the Christian Faith*. He was every inch a solid, mainstream Victorian. There were no skeletons in his cupboard, and, although he was a kindly man, his unbending Anglican sternness cost the 'immoral' author dearly. Under his régime, no grant was ever given to the widow of an author unless she could produce a marriage certificate; even if she had been living with her husband for thirty or forty years. Among those who were rejected was the widow of Cyrus Redding, who had lived with him as his wife for forty-nine years, and the daughters of Thomas Roscoe. Blewitt wrote in a memorandum: 'Mrs Roscoe was very seldom seen by friends of the family, and there always appeared to be an unwillingness to introduce her into Society. . . . I had entertained doubts whether they were married at all, and the alleged difficulty of producing the certificate now strengthened these doubts.' If an author was not considered by Blewitt and the committee to be of 'good, moral character' the application would be rejected, or worse – as the case of Thomas Macknight demonstrates.

In 1863 Macknight, a well-known biographer and political writer who had breakfasted with Gladstone and was a friend of F.D. Maurice, applied for a grant and was supported by his publishers Chapman and Hall, and the historian J.S. Brewer. Unfortunately for Macknight, Blewitt, who scoured the newspapers for literary gossip, discovered a press report relating to his divorce proceedings. It appeared that Macknight had deserted his wife and taken up with an actress. Later, when his wife came to visit him to demand restitution, 'she locked the door and took the key out of the lock. He listened to her for some time, and at last jumped out of the window.'[32] This account so shocked Blewitt that although the Fund had granted Macknight an irrevocable £50, he at once wrote to his sponsors to inform them of Macknight's 'highly discreditable character'. Brewer wrote back, protesting his ignorance of the business, 'Mr Macknight's conduct must . . . shut him out'. Chapman and Hall literally did shut him out: 'we were in negotiation with Mr Macknight for a new book, but under the circumstances we feel bound to have no further transactions with him'. At exactly the same time as Macknight's transgression, Chapman and Hall were negotiating a contract for *Our Mutual Friend* which, 'under the circumstances', they felt bound to proceed with, although Dickens had left his wife for the company of an actress.

The case of Macknight is revealing in that it demonstrates Blewitt's operating principle as secretary; where possible (not, for example, in the case of Thornton Hunt who, although he was the lover of Mrs G.H. Lewes, was too popular and influential a writer to be socially ostracised) applicants should possess both moral purity and literary merit. The *Athenaeum* noted on 8 September 1849: 'We believe the Secretary to be an upright and excellent officer; not, however, without strong personal feelings: political and religious – likings and dislikings, that have been but too manifest.' Jerdan, who had served on the committee for eighteen years and regarded himself as the Fund's most active supporter, also found Blewitt over zealous. When Blewitt pursued him for arrears in his subscriptions he resigned, contrasting the 'coldness and statistical economics of the present day' with the good old days of 'cordiality and humanity'.

In fairness to Blewitt, he was also a sympathetic and generous man; it was typical of him to take personal charge of the most wretched authors.

In 1856, for example, he reported to the registrar that Daniel Spillan and his family 'had been living on food cooked especially for them in my kitchen, and had been many times clothed by Mrs Blewitt'. Nevertheless his kindness was tempered by sternness and Mrs Spillan was refused a widow's grant on failing to produce a marriage certificate.

Blewitt's great achievement as secretary was to recognise, as early as 1839, the historical and literary value of the Fund's archive. His main efforts on his appointment were directed towards disentangling forty years of history; reorganising the archive, cataloguing applicants and analysing the grants and income. He was also responsible for the introduction of a printed form of application, which, although it was unpopular among the applicants, has proved to be of great value to historians and biographers. Another important innovation was his rearrangement of the annual reports to give a complete and detailed picture of the Fund's activities. In general he improved the Fund's affairs to such an extent that in 1840, only one year after his appointment, he was given a gratuity of £50 on top of his salary of £100 in recognition of his 'great zeal' and 'extraordinary exertions'. In 1842 his salary was increased to £150 and in 1846 it was increased to £200. Dickens, at the height of his dissatisfaction with the Fund, testified that the secretary 'was, at that time [1840], the right-hand of Reform; it was by his excellent arrangements of the documents that one-half of the shameful abuses which had disgraced the Society, were discovered; and he most justly entitled himself to . . . honourable recognition'.[33] In private, however, he referred to Blewitt as 'the pious B—'.[34]

DICKENS was first introduced to the Literary Fund in November 1836 when he attended a dinner of the Literary Fund Club, a monthly dining club attached to the Fund and presided over by John Cam Hobhouse, the Whig politician and friend of Byron. In May 1837 he accepted an invitation to become a steward at the anniversary dinner. Although he was the author of only one published book, *Sketches by Boz* (in which he included a satirical account of a charity dinner), and half the serialised *Pickwick Papers*, he was honoured by the toast 'Mr Dickens and the rising Authors of the Day' to which he gracefully responded, hoping 'that the rising authors would all feel it an honour to be connected with that institution'. It was his first public speech, appropriately addressed to about 120 of his 'literary brethren'.

In March 1839 Dickens joined the committee whose members included his friend William Jerdan, and his enemy and publisher

Richard Bentley. He did not attend the next few meetings of the committee, but after the completion of *Nicholas Nickleby* he found time to attend the meeting on 13 November 1839. It turned out to be the busiest meeting in the history of the Fund. Dickens had to sit through thirty-five separate cases, one of which he sponsored. The meeting ranged from the award of £50 to the comparatively well-known miscellaneous writer Thomas Roscoe, to the rejection of Matthew Ferstanig, self-styled 'Head of Oriental and Classical Literature in the Kingdom' – a madman who later published a bill poster indicting the committee, including Dickens, for keeping a 'seraglio of 82 women at that harem at No. 4 Lincoln's-Inn-Fields' and lavishing the Fund 'in gluttony and inebriation, at the Free Mason's and other Taverns'.

The range of misery and delusion that the committee dealt with that day could have been the raw material for a Dickens novel. One applicant had been imprisoned for debt for eight years; another, a clergyman, had embezzled Church funds to meet 'extravagancies in his style of living'; a third had been defrauded of his property 'through the perfidy of a pretended friend'. The worst case was probably that of the historian and editor John Watkins who had applied for the first time in 1831 on the death of his son, consumption of his daughter and lunacy of his wife, and was making his eighteenth application 'after it had pleased providence to take the last of my three sons'. His sponsor wrote: 'these are the appalling facts, and barely to be exceeded in human miseries'. Dickens's personal acquaintance with suffering was not negligible, but at this committee meeting he was brought face to face with the widespread suffering of authors, his 'literary brethren', and although he left no record of what he thought, it must have been both a depressing and a provoking experience.

Although he chaired the Literary Fund Club dinner the following March he attended only one committee meeting in 1840 and was therefore declared ineligible for re-election in March 1841. He did not serve again until his return from Italy in 1845. He was re-elected to the committee in March 1845, attended the December meeting, and five meetings in 1846, two meetings in 1847 and two in 1848. By 1849 his interest in the Fund's activities was at its height. He wrote anxiously to Blewitt in January 1849 to make sure that he was entitled to re-election, and throughout the year he attended all but two of the meetings. It was his most active year as a committee member, but he was already growing disillusioned with the management of the Fund. He attended his last committee in January 1850 and was elected to the council in

May 1851, claiming to be 'exceedingly sorry to have vacated my seat at the General Committee'. Over the years 1850 to 1855, as his efforts to reform the Fund were increasingly opposed, so his retrospective criticism became more vehement.

The Royal Literary Fund tended to reduce the bona-fide man of letters to the same level as the begging-letter writer, making tremulous appeals to its 'charity', 'munificence' or 'bounty'. Dickens believed that it must be possible to assist authors without crushing their pride. To that end, together with Bulwer Lytton, he founded the Guild of Literature and Art in November 1850. The principle of the Guild, unlike that of the Royal Literary Fund, was to honour professional writers by awarding them pensions ('salaries') and, if required, free purpose-built homes near Stevenage.[35] Applicants to the Royal Literary Fund were, perforce, begging-letter writers; pensioners of the Guild would be acknowledged as 'gentlemen'. In 1854 Bulwer Lytton introduced a bill to incorporate the Guild by Act of Parliament. Unfortunately the Act required the Guild to wait seven years before putting any of its proposals into effect.

The combination of the ineffectiveness of the Guild and the miserliness of the Fund (the average value of a grant was £30) led Dickens to consider ways of reforming the Fund by grafting on some of the functions of the Guild, which the Fund's charter of 1818 had in some respects anticipated though never put into effect. The better to press for reform, Dickens resigned from the council which, as a result of the cancellation of a bye-law in 1848, had no powers to meet and had lost all authority over the committee. C.W. Dilke, a member of the council and proprietor of the *Athenaeum*, who had kept up an attack on the financial management of the Fund from 1836, and John Forster, who was an ordinary subscriber, became Dickens's chief allies in the campaign that followed.

The reformers' principal objections to the Fund were that the council had no powers, and that the cost of administration was out of all proportion to the money distributed to the applicants. At the annual general meeting on 14 March 1855 Dickens and Dilke brought these charges before the subscribers. After much wrangling it was agreed that a special committee should be set up to examine the question of a new charter. Dickens was appointed chairman and both reformers and staunch committee members were represented. Dickens wrote optimistically to Wilkie Collins: 'virtually I consider the thing done'.[36]

It was a severe miscalculation. The special committee appointed a subcommittee to make a detailed proposal. The result was a plan for a radical extension of the Fund's policy. The subcommittee recommended that in addition to its charitable activities which should include the granting of pensions and loans to authors, the house of the Fund should become a literary club and hotel 'for the purposes of study, writing and consultation with one another', and a college should be founded 'for the honour of literature and the service of literary men'. To achieve all this the Fund should use its permanent fund which had accrued £21,000 since 1802 and launch a public appeal. The whole revitalised Royal Literary Fund would be renamed the Literary Institution of Great Britain.

The idea of providing club facilities for some of the richest authors in London appalled the conservatives on the committee. After taking legal opinions they won the vote against the proposal by a large majority. The council was not reformed, pensions were not awarded and the reformers found themselves criticised in the press. *The Times* commented:

We believe that there is room for much reform in the management of the funds of the society. The charge of £500 for administering £1500 seems preposterous; but we do not think that the best way to remedy this or any other abuse is to superadd to the present duties of the secretary the management of a cheap Literary Club [18 June 1855].

As a result of his unexpected failure, Dickens's attitude towards the Fund grew more belligerent. For some time, no doubt at Dilke's instigation, the *Athenaeum*, first under T.K. Hervey and then under Hepworth Dixon, had been the official critic of the Fund, but on 8 March 1856 Dickens took up the attack in *Household Words* as a prelude to the approaching annual general meeting. By the time of the meeting on 13 March he had succeeded in antagonising potential allies who were worried about the effect of unfavourable publicity. After delivering a facetious speech his resolution condemning the management of the Fund was defeated by 57 votes to 30. Crabb Robinson, who attended the meeting, gave a severe account of the affair: 'Dickens made a bold, clever, but imprudent speech which did harm. Forster was angry and Dilke coarse. On the other side, Bell was tedious and trickish – that is lawyerlike, evasive; Blackmore dull and offensive; Murray gave offence.'[37] Charles Macfarlane, author and Royal Literary Fund applicant, wrote to congratulate Blewitt on the result: 'surely Dickens was very shallow, and impertinent. He is inflated by his temporary prosperity.'

The attack was repeated again in 1857 and again defeated by an even

33

wider margin of votes. By now Dickens was furious with the Fund. He wrote to Macready: 'The annual fight at the Literary Fund came off last Wednesday. I am resolved to reform it or ruin it – one or the other.'[38] This bloody-minded resolve to ruin an organisation which he knew did a great deal of good for authors, was probably a symptom of his increasing paranoia. His domestic life was strained: he was soon to break with his wife and publish his notorious letter airing their marital difficulties. Other victims of his paranoia were his old friend Mark Lemon and publisher Frederick Evans, both of whom he accused of taking Catherine's side.

The battle for control of the Fund culminated in a pamphlet war. *The Case of the Reformers in the Literary Fund* was circulated to the press and all subscribers before the annual general meeting of March 1858. It repeated the criticism that the council was powerless and the administration burdensome, and it ended by quoting from Southey's attack in the *Quarterly Review*. The committee appointed Dickens's friend and fellow amateur actor Robert Bell to write a reply, *A Summary of Facts: Drawn from the Records of the Society*. Bell, briefed by Blewitt, was able to show that many of the allegations were unfounded. He did not explain that this was because the reformers had assumed the printed annual reports contained accurate information. At the March meeting, Dilke scored a moral victory: 'allow me to ask Mr Bell whether he has any better authority for what he is saying than the printed statements of the Society? It is from those statements that the account given in the pamphlet was drawn up, with the assistance of the Secretary. If the figures are false, I am not responsible for that.' In fact Bell made a Herculean effort to make sense of the pre-Blewitt accounts. He confessed to Blewitt: 'I have spent hours and hours over some perplexities in the accounts . . . I have no means of reconciling the enigmas, or rather of solving the enigmas which have arisen in my progress.'

A Summary, published after the annual general meeting, was not wholly convincing. To the charge that the Royal Literary Fund spent £532 on distributing £1,225, Bell wrote 'the comparison of the expenditure with the sum distributed is false in principle, because the expenditure is incurred in the creation, and not the distribution of the Fund'.[39] To this Dickens was able to reply that the greater part of the Fund's income was self-creating, dividends paid to the bankers, subscriptions paid through standing orders, and receipts from legacies. The committee also denied that David Williams had ever intended to enlarge the scope of the Royal Literary Fund: 'Mr Williams lived in the house of the Society from 1805 to 1816 . . . with the most favourable opportunities to carry out these views, he never took a single step to establish a Hall or College'.[40] John Britton had testified in his *Autobiography* that Williams was living in the house of the Fund because he was sick and senile: 'almost the "slippered pantaloon", he was wheeled into the Committee-room, where he seemed to revive from a semi-lethargy . . . at all times the amiable Chairman kindly appealed to the Founder for his opinion, who never differed from that expressed or implied by the former'.[41] This was hardly the energetic radical, capable of reforming or enlarging an established institution.

After the meeting Dickens wrote ominously, 'it is as certain as Death, that they must either set their house in order, or fall without their house, or fall with it'.[42] But ten years later the cost of administration was unchanged; the council remained powerless, and the Fund continued to function as an unreformed, unrepentant charity. As a result of Dickens's onslaught, the conservatives on the committee succeeded in resisting all and any change. The Fund had to wait over a century for a new charter which, had Dickens's tactics been more subtle, it might have had in 1855. As for the fate of the reformers, several of the writers who had supported Dickens ended up applying to the Fund.

Dickens made one last attempt to reform the Fund. In March 1859, at the request of an anonymous philanthropist, he offered the Fund 'a magnificent Library . . . and the sum of Ten Thousand Pounds for its maintenance and enlargement in perpetuity . . . conditional on the Literary Fund's obtaining an amended charter, and rendering other services to Literature than those to which it is, in its practice, at present limited'. The committee did not feel disposed to be bribed in this way, especially as the library would not pass to the Fund until the death of its unknown owner. In fact the library belonged to Forster who left it instead to the Victoria and Albert Museum.

Dickens's friends, and some partisan biographers and historians have characterised his war with the Fund as one of professional middle-class writers against upper-class and aristocratic amateurs.[43] It was rather more complex than that. Dickens understood the value of aristocratic support as his efforts on behalf of the Guild make clear. In 1854 the council of the Guild (its management committee) boasted a duke, an earl, a baronet and two knights, compared to the Royal Literary Fund's marquess, two baronets and one knight. And though Dickens was supported by writers of humble origin such as Forster and Wills, he was also supported by Charles Wentworth Dilke and Edward Bulwer

Lytton who were no less gentlemanly than the Fund's Thackeray and Richard Monckton Milnes.

To suggest the reformers were somehow full-time while the Fund's authors were part-time is equally misleading. Robert Bell was a full-time professional editor, writer and journalist of thirty years standing; Thackeray was as voluminous an author as Dickens. Lytton, on the other hand, was a busy politician, and Forster abandoned journalism in 1855 – at the start of the campaign against the Fund – to become the salaried secretary of the Lunacy Commission. And among those 'professional' writers who remained neutral were Leigh Hunt, who had been helped by both Dickens and the Fund, and Thomas Carlyle, who subscribed five guineas in 1853 when the Fund gave his friend William Maccall a generous grant.

The main difference between the Dickensians and the Fund committee was in their choice of literary activity. There were few novelists or poets on the committee; the majority of its members were reputable writers of non-fiction: Henry Hallam, historian; Henry Reeve, *Times* leader writer and editor of the *Edinburgh Review*; William Smith, classicist and lexicographer; John Gough Nichols, antiquary and editor of the *Gentleman's Magazine*; P.M. Roget, scientific writer and compiler of the *Thesaurus*. The committee was undeniably establishment – the Headmaster of Charterhouse (Russell); the principal librarian of the British Museum (both Ellis and Panizzi); the Dean of Westminster (Stanley) and a cabinet minister (Cardwell) – but then committees are never anything else. There is certainly no evidence that any committee member, Thackeray included, plotted to diminish or contain the social aspirations of men of letters.

At the anniversary dinner of 1859 Thackeray alluded to the trouble Dickens had caused which had earned the Fund the nickname of the 'Rupture Society': 'Gentlemen, I do not know for what earthly reason people are perpetually flinging mud at us. It was not as a literary man, not merely as a writer of novels, that I came here, but as a supporter, as an admirer, and a cordial friend of this Society.' Unfortunately he too was prickly. In 1861 he took umbrage at an unintentional slight and resigned: 'At a dinner, where men of letters and their friends assemble, I don't choose to be made to sit at a side-table and to be forced to speak against my express desire. I will distribute my own little Literary Fund henceforth.' Thackeray died two years later and at the anniversary dinner of 1864 Anthony Trollope, who had just been elected to the committee, paid graceful tribute to his memory: 'I do not think that we yet know how great that man was'. Trollope also spoke at the anniversary dinner of 1871 where no allusion at all was made to the death of Charles Dickens.

It was left to Milnes, recently elevated to the peerage as Lord Houghton, to sum up his impression of the campaign for reform, when he presided over the dinner of 1866:

We had indeed one considerable storm. We got into conflict with a very important portion of the literary interest of England. That interest was headed by one of the most distinguished, one of the most disinterested, one of the most noble men of English Literature . . . Well, the issue of that conflict has been that we are as strong and as well as we ever were, and that we at least maintain our position. And now I shall be most happy to see all these wounds healed – all that difference forgotten; and that it should be clearly understood that any position we took, we did not take individually or even theoretically, but because we believed that acting on the old ways of this Society, we were doing what was best to enable us to get a large portion of the public to contribute to the necessities of the literature of England (cheers).

It was an involuntary admission that writers were still necessitous, and that their occupation was still uncommonly risky. However, in retrospect, it seems unlikely that a reformed Royal Literary Fund would have made the slightest difference. Trollope, Thackeray's successor as the Fund's celebrity novelist, drew a very un-Dickensian moral from his eighteen years on the committee: 'in that capacity I heard and saw much of the sufferings of authors . . . the experience I have acquired by being active in its cause forbids me to advise any young man or woman to enter boldly on a literary career in search of bread'.[44]

37

2

FROM PRISONS TO PENSIONS:
GRUB STREET AND ITS INSTITUTIONS

WILLIAM JERDAN, committee member of the Literary Fund and editor of the *Literary Gazette* for a third of a century, wrote of authors

That most have been steeped in poverty; that a few have barely contrived to subsist; that not one in a hundred, who were without private and extrinsic resources to fall back upon, have succeeded to the realisation of a moderate independence; and that, perhaps, one in five hundred, the exception to the rule, has reached a goal almost as satisfactory as he would have done had he been, with a tolerable capacity, a divine, a lawyer, or a physician.[1]

This picture of almost certain literary failure had been constantly before the aspirant author since the foundation of the Literary Fund. Every year at the anniversary dinner one of the speakers would draw attention to the foolishness of embarking on a literary career. And in almost any daily newspaper there would be an item about a decrepit author applying for poor relief or soliciting public charity. Literature itself, from D'Israeli's *Calamities of Authors* to Gissing's *New Grub Street*, could hardly have left the prospective author with any illusions.

But it is not easy to give up a sense of vocation, or visions of fame and fortune. The majority of writers accepted that literature was a lottery, but if the odds against success were high, the prizes – wealth and/or immortality – were worth the risk. Writers were, and are, literary speculators. Dostoyevsky's brilliant study of the psychology of the gambler also amounts to a study of the psychology of the author:

I would not leave Roulettenburg the same man as I arrived there; some radical and decisive change in my destiny will inevitably take place. It must and will. However comical it may be that I should expect to get so much out of roulette, the routine opinion, accepted by everybody, that it is absurd and silly to expect anything at all from gambling seems to me even funnier. . . . It is true that only one person in a hundred wins. But what do I care about that?[2]

More often than not, speculation leads to debt. However, writers' debts were only occasionally the result of extravagance. It is difficult to be extravagant on £100 a year. Most writers found themselves in debt because they could not earn enough to pay even modest bills. In all this, they were no different from the rest of the nineteenth-century poor, except that they were supposed to be able to equip themselves in the manner of other professions. This was a costly business and led to the pawnbroker, the bailiff, the sheriff's officer and the jail.

ALTHOUGH debt had been an imprisonable offence since the reign of Edward I, Thomas Dekker was the only famous writer to be imprisoned on such a charge until the eighteenth century. After 1700 as authorship began to establish itself as a paid activity so imprisonment for debt became an occupational hazard. No doubt scores of Grub Street hacks found themselves in and out of prison but the first notable writer debtor was Richard Savage. Savage lived 'within the liberties of the Fleet' in 1738 and died in 1743 in the Bristol Newgate where he had been imprisoned for a coffee house debt of eight pounds. Compared with the rest of his turbulent life he found his imprisonment relatively congenial. 'I enjoy myself with much more tranquillity than I have known for upwards of a twelvemonth past; having a room entirely to myself, and pursuing the amusement of my poetical studies, uninterrupted.'[3]

Samuel Johnson's *An Account of the Life of Mr Richard Savage* (1744) marks the beginning of over a century of literary references to debtors' prisons which culminate in the novels and biography of Charles Dickens. Johnson's Savage was followed by a spate of fictional accounts in which hardly a picaresque hero escapes imprisonment. The most important novels dealing with life in debtors' prisons, not least because of their influence on Dickens, were by Fielding and Smollett. Fielding, a Bow Street magistrate, set a large part of the action of *Amelia* (1751) in the debtors' side of Newgate and in a sponging house, a kind of grim hotel for debtors run by sheriffs' officers for their own profit. Smollett's heroes invariably ended up in debtors' prisons; Roderick Random was imprisoned in the Marshalsea in 1743, Peregrine Pickle in the Fleet and Count Fathom and Launcelot Greaves in the King's Bench. *Roderick Random* (1748) contains a prison episode which made a profound impression on the young Charles Dickens/David Copperfield. When visiting Micawber in prison, Copperfield remembers with 'dimmed eyes' and a 'beating heart' Roderick Random's encounter in the Marshalsea with a debtor who is naked but for an old rug. This half-starved, half-carpeted debtor turns out to be an author.

So many hacks were incarcerated in debtors' prisons during Smollett's day that the very title of author became synonymous with debt.

When Peregrine Pickle loses his fortune he turns to authorship to recoup it but he soon discovers that the fraternity of authors at liberty spend most of their time commiserating with 'those members who were confined in the prisons of the Fleet, Marshalsea, and King's Bench'.[4] In *Humphrey Clinker* (1771) a similar society of scribblers includes a stuttering hack who 'had almost finished his travels through Europe and part of Asia, without ever budging beyond the liberties of the King's Bench'.[5] The one distinguished author imprisoned for debt at this time was the poet Christopher Smart. He was imprisoned in the King's Bench in 1768 and died there, half-crazy and wholly drunk, in May 1771.

The laws which enabled creditors to imprison debtors were so tangled and convoluted that it took half the nineteenth century to unravel them. In theory the creditor, by arresting the debtor, could keep an eye on the debt and eventually obtain its recovery. The imprisoned debtor could attempt to satisfy the creditor by working – cobbling, sewing, writing – or by selling up, if the amount realised would be enough to settle the debt. Alternatively, debtors could declare themselves insolvent under the Insolvency Act as long as they could prove their indebtedness was unintentional. This obliged creditors to settle for the value of the debtor's worldly goods (not, of course, those that had been stashed away).

For many creditors, if the debt was small and the debtor unscrupulous, it was often better to accept the loss, rather than prosecute. Sir Samuel Romilly, a prime mover in the campaign to reform the law, noted that 'a debtor might, at the expense of five guineas to himself, put his creditor to the expense of £100; and for £24 and a fraction, oblige him to pay, in fees and expenses, above £300.'[6]

But usually it was the debtor who was the victim. It was quite possible to secure an arrest merely by alleging a debt. The scope for malice, extortion, revenge and profit was considerable. The writer and veteran debtor R.P. Gillies calculated the annual costs of arrest for debt were at least £2 million. By 1837 there were, according to Gillies, between 30,000 and 40,000 annual arrests for debt with a further 80,000 dependent relatives affected.[7] Arrest for debt was almost as common as twentieth-century parking fines.

The opponents of reform were all those who earned a prosperous living from the system. All the officials connected with the debtors' prisons received their incomes from fees extracted from the debtors. Lord Ellenborough, when Lord Chancellor, was an implacable enemy of reform, largely on the grounds that imprisonment for debt was self-financing; he had personally benefited from the system as Clerk to the Court of the King's Bench – earning some £9,625 a year in fees. It was graft from the Woolsack down to the turnkey.

In 1869, after a long and arduous campaign and much unnecessary misery, imprisonment for debt was abolished except for defaulting solicitors, trustees and debtors to the Crown. As with other important social questions writers were in the vanguard of reform. But on this question they were not merely committed sympathisers, they were very much among the victims. Dickens, whose first-hand experience of imprisonment for debt lasted from February to May 1824, when his father was in the Marshalsea, began his career as a novelist with an attack on debtors' prisons at the precise moment that reforming legislation was running into opposition in Parliament. So *Pickwick Papers*, a work of comic genius, was also one young writer's attempt to lobby for the Judgments Act of 1838, which was to prevent creditors from imprisoning debtors merely to insure their eventual appearance in court. Authors were very much among the beneficiaries of the Act. Between 1800 and 1838 over a hundred authors applied to the Literary Fund from debtors' prisons. After 1838 there were less than a dozen such applications.

The literary campaign was led by Robert Gillies. Gillies, who had first been imprisoned in the King's Bench in 1831, claimed the unusual distinction of having been arrested more than anyone else for the same debt. In August 1836 he published a King's Bench tale 'O'Hanlon and his Wife' in *Fraser's Magazine*. Sir John Campbell's proposed bill to reform the laws of debt had just been lost through the dissolution of Parliament. Gillies was imprisoned a second time in September 1836 and again from May 1837 to April 1838. In the summer of 1837 J.M. Kemble, editor of the *British and Foreign Review*, paid him £36 for a slashing attack on the existing laws, 'The Law of Debtor and Creditor'. On 15 July the *Athenaeum* published a long review of J.B. Bayle-Mouillard's *On Imprisonment for Debt* which unfavourably contrasted the British system with the more humane French laws. But undoubtedly the most influential literary attack on conditions in debtors' prisons was the Fleet number of *Pickwick Papers*, also published in July, which achieved a sale of 40,000 copies.[8]

Dickens's timing illustrates the propaganda value he attached to *Pickwick*. On 24 November the House of Lords gave the proposed legislation its first reading. At the second reading on 5 December the

41

Lord Chancellor confessed 'he did not believe that there were many persons who were not in the situation of either debtor or creditor'.[9] On 15 December the real Fleet debtors petitioned their lordships for the speedy passing of the bill. Six months later, on 14 June 1838, the Judgments Act became law and some 3,000 to 4,000 prisoners prepared for release. The *Edinburgh Review* commented 'the imprisonment of Pickwick affords an opportunity of depicting the interior of a debtors' prison, and the manifold evils of that system, towards the abolition of which much, we trust, will have been affected by a statute of the past session'.[10]

The battle was not quite over. The immediate effect of the Judgments Act was to reduce the prison population. The Fleet and the Marshalsea were shut down for lack of customers under the Queen's Prison Act of 1842, and the remaining debtors were transferred to the Queen's Prison at Southwark or to Whitecross Street. From 1842 to 1869 debtors were treated much as other criminals in Victorian penitentiaries; imprisonment had lost its careless side.

Dickens was twelve years old when his father was imprisoned in the Marshalsea and nineteen when he passed through the Insolvency Court a second time. Many of his friends and acquaintances, including fellow writers, had similar experiences. From the Fleet chapters of *Pickwick Papers*, through the more relaxed King's Bench scenes in *David Copperfield* to the depiction in *Little Dorrit* of the Marshalsea prison as a whole sordid world, debt and its consequences was a recurring theme in his novels.

Debtors' prisons were a major part of the social landscape. They were the bane of writers and the stuff of fiction. The experience of the one provided the material for the other. Below Dickens there was a sub-genre of debtors' fiction, now of sociological rather than literary interest. Among the better-known writers who tackled the subject were Charles Rowcroft in *Chronicles of the Fleet Prison* (1844), Charles Whitehead in *Richard Savage* (1842) and W.H. Ainsworth, G.W.M. Reynolds, Theodore Hook, G.P.R. James, Pierce Egan and Douglas Jerrold. Almost every low-life novel up to the 1860s had its debtors' prison scene, as did many of the early Victorian novels on the popular theme of disputed inheritance.

The most famous fictional account of an author in prison is in *Pendennis*, where Thackeray portrays his old mentor William Maginn as the irrepressible Charley Shandon. Maginn was an inveterate debtor, quite outside the scope of the Judgments Act. He was first imprisoned in the Fleet in the summer of 1839. E.V. Kenealy, friend and biographer of Maginn, wrote: 'From this time until 1840, the condition of Maginn was one of wretchedness. . . . He was arrested and thrown into jail . . . yet in all his misfortunes he retained his serenity of mind.'[11] And just as Shandon busily scribbled 'slashing articles' for the *Pall Mall Gazette* from prison, so Maginn carried on his connection with *Fraser's*.

Maginn's second period of imprisonment in 1842 was altogether a more sombre affair than Shandon's. Lockhart, allowing for poetic licence, draws a credible picture of the broken-down soak:

> But at last he was beat, and sought help of the bin,
> (All the same to the Doctor, from claret to gin),
> Which led swiftly to gaol, with consumption therein.

Drink may have confused Maginn's affairs but it was literature that ruined him: 'In the early part of 1842 Dr Maginn was thrown into prison for the expenses incurred by the publication of the ten numbers of his 'Miscellanies' . . . Here [in the Fleet] he continued to write for *Fraser* and the newspapers.'[12] Unlike Shandon, Maginn was not released through the generosity of his publisher but through a degrading appearance before the Insolvency Court.

Maginn's efforts to clear his debts and to provide something for his family by writing were typical of imprisoned authors. Although many authors managed to write themselves into prison through debts to printers and stationers, few succeeded in writing themselves out again. Indeed the consequence of authorship in prison was often further debts.

Robert Huish was a contemporary of Micawber's in the King's Bench. A bookseller's hack, Huish blamed his publisher for his frequent imprisonment. In 1824 he was imprisoned 'at the suit of the late John Debrett'[13] for an alleged debt of £20. If Huish's story is to be believed, Debrett had introduced him to the publisher Thomas Kelly who promptly commissioned him to write a popular biography of Princess Charlotte for £3 per 24-page number. When the work appeared, Debrett demanded an agent's commission of £90 which Huish refused to pay. Both parties submitted to arbitration which found in Debrett's favour. Huish managed to pay £75 but was arrested by Debrett for the remainder in 1819. When Debrett died intestate in 1822 Huish was released from the King's Bench, but he was soon re-arrested by Debrett's creditors for £15 plus costs. Meanwhile Thomas Kelly had been making a fortune on the *Memoirs of Princess Charlotte* amounting, so Huish claimed, to some £30,000.

While in prison, Huish, like John Dickens, had a wife and five
children to support although, unlike John Dickens, he did not have an
income of £6 a week. Instead, perhaps encouraged by the success of *John
Bull*, which Theodore Hook was editing within the rules of the King's
Bench, he attempted to support his family by launching his own
magazine:

he was induced to enter upon the Publication on his own Account of a periodical
work entitled The Sabbath . . . instead of turning out a profitable concern, it has
been the cause of considerable loss, and has reduced him to a state of complete
Indigence. That having carried on the work to 18 numbers entirely written by
himself, the copies unsold were taken under a distress for rent and sold as Waste
Paper [July 1824].

As others had found before him, so Huish found that 'the Mind
absorbed in the Reflection of this destitute Condition, loses that Tone
and Vigor which are so requisite for literary labor'.

A prerequisite for authorship was peace and quiet. If they could
afford to, most authors preferred to live within the rules rather than be
locked up in prison. The 'rules' referred to an area extending in
circumference for two and a half miles around the prison where debtors
could live free from arrest upon paying a few guineas as security, or a
fixed percentage of their debts, whichever was the larger. It gave them a
temporary respite from creditors (although they still ran the risk of
incurring new debts to their landlords) and provided marginally better
conditions for continuing with their authorship. William Combe wrote
most of *Dr Syntax* while living within the rules of the King's Bench, and
Eliza Parsons wrote a four-volume novel. William Hone completed his
Every Day Book while lodging with a tobacconist in Suffolk Street. When
Theodore Hook was imprisoned in Hemp's Sponging House, a 'vile,
squalid place, noisy and noxious, apparently almost inaccessible either
to air or light, swarming with a population of thief-catchers, gin-sellers,
and worse', he was unable to write a line. But when, in April 1824, he
was released into the rules of the King's Bench he entered on 'the busiest
period of his literary career'[14] as editor of *John Bull*.

The priority of imprisoned authors was to avoid sharing or 'chum-
ming' with other prisoners. Thomas Ashe wrote to the Literary Fund in
1810:

The *Bench* is so crowded that there are from three to six persons in a Room; therefore,
instead of enjoying that calm which I contemplated with so much hope, I find I have
to live in a Storm; in a Whirlwind which blots out the intellects, and destroys and
dissipates the works of the imagination and the light of the mind. – And yet there is a

way of obtaining a *Separate Apartment*, and of enjoying all that leisure and serenity which are essential to literary pursuits. . . . by paying persons a certain Sum per Week to quit an Apartment and provide for themselves elsewhere.

Ashe required a guinea a week for the purpose. Once installed in his 'very elegant and convenient chamber'[15] he was able to settle down to editing the *Phoenix* at a salary of 3 guineas a week. Over the next six months he claimed to have ghost written a pamphlet on the state of Ireland for Sir J.J.W. Jervis, a work on political reform for W.H. Yate, and a history of the Azores. He also obtained £50 from his creditor for agreeing not to publish a scurrilous satire against him. In all he reckoned he had earned over £700 through literary work.

Not all writers were so fortunate or so brazen. Thomas Kibble Hervey, later editor of the *Athenaeum*, was imprisoned in the Queen's Bench for nearly two years from 1837 to 1838. Although he managed to afford a room, he could not afford to furnish it. A visitor wrote:

I was much shocked to see him in a room totally unfurnished (the person from whom he had hired a few necessary articles having removed them because he could not pay the arrears that were due for the use of them) and also to learn that he had been in that state for ten days, obliged, for want of a bed, to pass the nights in a chair which, together with a table, had been lent to him by a fellow-prisoner, without money, and almost without necessities of life.[16]

The worst prison for writers was Whitecross Street. Built in 1815 it had common wards instead of individual rooms. The prison inspectors thought that 'the crying evil of Whitecross-Street prison is that the well-disposed debtor, when so inclined, has no means of protecting himself from association with the depraved'.[17] It was certainly difficult for the author. Gillies was imprisoned in Whitecross Street from May 1848 to August 1849:

as to writing books, I had not a moment of solitude or peace night nor day, to collect my thoughts, and could not finish a coherent page. Besides, if I laid papers on any of the tables (which were all common), this, of course, was voted a bore, and if I turned off my eyes for a moment, they were liable to be seized and hidden by some facetious fellow-prisoner. . . . A little gasp of quiet, however, was allowed me even in that prison, where, by chance, one morning I got possession of what was called the fever-ward, or 'dead-room'. . . . It was a garret, from a window of which a prisoner had thrown himself not long before, his body being smashed on the pavement beneath.[18]

Despite the considerable amount written in debtors' prisons – including Gothic novels by Mrs Parsons, political economy by Thomas Ashe and William Playfair, poems by Thomas Dermody and T.K. Hervey, plays by George Soane and T.J. Dibdin (who owed over £17,000), and journalism by Maginn and Gillies – none of it was very memorable, not nearly as memorable as the literature about debtors' prisons. It is not hard to see why. Authors imprisoned for political reasons for a fixed period of time, such as Leigh Hunt and Thomas Cooper, managed to write some of their most successful work in the prison cell. Authors in debtors' prisons, however, had no idea when they would get out and were obsessed and oppressed with financial worries. Gillies's prison writings clearly demonstrate the overriding concerns of the indebted author. In 1837–8, while he was in the Queen's Bench, he wrote three general articles for *Fraser's*. Other than this, Gillies's entire prison opus for that year consisted of prison literature – an article on the law of debtor and creditor for the *British and Foreign Review*; a pamphlet 'Legality and Illegality of Arrest for Debt'; a letter to Lord Lyndhurst on the same subject, and a 'Petition of the Prisoners for Debt in the Queen's Bench'. When he published his three-volume autobiography in 1851, almost the entire third volume was devoted to scenes of prison life.

One of the last writers to be imprisoned was Elizabeth Hardy. Her story serves as an appropriately pathetic conclusion to the literature of debt. Born in Dublin in 1786, she inherited a small income which she invested in a joint-stock bank which failed. Most of the little she had left was then embezzled by her solicitor, and so, in 1830, she turned to authorship. She published four novels totalling eight volumes between 1831 and 1845, none of which made her any money. In 1848 she began to write what was intended to be her masterpiece, a fictional account of the life of Owen Glendower, 'while writing Owen Glendower I gave myself to research . . . I lived – alas! for the *ideal* – I forgot reality. Difficulties pressed me hard – I had recourse to Irish bills of exchange.' Pressed by her creditors Hardy was obliged to conclude a not very favourable contract with Richard Bentley for half-profits on an edition of 500. Only 250 copies were sold and Hardy was left with a debt of £5 for her share of the production costs. Her creditors were unwilling to allow her to begin work on another 'bestseller', and in 1852 she was arrested and imprisoned in the Queen's Prison for debts totalling £280. The Literary Fund granted her £40 which was seized by her creditors. She died in prison two years later. At the coroner's inquest, her pitiful attempts to continue her writing were reported with melancholy exactness:

Eliza Tyler, a nurse, said she had attended the deceased on and off for the last two years. She never complained of being ill-used by any one, and she had every necessity in the prison. She had a pint of brandy allowed to her at a time . . . William Gore Pearce, a debtor, and inmate of the prison, said he had known the deceased for some years. . . . His impression was that her death was produced by her age, debility, and the length of her confinement. She would be up before daylight, writing as an authoress, and would frequently sit up to a late hour at night engaged in a similar way.[19]

Needless to say, none of Elizabeth Hardy's prison writings were published.

In *The Vanity of Human Wishes* (1749) Johnson sums up the prospects of the eighteenth-century writer, 'Toil, envy, want, the patron and the jail'. While imprisonment for debt was commonplace, patronage – even in the age of Johnson – was rare. The bookseller had, in most cases, taken over from the patron as the author's paymaster and taskmaster. However, the poor yet talented poet whose works were unattractive to booksellers, could still expect to be encumbered with patronage. Of the authors who applied to the Fund before 1800, the careers of Thomas Dermody and S.T. Coleridge best illustrate the hazards of unremunerative and erratically patronised authorship.

Thomas Dermody, 'the Irish Chatterton', provides a striking example of the failure of private patronage to benefit an author. Dermody was born in County Clare in 1775, the eldest son of a tipsy schoolmaster. At the age of nine he became assistant classics master at his father's school; the following year he ran away to Dublin. There he met Robert Houlton, author and physician, who was so impressed by the boy's knowledge of Homer and Horace that he took him in to live with his family. Under Houlton's roof Dermody became a spoilt party performer, dazzling the dinner guests with his Horatian renderings and classical compositions. Houlton's patronage, however, did not last. He left Dublin without making any adequate provision for Dermody, who, at the age of eleven, found himself once more on the streets. He met his next patron, the actor Robert Owenson, through frequent visits backstage at the Theatre Royal. Owenson's son had just died and Dermody became a replacement playmate for Owenson's daughters, the eldest of whom was later to become the popular novelist Lady Morgan. Although Owenson was kind to Dermody he treated him with a curious lack of judgment. J.G. Raymond, Dermody's biographer, records: 'Mr Owenson always introduced him in rags, that his appearance might excite both wonder and compassion'.[20] In 1798 Owenson sent his infant prodigy to board at the Rev. Gilbert Austin's school. A year later Austin collected £150 from subscribers to Dermody's first collected book of poems, a significant sum for a fourteen year old poet.

It would seem that his better star had now the ascendant, had he but known how to estimate the value of his situation. . . . He had the opportunity of acquiring the most polished manners, from the elegant company of both sexes resorting to the house of Mr Austin; of forming connections, though not numerous, among the sons of some of the first families in the kingdom placed there for their education; and of cultivating his taste for literature under a kind and able preceptor. His days, for a considerable time, were thus spent in the happiest manner; and his evenings were generally devoted to the circles of taste and fashion, for it became the rage of the day to have 'the little poet' at all the parties of any style or consequence.[21]

But the little poet was insufficiently grateful for this munificent pampering and preferred the company of the riff-raff he met on the streets and in the Dublin taverns. Too much patronage had already taught him to despise his patrons. When Austin discovered that he had been made the subject of a satirical squib by Dermody, his anger was Olympian. He destroyed all the printed copies of Dermody's poems, returned the entire £150 to the subscribers, publicly denounced his former protégé as a 'monster of ingratitude' and peremptorily expelled him from school and shelter.

Without patrons Dermody had only one recourse – to sell his facile writing skills in the literary market-place. He became a hack writer for a Dublin newspaper. He did not have to remain long on the paper for, rediscovered by Owenson, he was introduced to 'the glory of her country', the dowager Countess of Moira. She patronised him at arm's length, buying his clothes and books and sending him to a country school to complete his education. But Dermody's antipathy to the schoolroom had been confirmed by his experience of Dublin lowlife. Despite Lady Moira's threats he left the country school for the city tavern in high spirits:

> If to old Lory's you repair
> To tipple off the fortnight's care
> Still Tom shall steal upon you there
>   And prompt each wish:
> Tom, that would smoke like a lord-mayor
>   Drink like a fish.[22]

Lady Moira wrote icily: 'As Dermody has thought proper to withdraw himself from her direction and protection in a manner equally ungracious and absurd, Lady Moira informs him that the donation which accompanies this note is the last attention or favour that he is ever to expect from Lady Moira, or any of her family.'[23] Tom then repaired to old Lory's with her gift of ten guineas and drank like a fish until his debt to the landlord forced him to work at 'a little fugitive lucubration for a magazine'. When he was not writing to order, he sent begging letters to his former patrons, usually enclosing a panegyric on their personal qualities which nearly always elicited a few guineas accompanied by some finger shaking. One of his patrons, Edward Tighe, tried to bribe him to write for the temperance cause. Instead he wrote a pamphlet on 'The Rights of Justice, or Rational Liberty', hailing the French Revolution and praising the storming of the Bastille.

At the outbreak of war with France, Dermody was able to realise his greatest ambition, to travel to England. He enlisted in 1794 and crossed the Irish Channel as Sergeant Thomas Dermody, aged nineteen. The company of young men of his own age and inclinations, combined with military discipline as opposed to the discipline of the schoolroom, seems to have been to Dermody's liking. His comparative success in the army was noticed by the Commander-in-Chief, the Earl of Moira, Lady Moira's son. Moira had Dermody gazetted a second lieutenant and he was to spend the next four years fighting the French. He returned to England sometime in 1799, battle-scarred but pensioned on the half-pay list. For the first time in his life he had a small but regular income that was free from the strings of patronage. It was just enough money to enable him to appreciate the camaraderie of the London underworld, and his transition from poet to rake was complete.

In 1800 at the intervention of J.G. Raymond, who was shocked by Dermody's way of life, the booksellers Vernor and Hood brought out a two-volume edition of his poems. It was the first time his work had been published in London and for a brief period Dermody had to leave his den in London's notorious Strutton-ground and walk around in a new suit of clothes. But the renewed celebrity his poems brought him drove him once more underground. His life was now set in a cycle of poverty, patronage, and debauch. By 1800 he was a beggarly rake; scribbling letters and poems to any rich man who might be touched by his appeal. In this way he managed to live off the guineas sent him by – among others – Moira, Henry Addington and Sir James Bland Burges, whose epic poem *Richard the First* in eighteen books, earned Dermody's most extravagant praise:

> Lo! from the ruins of the 'mighty dead'
> Once more English Genius lifts his head
> Britain once more with partial transport views
> Th'appropriate honours of the epic muse.[24]

In May 1800 Dermody addressed a sonnet to the subscribers of the Literary Fund, 'Oh! may a young advent'rer woo your aid'.[25] It was accompanied by a letter which made it clear that he regarded the Literary Fund as existing to respect the rights of authors: 'Individual patronage, however munificent, must appear casual and confined, when compared to the liberality of a fund open to the appeal of every embarrassed child of Merit, unbiassed by the narrow views of party, and unalterable through deviation of sentiment or critical opinion.' Pye and Fitzgerald reported on Dermody's literary claim and recommended him for a grant. He was awarded 10 guineas – the kind of sum he was, at this stage in his career, accustomed to spend in a fortnight in the company of his Strutton-ground friends. Other grants followed despite the one-year rule of the Fund. By December 1800 he had received 20 guineas, quite enough by the standards of the day to keep an artisan, his wife and four children in relative comfort over a six month period. In March 1801, at the recommendation of Burges, Dermody was awarded another 20 guineas which he managed to lose or spend in a week before bursting into Burges's library 'literally in rags, [he] was covered with mud, had a black eye, and a fresh wound on his head from which blood trickled down his breast; and, to crown the whole, was so drunk as to be hardly able to stand or speak'.[26] Burges gave him yet more money and discharged his debts. His case was once again brought before the Literary Fund who granted him a further sum of 10 guineas making a total of 50 guineas in a year, a respectable salary. Unfortunately Dermody thought that in Sir James he had found a source of income that would never dry up; he became so importunate that the irate baronet shut him out of his house.

In June 1802 Raymond discovered Dermody living in wretched poverty. He immediately raised a subscription to which Moira and Burges each contributed £10. But the total subscriptions barely covered Dermody's debts and he was anyway too ill with malnutrition, alcoholism and other, unspecified, consequences of dissipation for the money to be of any use. He died on 15 July and the Literary Fund paid his funeral expenses.

Raymond's biography of Dermody was written with the cooperation of the Fund. On its publication many poor authors applying for grants could not restrain their jealousy. The Rev. David Rivers, on being awarded a grant of 3 guineas, wrote in frantic indignation, 'In perusing lately the life of Dermody, an Irish poet as written by Mr Raymond I find that he received in no less than two years the enormous sum of £56

. . . tears of indignation start from my eyes – God of mercy – shalt thou bestow thy blessings on the debauched and extravagant whilst thou sufferest the Literary man with a Family to die with want.'

Undoubtedly Dermody was self-destructive; he was neither prudent nor enough of an opportunist to build on his good fortune. By his own admission he preferred shillings to pounds because they jingled prettily in his pocket. All his weaknesses were magnified by indiscriminate patrons who, shuddering at the monster of pride and ingratitude they had created, left him to sink in the slum of his choice.

The year Dermody applied to the Fund, David Williams wrote in *Claims of Literature*, 'Patronage is the price of an unfortunate man's liberty; it is the prerogative of insolence and outrage; it is despotic sovereignty over an abject dependent, whose abuses are, to the last degree, humiliating and oppressive', and he described patrons as 'half-learned, demi-connoisseurs open to gross flattery on account either of birth, fortune, or other circumstances, which neither bestow, nor exclude, talents, virtue, or merit'.[27] George Crabbe, himself no stranger to patronage, best described the duties of a poet towards his patrons:

> The real favourites of the great are they
> Who to their views and wants attention pay
> And pay it for ever.[28]

Although the writings of Thomas Dermody were deservedly well known, he suffered every indignity from exploitation to imprisonment. His fate was not uncommon. Most authors had similar experiences and even the very best, like Coleridge, had moments of hardship. But Coleridge was never bankrupt, imprisoned or destitute and although he undoubtedly deserved his modest material success he was also, by the standards of the time, very lucky.

Like Dermody, Coleridge was left without parents at the age of nine. Unlike Dermody he did not have to fend for himself; he was sent to Christ's Hospital School and then to Cambridge. He was a precocious boy, though no prodigy, and his relatively normal youth was free from patronage. He enlisted in the army at the same time as Dermody but was an indifferent soldier and, moreover, a pacifist. Like Dermody he was an addict – of opium rather than alcohol – and his addiction excused his shortcomings.

'Money and immediate reputation form only an arbitrary and accidental end of literary labour'[29] Coleridge wrote in 1816, and although he was often paid reasonable sums for his poetry his annual

51

income was largely made up of donations and annuities from his friends. De Quincey summed up Coleridge's ability to survive his lack of private means:

If, generally speaking, poor Coleridge had but a small share of earthly prosperity, in one respect at least, he was eminently favoured by Providence; beyond all men who ever perhaps lived, he found means to engage a constant succession of most faithful friends; and he levied the services of sisters, brothers, daughters, sons, from the hands of strangers – attracted to him by no possible impulses but those of reverence for his intellect, and love of his gracious nature.[30]

The catalogue of Coleridge's faithful friends begins with Joseph Cottle who loaned him £5 when he first arrived in Bristol in 1795 and ends with John Hookham Frere who gave him £100 a year from 1830 onwards.

1796 was the first year of real hardship for Coleridge. He was twenty-six years old, had just married and had very little money; nevertheless with a loan from Cottle he founded the magazine the *Watchman* which ceased publication after only ten issues. He found himself about £40 in debt to Cottle and £5 in debt to his printer Nathaniel Biggs.

His friend Thomas Poole set about raising a subscription on Coleridge's behalf. He persuaded a few friends to contribute 5 guineas each to an annuity which continued until 1798. At the same time as Poole's fund-raising activities, James Martin, MP for Tewkesbury and a friend of David Williams, wrote to the Literary Fund:

Having been informed, that Mr Coleridge, a man of genius and learning is in extreme difficulties, proceeding from a sick family, his wife being ready to lie in, and his mother in law whom he has supported, being, as is supposed, on her death bed, I undertake to lay his case before you. Mr Coleridge is of that description of persons, who fall within the notice of your benevolent Institution. He is a man of undoubted talents, though his works have been unproductive, and, though he will in future be able to support himself by his own industry, he is at present quite unprovided for, being of no profession [13 May 1796].

Coleridge was awarded 10 guineas, enough to enable him to pay off his printer's bill. On 10 June he wrote a letter of acknowledgment promising that 'in happier circumstances I shall be proud to remember the obligation'. He never felt quite happy enough to express his pride.

As a result of his difficulties with the *Watchman*, Coleridge's circumstances – his 'lack of profession' – attracted the practical sympathies of his friends, and he succeeded in turning a £5 deficit into a £30 or £40 profit. The money he owed Cottle for helping him establish the *Watchman* was never repaid. Having overcome his temporary difficulties, Coleridge went to Nether Stowey in December to live under the protection of Thomas Poole, and to cultivate vegetables instead of fastidious subscribers to a motley newspaper.

In 1798 Josiah and Thomas Wedgwood offered Coleridge £150 a year to enable him to devote his time to poetry and philosophy instead of becoming a Unitarian minister. By 1802 Coleridge was giving most of the Wedgwood annuity to his estranged wife, but other private gifts together with his journalism kept him solvent. In 1800 he had become a professional journalist writing for the *Morning Post* for a few guineas a week. Coleridge claimed that Daniel Stuart, the proprietor, was so pleased with the quality of his contributions that he offered him shares in the paper worth £2,000 a year. However he declined the offer, telling Poole: 'beyond £250 a year, I considered money as a real Evil'.[31]

In 1804 Coleridge became private secretary to the British High Commissioner in Malta which led to the lucrative, though temporary post of acting Public Secretary. This was the only professional appointment Coleridge ever held and he did not enter it with any great enthusiasm. By September 1805 he was on his travels again, returning to England in the summer of 1806. From then on he lived in the homes of his friends, earning a patchy living by journalism, poetry and lectures. His poetry brought him fair rewards by the standards of the time, £80 for 'Christabel' for example, but he could not compete for the growing popular market. His work, however much admired by his fellow poets, was esoteric and not worth anything like the £3,000 John Murray paid Byron for the first five cantos of *Don Juan* or Crabbe for his *Tales of the Hall*.

Frequent illnesses, opium addiction and an impractical metaphysical disposition handicapped Coleridge's ability to earn his living by his pen. That time of literary self-sufficiency which he and James Martin had looked forward to in 1796 never arrived. He was always dependent on the generosity and goodwill of his friends. De Quincey gave him £350, Basil Montagu paid for his son's education and even Wordsworth lent him money. But such support was haphazard: it depended on an identifiable crisis. One such major crisis occurred in 1816.

Since 1810 he had been living with the family of John Morgan, a retired lawyer who acted as his unpaid amanuensis. But in 1815, half way through the composition of *Biographia Literaria*, the Morgans, heavily in debt, were forced to give up their London home for a cottage at Calne in Wiltshire. Coleridge went with them, completing *Biographia Literaria* at the end of the year. He was impatient to realise a profit on the work, the more so as his future with the Morgans was uncertain. It came as an unpleasant shock to be told by his printer J.M. Gutch that because of a miscalculation of pagination he had to write an extra 150 pages. Under these circumstances Coleridge felt he needed the moral support of financial assistance. He wrote to Gutch on 25 January to ask him for the names of the secretaries of the Literary Fund. On hearing of his difficulties, William Sotheby, an old friend who also happened to be on the council of the Fund, wrote to sponsor his application. On 14 February Coleridge was granted £30. At exactly the same time Byron sent him £100. Byron's handsome gift displayed the weakness of the Literary Fund: although patronised by dukes it could not compete with the private patronage of even the poorest lord. The Fund's grant was undoubtedly useful, but it was far from being vital. On 15 April Coleridge found himself a new home, doctor and family at the same moment, when Dr James Gillman accepted him as an honoured guest at his house in Highgate. John Morgan became an inmate of a debtors' prison.

Coleridge's last years were spent under the care and kindness of Gillman and his wife. He was not entirely without financial worries and in 1819 he lost heavily by the bankruptcy of his publisher Rest Fenner. However, in 1824 George IV gave 1,000 guineas to the Royal Society of Literature for the benefit of ten associates, who were, in effect, literary pensioners; Coleridge, together with Thomas Malthus and William Roscoe were among the authors who received 100 guineas a year. The pensions were discontinued on the accession of the philistine William IV but Coleridge's was kept up by John Hookham Frere who had long admired his work.

In 1850, after the publication of Leigh Hunt's autobiography, there was a correspondence in *The Times* relating to Coleridge's habit of 'availing himself of eleemosynary aid on all sides'.[32] The charge was vigorously denied by his son Derwent, who wrote that 'whatever pecuniary aid he at any time received was from private friends, who held themselves indebted to him in a way and to an extent which money could neither measure nor repay'. While inaccurate, the defence is substantially correct. Although Coleridge had received assistance from the Literary Fund on two pressing occasions, he could have done without it thanks to the generosity of his friends. Moreover his pension from the Royal Society of Literature was no more than he deserved and considerably less than the Civil List pension of £300 a year granted to Dermody's old playmate Lady Morgan. The striking difference between Coleridge and his friends – De Quincey, Wordsworth, Byron, Montagu – was money: they all had private incomes, he did not.

COLERIDGE had been able to take advantage of two newly founded authors' societies: the Literary Fund (1790) and the Royal Society of Literature (1823). This latter society was almost universally despised. William Jerdan of the *Literary Gazette* and Literary Fund committee took the lion's share of the credit for founding the society. With James Christie, another Literary Fund committee member, he assiduously canvassed support for a society devoted to the 'advancement' of literature. Thomas Burgess, Bishop of St David's, accepted the presidency in 1823 and secured the patronage of George IV. Scott was approached but characteristically refused to have anything to do with the enterprise – 'Let men of letters fight their own way with the public.'[33] According to Jerdan, the King told the Bishop of St David's that 'he knew Scott very well, and that where he did not lead he was not much inclined to co-operate, and far less to follow'.[34] Younger writers were just as antipathetic as Scott. Macaulay wrote in *Knight's Quarterly Magazine*, 'To be the most absurd institution among so many institutions is no small distinction; it seems however to belong to the Royal Society of Literature.'[35]

The two objects of the society were to 'reward literary merit' and 'excite literary talent'. The rewarding of merit was in part achieved through George IV's generous annual donation of 1,000 guineas, though apart from Coleridge and Malthus the other eight 'royal associates' were worthy and dull and are now forgotten. James Hogg, the Ettrick Shepherd, failed in his bid to be nominated; Sir William Ouseley, Persian scholar, whose brother Sir Gore was a vice president of the society, succeeded. The second object – the exciting of literary talent – was achieved by awarding a prize of 50 guineas for the best poem on the subject of Dartmoor. It was won by Mrs Hemans out of seven entries. After the accession of William IV in 1830, the Royal Society of Literature lost its patron and its pretentions, and became a transaction society noted for its harmless, if tedious, antiquarian and philological proceedings.

Because of the failure of the Royal Society of Literature to live up to its name there were repeated attempts to found a literary institution that would offer tangible benefits to all members – not just those who were bankrupt or decrepit. In part these were all attempts to improve the contractual terms between authors and publishers. Walter Besant noted in his account of the ill-fated Society of British Authors of 1843, 'Unfortunately a profound ignorance of everything connected with their own trade, such as the cost of printing, paper, binding, advertising, and wholesale prices, made the murmurings of authors as useless as the rolling of distant thunder.'[36]

The attempt to found a Society of British Authors followed closely on the failure of the Milton Institute, a literary union proposed by Charles Mackay and others in 1842 as 'an association, in which authors, journalists, and critics might meet daily for natural support and assistance in the battle of life'.[37] Mackay seems to have forgotten that there was no shortage of clubs for literary men in London. The Literary Union Club founded by Thomas Campbell and Cyrus Redding in 1831 had much the same aims as the Milton Institute, though its members were only interested in the extent of its club facilities – it became the Clarence with premises in the West End. Also in 1831 several members of the Literary Fund including Jerdan and R.H. Barham founded the Garrick to enable men of culture to take daily pleasure in each other's company.

Both the Milton Institute and the Society of British Authors failed because authors could not agree on the fundamentals so necessary to the success of professional associations, such as collective responsibility. Authors were a disunited body of vain and self-seeking individualists who lacked leadership. As Besant put it, 'In every new society it is one man, and one man alone, who at the outset determines the success and the future of the association. It is one man who rules, infuses spirit, collects ideas, orders the line of march, lays down the policy, and thinks for the society.' For ninety-four years, between Williams's Literary Fund of 1790 and Besant's Society of Authors of 1884, the literary profession lacked a practical champion. John Robertson, who had been sub-editor of the *Westminster Review* under J.S. Mill, was the moving spirit behind the Society of British Authors and did not possess the intellectual calibre and dogged determination of a Williams or Besant. About the only author who might have pulled the profession of letters together was Dickens. But he found novel writing too time-consuming and his efforts on behalf of his fellow writers were random and part-time, as demonstrated by the failure of the Guild of Literature and Art, discussed later in this chapter.

If authors lacked a society, the founding of charitable funds to which they could apply continued apace – sometimes as a direct result of the example of the Literary Fund. The first benevolent organisation to follow the pattern set by the Fund was the grandly named National Benevolent Institution (NBI) founded in 1812 by Peter Hervé, an obscure miniature painter.[38] Hervé wrote to David Williams in 1813 'I have long felt desirous of meeting you, being myself engaged in . . . the alleviation of distress among the middle Ranks of people in general'. This amounted to the award of small annual pensions to impoverished gentlefolk over the age of sixty. Pensions varied in value from £12 to £30, the higher sums going to older pensioners. By 1850 there were 230 pensioners costing the NBI £5,000 a year. The subscribers to the NBI, who included Byron, were entitled to buy pensions for their protégés. One benefactress, Mrs Partis of Bath, gave 1,000 guineas to the Institution which bought her the right to 'elect' five pensioners. One of her nominees for 1828 was Catherine Hyde, the Marchioness Solari. She was the widow of a Venetian nobleman, an attendant of Marie Antoinette and the author of a series of court memoirs published by Henry Colburn. This lady was imprisoned on several occasions for small debts and was a frequent applicant to the Literary Fund. She was an NBI pensioner for at least fifteen years. Camilla Toulmin met her in 1843 and was entranced by her Napoleonic anecdotes. Claiming to be ninety-five years old, 'the one-time companion of princes now lived in rather humble lodgings near Fitzroy Square'.[39]

If authors were poor and well-bred they could apply to the NBI for a pension. That few did so may be a reflection on their breeding, though it is more likely that the NBI's system of election and public notification of results was too much for their self-esteem. Among the authors who swallowed their pride in return for a pension were John Watkins, historian and one-time editor of the *New Monthly Magazine*, and an obscure but genteel poetess Sarah Burdett, daughter of Sir Charles Burdett Bt. The radical William Hone applied for election but died before he could be turned down and William Godwin's widow was rejected.

One of the NBI's first committee members was the auctioneer James Christie who seems to have been one of the busiest committee men in London. He joined the Literary Fund in 1800 and became its registrar; he was a co-founder of the Royal Society of Literature; was elected to the Dilettante Society and the Athenaeum Club, and in 1810 helped to establish the Artists' Benevolent Fund whose anniversary dinner he chaired in 1812. The Artists' Benevolent Fund owed its existence to a destitute engraver named Tagg who was thrown out of his lodgings for non-payment of rent.[40] A fellow engraver, Edward Scriven, set about raising a subscription for his relief. The success of the Tagg fund led Scriven to propose a general benevolent fund for artists. The first meeting was held on 10 January 1810 with Valentine Green, Keeper of the British Institution, portrait painter and mezzotint engraver, in the chair. Green provided another link with the Literary Fund as six years earlier he had been awarded the large sum of £30 when in temporary financial difficulties. Indeed until 1810, the Literary Fund was the first recourse for artists whose work had also been printed, including two academicians – James Barry and William Hodges – as well as less famous artists and engravers. Even after 1810 artists who were also writers, notably B.R. Haydon and the water-colourist W.H. Pyne, were helped by the Fund.

The extension of the Literary Fund to allow applications from artists was confirmed by the charter of 1818 which defined eligible applicants as 'persons of genius and learning'. Scientists as well as artists benefited from this catch-all phrasing. Just as the venerable Royal Society had once admitted literary men to its Fellowship so the Literary Fund, at rather more cost, accepted applications from poor scientists. In the first half of the century mathematicians were particularly favoured: grants were given to James Glenie FRS, John Hind, John Radford Young, and to the émigré mathematicians Theophilus Holdred and Hoehne Wronski. Other scientists who posed as indigent authors included John Millington, Professor of Mechanics at the Royal Institution, chemist and inventor William Nicholson and Stephen Lee, Secretary of the Royal Society. Several Fellows of the Royal Society were among the most active members of the Literary Fund committee, including Francis Baily, founder and President of the Royal Astronomical Society; Sir Roderick Murchison, President of the Royal Geographical Society and the British Association; P.M. Roget, Secretary of the Royal Society; George Busk, President of the Royal College of Surgeons, and Richard Owen, anatomist and antagonist of Darwin. Owen had been a subscriber to the Fund since 1845 and had sponsored a number of applications which 'met, not merely with quick and immediate, but with ample, and I must say generous relief'. In a speech at a Fund dinner in 1859 Owen, in what may have been intended as a dig at Darwin's recently published *Origin of Species*, referred to the inevitable growth of specialisations, 'all these evolutions are attended with concomitant casualties, increasing instances of failure and distress, and require corresponding expansions of means of relief'. The Royal Literary Fund was no longer enough to protect scientists from the struggle for survival:

There has lately risen among men of science, a movement tending to the development of an organisation, for the more immediate and express application to the needs and distresses of fellow-labourers. This has not arisen from any sense of deficiency in the application of your funds to our relief; it has arisen rather as a natural consequence of your beneficent example. You have taught us what to do.

The founding of the Scientific Relief Fund in 1859 did not stem the flow of scientific applicants to the Royal Literary Fund. In November 1859, before the new fund was operational, T.H. Huxley and Joseph Hooker applied on behalf of the widow of Arthur Henfrey FRS, Professor of Botany at King's College London. 'There is no other author to whom continental botanists are so deeply indebted' Hooker enthused. The Fund gave Mrs Henfrey £100 which Huxley took as 'proof. . . of the unity of science and literature'.[41] It was a unity which was to last for the rest of the century. Among the more distinguished scientists who were able to apply to both the Scientific Relief Fund and the Royal Literary Fund were James Croll, geologist and climatologist; the chemist Walter Weldon; entomologist E.C. Rye; and the widows of mathematician W.K. Clifford, zoologist G.R. Gray, chemist F. Guthrie and geologist P.M. Duncan.

In many instances it is possible to date the self-confidence of an occupational group by the founding of their benefit societies and pension funds. When the members of a profession felt they had achieved a modest prosperity and a recognised social status they were prepared to dip into their pockets for the relief of their poorer brethren – if only to protect their occupation from disrepute. If scientists seem to have been meaner for longer – it was 199 years between the founding of the Royal Society and its Scientific Relief Fund – it may be because even in the nineteenth century science was regarded as natural philosophy with a claim on the Literary Fund. The clergy achieved this self-confidence in 1678 (Dissenting ministers in 1733); musicians in 1738 (female musicians in 1839); schoolmasters in 1798; commercial travellers in 1800; artists in 1814; lawyers in 1817; pawnbrokers in 1823; actors in 1839; dancers and governesses in 1843; and architects in 1850.

Although book writers had made a provision for the hazards of their trade as early as 1790, through the founding of the Literary Fund, journalists who did not write books had no purpose-built refuge in times of debt or sickness. As late as 1864 the *London Review* complained, 'The Royal Literary Fund . . . excludes newspaper editors, reporters, and contributors as such. If they have ever written a dull book they may be relieved from the fund; but if they have written nothing but brilliant leading articles, discriminating literary reviews, and accurate Parliamentary reports, the Royal Literary Fund will have nothing to say to them.'[42] In fact Robert Bell, the editor of *Atlas*, had passed a motion in 1858 extending the Fund to authors 'of important contributions to Periodical Literature', but this still excluded routine newspaper work. In 1861 James Sutherland Menzies was rejected, although he was editor of the *Court Journal* and *St James' Magazine* and a regular reviewer for the *Daily News*, yet in 1866 he was awarded £50 as the author of a trashy book *The Royal Favourites* (1865).

There had been an unsuccessful attempt by a group of London journalists to run a mutual assistance scheme called the Newspaper Press Benevolent Association (NPBA). The Association, founded in 1837, was the brainchild of the editor of the *Morning Advertiser*, a Mr Anderson. Robert Knox, later editor of the *Morning Herald*, was the honorary secretary and W.H. Watts, parliamentary correspondent of the *Morning Chronicle* was the first chairman. The association aimed to provide 'decayed' journalists with annual pensions of £52 10s and to make small grants to relieve temporary distress. Only members who had paid their subscriptions for five consecutive years were entitled to relief. The membership fee was high, and although it was quickly reduced from four guineas to two guineas a year it was still twice the usual subscription for such enterprises. At first the new fund prospered to the extent of banking some 300 donations and making a few small grants. In 1839 it was worth £900. The Duke of Sussex had accepted the presidency, the vice presidents included Palmerston, Lyndhurst and George Birkbeck, and among the subscribers were Dickens, Disraeli, Talfourd, Macready, Charles Knight, Henry Colburn, Lord Brougham and Edwin Chadwick. By 1847, however, the number of members had dwindled to a mere eighteen, three less than the number required to form a management committee. The surviving members considered making the fund over to an appropriate charity, but as 'neither the Literary Fund nor any existing society answered the required conditions', with great regret they divided the balance among themselves agreeing to assist other charities 'upon the conscience of each'.[43] The activities of the Newspaper Press Benevolent Association, though not technically fraudulent, were hardly praiseworthy and almost certainly prejudiced several prominent newspapermen against attempts to establish a press fund in 1858.

In April 1858 at a routine meeting of parliamentary reporters the idea of establishing a 'Provident and Benevolent Fund in connexion with the Newspaper Press' was again considered and met with general approval. The provisional committee felt that little could be achieved without the sanction of the proprietor of *The Times*. John Walter, however, was unenthusiastic. He wrote to the committee on 10 July 'I consider it unworthy of the character and position of the Press, and inconsistent with its independence'.[44] Quite how the independence of the press would be compromised was not quite clear. When the Fund was eventually established Dickens defended it against such criticism with all the authority of a former *Morning Chronicle* reporter: 'Is it urged against this particular Institution that it is objectionable because a parliamentary reporter, for instance, might report a subscribing M.P. in large, and a non-subscribing M.P. in little? . . . I reply that it is notorious in all newspaper offices that every such man is reported according to the position he can gain in the public eye, and according to the force and weight of what he has to say.'[45] Maybe so, but some MPs, it seems, left nothing to chance. The most generous political benefactor to the Fund was the Marquess of Salisbury, three times Prime Minister, who subscribed over £235, twice as much as his contribution to the Royal Literary Fund.

Such arguments failed to convince the pompous Walter, and neither he nor his paper nor its editors made the smallest donation to the Fund but instead kept up their criticisms during its formative years. In August, following the rebuff from Walter, came an equally curt note from Macaulay declining to accept a vice presidency, 'I will frankly own that I do not like the plan of your Institution'. Others who declined the privilege, partly no doubt because of their unhappy memory of the NPBA, were Brougham, Lyndhurst and Disraeli (who later changed his mind). The committee's first success came at the end of July when Lord Campbell and C.W. Dilke II agreed to become vice presidents, and Herbert Ingram, owner of the *Illustrated London News* became a trustee. Eventually Lord St Leonards, a former Tory Lord Chancellor, was prevailed upon to become president but the office did not suit him; he resigned in 1864 and was succeeded by the much more literary and less political Lord Houghton. In the same year Dickens became a vice president and the country's most famous correspondent, W.H. Russell of *The Times*, braved Walter's displeasure and became one of four trustees.

After six years of patient and sometimes plodding effort the

Newspaper Press Fund held an 'inaugural dinner' on 21 May 1864, with Lord Houghton in the chair. The Fund had raised £1,442 from a hundred or so members, donors and vice presidents. The literary vice presidents included J.A. Froude, Shirley Brooks, Mark Lemon, Charles Reade, G.A. Sala, Robert Bell, Trollope, Tennyson and Bulwer Lytton as well as Dickens. The annual membership fee was a guinea and life membership was set at 10 guineas. Except in the case of honorary members – the benevolent rich, cabinet ministers and bishops – membership was confined to paid 'contributors to the Press' on the production of satisfactory references. To begin with only members were eligible for grants but within a few years small grants were also available for needy non-members who were bona-fide journalists. The first grant of £20 was made to the widow of Washington Wilks of the *Morning Star* in August 1864.

The tenth annual dinner, held in May 1873, was a fair celebration of the institution's success. Froude presided over the usual 'numerous and brilliant company of gentlemen distinguished for their achievements in the literary, artistic, and political world'. Literature was represented by Anthony Trollope, R.H. Horne, S.C. Hall and Edmund Yates. Lord Houghton, in his presidential address, regretted that the Fund had not made more of an impact: it counted 300 members out of a potential membership of many thousands. It had, however, secured the patronage of the Prince of Wales and achieved its first object of providing an 'insurance fund' for its members. £2,282 had been shared out among more than 100 applicants. Thomas Littleton Holt, a vigorous campaigner for the repeal of the Stamp Act, opportunistic editor of the *Iron Times* (c. 1840s) and the *Army and Navy Dispatch* (1854) and, after a spell in a debtors' prison, of the *Morning Chronicle*, was awarded the Fund's highest grant of £50 in 1868. £30 was given to the Mark Lemon Fund, and J.H. Stocqueler, a disreputable adventurer and editor of the *Calcutta Englishman* and the *English Gentleman*, received £25 in 1871, £15 in 1872 and £25 in 1875.

The work of the Fund was undertaken by a committee of professional journalists. In the first ten years committee members included Justin McCarthy, editor of the *Star*; William Saunders, founder of the first press agency, the Central News Agency (1870); Edward Russell, editor of the *Liverpool Daily Post*; Richard Gowing of the *Gentleman's Magazine*; S.C. Hall, editor of the *Art Journal*, and J.M. LeSage, managing editor of the *Daily Telegraph*. The *Daily Telegraph* was the chief supporter of the Fund, subscribing nearly £1,000 by 1900, four times more than any other paper. The owner and editor of the *Daily Telegraph*, Edward Levy (later Lawson), was a vice president and a generous donor. The most generous press baron was Sir Algernon Borthwick, owner of the *Morning Post*, who succeeded Houghton as president in 1885 and subscribed nearly £4,500.

By the end of the century the Newspaper Press Fund had over a thousand members of whom nearly half were provincial journalists; only twenty years earlier less than one in three of the Fund's members worked outside London. The accounts for the financial year ending January 1899 show that the thirty-five year old Press Fund was worth £27,631, had an income of £4,521, and spent £2,088 on grants compared with the century-old Royal Literary Fund worth £56,269, with an income of £5,192, and a grant expenditure of £1,905. Although the Royal Literary Fund made fewer grants the value of its awards was considerably higher. In 1899, for example, its grants ranged from £10 to £250 shared out between twenty-seven applicants. In the same year 112 Press Fund applicants received sums ranging from £5 to £75.

Although only a fraction of journalists wrote books and were eligible for Royal Literary Fund grants, a much larger number of book writers wrote for newspapers and magazines. The founding of the Newspaper Press Fund in 1864 offered a welcome supplement to the charitable earnings of indigent writers – always supposing they could afford the guinea a year membership fee. Writer and journalist Henry Barton Baker had a policy of applying to both funds in turn. In 1896 the Royal Literary Fund granted him £80 and in 1897 the Press Fund gave him £75. He ended up on a small Press Fund pension of £30 a year, supplemented by occasional Literary Fund grants. Such double applications were quite common and usually openly admitted. Novelist and *Times* special correspondent David Christie Murray received £100 each from both charities in 1893. Others who claimed on both funds were the widows of Henry Kingsley, R.H. Horne and Sir Frederick Wraxall; Bohemian journalists Percy St John and George Hodder; boxing correspondent H.D. Miles; publishers and translators Henry and Ernest Vizetelly; press historian and editor of the *Fortnightly Review* T.H.S. Escott; and the Chartist and provincial editor Thomas Frost.

It is clear that the vast majority of Press Fund applicants were reporters and editors with no pretensions to authorship. The historical interest of the Fund lies in the light it casts on journalism as a profession. In the last quarter of the nineteenth century applications to the Royal Literary Fund decreased while applications to the Newspaper Press

Fund increased. Probably the majority of the young men and women who earlier in the century would have chanced a literary career were opting for the narrower profession of journalism. The size of a benevolent fund is a sure indication of the prosperity of a profession: the larger the fund, the more prosperous its members. By the end of the First World War the Press Fund had caught up with the Royal Literary Fund. Today it far outstrips it.

In 1836 John Brownlow, the secretary of the Foundling Hospital, whose name Dickens may have borrowed for Oliver's benefactor in *Oliver Twist*, compiled *A Pocket Guide to the Charities of London*. It was an early attempt to list the ever increasing number of charities in the capital. By 1850 Sampson Low's extensive survey of the same subject, *The Charities of London*, was too bulky for the pocket. Low counted 491 general charities (excluding trusts established by City companies) of which 294 were nineteenth-century foundations. These charities had a combined income of £1.76 million; the richest by far were the Church charities and missionary and bible societies whose income exceeded £875,000. By 1854, when Low published a second edition, there were 530 charities in London which disbursed £1.8 million out of a larger, though unspecified income. On 11 February 1869 *The Times* published a report on charities by G.M. Hicks as part of a campaign to influence the incoming Liberal administration to reform the Poor Laws and to relieve 'voluntary effort . . . from some of the burdens which inefficiency has so long thrown upon it'. Hicks listed some 360 London charities which provided details of their operations in published reports. His analysis showed that 'voluntary effort' was well rewarded. His list of selected charities had a turnover of more than £2 million a year. £281,620 was spent on salaries, and by the time rent, furniture and housekeeping were added to the charity bill, it cost £800,000 to give away £750,000 to the poor and sick. Charity was a lucrative business, at least for charity officers.

With five hundred charities to choose from, all conveniently listed in well-researched books, begging-letter writing became a trade – even an art. The division between a justified, if pathetic, appeal and a begging letter was a fine one; so fine that the Mendicity Society was founded as early as 1818, to 'detect and repress' professional beggars. Successful authors and philanthropic peers were obvious targets. Among authors, Dickens, Lytton and Macaulay were frequently pestered and if they refused to donate a few pounds they were liable to be harangued. A Mr

H. Wall, who had written to Dickens in 1858 on behalf of a Prussian refugee, Ernst Stein Von Skork, was astonished by Dickens's unhelpful reply, 'I wrote to Mr Dickens for him[Von Skork]; but to my surprise he states not knowing him, he cannot assist him, poor excuse from a gentleman, who uses in his writings to the world such expressive language of feeling and sympathy towards his fellow creatures.' Authors, or bogus authors, believed they had a special claim on Dickens and he often forwarded their appeals to the Royal Literary Fund. In February 1849, for instance, he referred the case of an 'adventurer' and sporting writer, Frederic Tolfrey, to the Fund, '[he] has written me a couple of very defiant epistles, because I have felt it necessary to decline to 'lend' him ten pounds'. Tolfrey was well known to the Mendicity Society's begging-letter department.

After fourteen years as their victim Dickens's patience snapped. On 18 May 1850 he published a blistering attack on 'Begging Letter Writers' in *Household Words*, ending with the rallying cry 'we must resolve, at any sacrifice of feeling, to be deaf to such appeals, and crush the trade'. His description of the begging-letter writer's character may have been partly modelled on Tolfrey and on Daniel Tobin, an old schoolfellow. His particular model, however, has been identified as Edward Youl, who wrote to Lords Lansdowne, Denman, Brougham and Macaulay among others, passing himself off as the Quaker writer Mary Howitt in desperate circumstances, much to her dismay.[46]

Many authors, particularly if they were working class and had been encouraged in their authorship by misguided patrons, wrote genuine appeals for 'temporary relief'. Macaulay's biographer noted: 'To have written, or to pretend to have written, a book, whether good or bad, was the surest and shortest road to Macaulay's pocket. "I sent some money to Miss —, a middling writer, whom I relieved some time ago, I have been giving too fast of late; – forty pounds in four or five days. I must pull in a little." '[47] Thackeray's annual charitable budget reached £500, much of which he gave to fellow authors. George Hodder recalled that 'like many other generous men he had always a few pounds floating about amongst friends and acquaintances whom he had been able to oblige in their necessity'.[48] Lord Derby, when president of the Royal Literary Fund, gave away at least £500 a year at £5 or £10 a time to needy writers and others whose hard luck stories impressed him. Even Octavian Blewitt, as secretary of the Fund, received his share of unsolicited appeals. Samuel Langley, author of a concordance to Tennyson's poetry, apologised for asking Blewitt for a £5 loan, 'not having fully realised your real position compassed round by a ravenous crowd of impecunious scribblers'.

Authors were undoubtedly the most successful begging-letter writers. Not only were they professional story-tellers, the tools of whose trade were literacy and imagination, but it was a truism that their's was a hand-to-mouth existence, littered with bankruptcies and small debts. One of the most disreputable writers to apply to the Fund was the journalist John Horatio Leigh Hunt, who used his father's name and friendships to appeal to everyone from family friends to Prince Albert. Blewitt reported to Albert's private secretary:

Mr John Leigh Hunt . . . has been for many years one of the most systematic begging-letter writers in London. In fact he lives by it – and I believe lives well, for he obtains contributions from all quarters by using the name of his father who is both injured and annoyed by these proceedings . . . I understand that he takes the Court Guide and applies to everyone whose name occurs in the portion he selects. Latterly he has been applying to the members of the British Archeological Society having obtained a copy of their list of members [24 July 1845].

Although Blewitt was vigilant he was occasionally duped by a charlatan of the first class such as Henry Molineaux Wheeler. Wheeler had founded and edited *The Vineyard: a Journal for Clergymen's Wives*, and also written devotional works published by Longmans; perfect credentials for the pious fraud. Longmans recommended Wheeler to the Royal Literary Fund who granted him £30. A further sum of £40 was granted on the recommendation of the much deceived Miss Howitt. After the grant Blewitt read a press report in *The Times* entitled 'Wholesale Swindling' which stated that Wheeler had been sentenced to three months imprisonment:

For the past 11 years these people [Mr & Mrs Wheeler] have obtained a substantial income by practising a deceit upon the benevolent. Wheeler has represented himself as the author of several religious works, and they appear to have lived at the rate of between £300 and £400 a year. . . . All kinds of Directories, with a record of begging letters sent, and the replies thereto, were discovered by the police, and some thousand of those missives, most of them containing help for the afflicted Mr and Mrs Wheeler were recieved. An album full of autographs, headed by that of the Archbishop of Canterbury, testified to the high personages who had listened to this tale of woe told by these dexterous swindlers [26 August 1870].

A less self-abasing system of fund raising than begging on one's own behalf was to persuade friends and admirers to form a committee to write official begging letters. The receipts from such activities were known as 'testimonial funds'. In the Dickensian age testimonial funds were the preferred way of enabling richer authors to subsidise their poor friends, without the smack of patronage that had accompanied the largesse of a Rogers or a Shelley. The testimonial fund could be as discreet or as public as desired. In 1849, for example, a committee of brother authors was formed to help J.A. Heraud on his insolvency. John Forster was chairman, T.K. Hervey was treasurer, and Westland Marston was secretary. About £400 was raised through private letters to sympathetic members of the literary world. Heraud was spared unwelcome publicity.

Other testimonials relied upon publicity to achieve the maximum effect. When Mary Russell Mitford's notoriously speculative father died in 1842 bequeathing her his debts, a public appeal, headed by Lord Radnor, was circulated to the daily newspapers in February 1843. *The Times*, whose owner John Walter was one of the signatories, solicited contributions to the appeal through its leader columns. The sum raised was sufficient to clear her father's debts of over £900 and reimburse her for the several hundred pounds she had lost through the failure of the engraver William Finden. She did not seem to mind being described in the published appeal as 'one solitary and almost destitute woman'.

Where the author was unknown the public appeal was often anonymous, relying on the pathos of the tale for a sympathetic response. John Elliotson wrote to *The Times* on 28 January 1854 to open a public subscription on behalf of a literary lady whose father had been a rich city entrepreneur, but who was then living in very reduced circumstances. By way of a testimonial she was referred to as the author of 'a small volume of poems, published at a shilling, and dedicated to my friend Mr Dickens'. From this description the curious could discover that she went by the unlikely name of Maria Goodluck. Elliotson's appeal raised £370 in six months which was used to buy a government annuity of £20 a year. Dickens contributed his standard £10. Most of the subscribers preferred to remain anonymous – to avoid begging-letter writers – calling themselves by their initials or by such affected designations as 'a Fortunate Citizen', 'a widow's Mite'. The Goodluck Fund was an outstanding example of Victorian sentimentality. The honorary treasurer, one of whose functions was to print acknowledgments of the subscriptions, reported:

the donations in this case have represented every grade of society, from the President of Her Majesty's Council down to the poor seamstress. Every part of the United Kingdom sent its contribution, India and America most generously expressed their sympathy, thus forcibly proving to us how a genuine tale of distress gives that touch to our nature which makes the whole world kin [28 January 1854].

Goodluck's anonymous appeal was, in effect, sponsored by Elliotson and Dickens, both well-known public figures who could be relied upon to investigate the merit of a case before allowing their names to be used. Authors often admitted to receiving help from the Royal Literary Fund as a way of establishing their credentials. If a case had been investigated by the Fund's committee and found worthy, then the fact was worth advertising. Effingham Wilson wrote to *The Times* on behalf of the persistently impoverished Miss Goodluck on 12 February 1869: 'The fact that this lady has been repeatedly assisted by . . . the Royal Literary Fund, furnishes at once a guarantee of her deserts.' Where possible the Fund refused to endorse such appeals. Blewitt wrote to the organisers of an appeal in 1840 on behalf of the family of the journalist James Philpott: 'The Committee feel that they cannot . . . lend the name of the Society to promote the private views of parties they have relieved.'

Some testimonial funds ran for several years. Charles Mackay's testimonial lasted from 1874 to 1877 and earned him £770. John Kitto, the biblical scholar, received a £1,250 testimonial collected between 1854 and 1856. Francis Espinasse recalled that the friends and admirers of the Lancashire poet Edwin Waugh 'raised for him during some ten years an annual £200. In order to save his self respect it was called the Waugh Copyright Fund.'[49] A rather more modest and more typical testimonial was the £158 raised for the Bohemian journalist John Valentine Bridgeman in 1876, to which the Royal Literary Fund added £50.

Although they were commonplace, testimonial funds were also a nuisance. Someone had to be prepared to act as secretary, someone else had to receive and bank the money as treasurer. Leaflets and advertisements had to be printed; friends had to be cajoled into making contributions, and all too often the recipients of all this kindness were ungrateful and plain feckless.

A much more enjoyable, though less common, fund-raising activity was the staging of a play for the benefit of an author, often a dramatist. These benefit performances had a long and involved stage history. The first benefit appears to have been for the actress Mrs Barry in 1686, and throughout the eighteenth and nineteenth centuries special perform-ances where the profits went to a particular actor or actress were commonplace. Dickens describes a provincial benefit for Miss Snevel-licci in *Nicholas Nickleby* (1838). Miss Snevellicci lives off such charity performances which are staged on her behalf on the feeblest pretexts. George Augustus Sala's mother, a singer and actress, held regular benefits to support herself and her family. Her first public appearance, in 1814, was in a benefit concert on behalf of Peter Hervé who had failed to look after his own interests while energetically promoting the National Benevolent Institution. Mrs Sala, Madame Vestris and other members of the cast gave their services for nothing. Unfortunately the manager of the King's Theatre was not so generous, and charged Hervé £230 for 'house, wardrobe, and scenery, the services of the different workmen and people employed behind the curtain, the attendance of the box keepers, money takers, police, guards, and the whole of the theatre lighted complete'.[50] Hervé's profit was £14 7s.

Until the Victorian period it was comparatively rare for a benefit to be staged on behalf of an author. In the eighteenth century, dramatists often received the profits of the third night, or 'author's night', but this was in payment for the author's work and was not a benefit as such. In 1733 a benefit was staged at the Haymarket for the decrepit seventy-six year old critic and dramatist John Dennis, and in 1744 the blind Irish dramatist Michael Clancy acted the blind prophet Tiresias in a production of *Oedipus* for his own benefit; the novelty of the spectacle attracted a large audience.

As the nineteenth century progressed the practice of staging benefits for dramatists became less infrequent. One of the most notable occasions was a performance of the *Beggar's Opera* held at Drury Lane on 25 July 1849 to benefit James Kenney. Unfortunately he died a few hours before the curtain went up. The £500 proceeds went to his widow and children. Such performances – a musical for a paralysed playwright, a farce for a young widow – were in questionable taste, but they served their purpose.

In November 1845 Charles Dickens made his first public appearance on the London stage as Captain Bobadil in Jonson's *Every Man in His Humour* at St James's Theatre. The performance was in aid of Dickens's latest project, the Sanatorium Hospital, which was to fold for lack of funds a year later. Members of the cast included the *Punch* writers, Lemon, Jerrold and À Beckett. This was the first of a string of benefit performances staged by Dickens and his 'Amateur Company'. His second attempt to raise money for a worthy cause by enjoying himself was in July 1847, when the Amateur Company performed in Manchester and Liverpool for the benefit of Leigh Hunt and John Poole. Forster records that though the performances raised £904, they cost nearly £500 to stage. Testimonials were much cheaper to operate, though they were not so much fun.

The Amateur Company's next public appearance was in 1848, when they put on a production of *The Merry Wives of Windsor* with Mark Lemon as a pot-bellied Falstaff and Dickens as Shallow. After nine performances the play grossed £2,500. The beneficiaries were supposed to be Shakespeare's House at Stratford, and its curator designate Sheridan Knowles. After the expenses had been deducted the house received nothing; Knowles, who did not become curator, was paid the balance of about £1,500.

Dickens liked to think his theatricals were both necessary and opportune. At a public dinner in 1852 he boasted that 'every one of the three eminent writers to whom we had the high gratification of rendering most timely assistance by our theatrical performances . . . has since been placed on the Pension list.'[51] This was a misleading claim as Hunt and Knowles had been awarded Civil List pensions before the performances on their behalf, though the official announcement was not made until afterwards. In at least one instance Dickens organised a benefit that was publicly repudiated by one of the patronised relatives. When Douglas Jerrold died in 1857, Dickens busied himself in promoting all kinds of entertainments on behalf of the bereaved family and raised some £2,000 above expenses. But Mrs Jerrold had a life insurance policy of £1,000 and her son wrote angrily to the *Morning Post* on 10 October 1857, to protest at the inference that his father had left her penniless. However, the family accepted the money.

Probably more than anyone else, Dickens was responsible for the flurry of well-publicised mid-Victorian benefits, usually involving Amateur Company actors who were also *Punch* men. There were performances for George Stephens in 1850, for Angus Reach in 1855, for Mrs Bayle St John in 1859, Mrs Robert Brough in 1860, and Mrs Charles H. Bennett in 1867. There was even a benefit in 1874 for the widow of *Punch* editor Shirley Brooks whose estate was valued at just under £6,000.

ONE OF the most interesting attempts to support hard-up writers owed its long and almost useless existence to Dickens's passion for play-acting. Over a forty-eight year history the Guild of Literature and Art appointed just three pensioners and made a handful of grants. Its beginnings, however, were grandiose. The idea of a self-help provident society for writers and artists took shape at Knebworth in November 1850 when Dickens and Bulwer Lytton were entertaining the county of Hertford with three performances of *Every Man in His Humour*. The Amateur Company did not have a large repertoire. The Knebworth theatrical gave Dickens a welcome chance to act again in his favourite rôle as the braggart Captain Bobadil, and it provided Bulwer Lytton, as Member for Stevenage, with the opportunity to dazzle his constituents. The event was such a success that Dickens, loath to retire from the stage for lack of a cause, suggested that the cast should direct their acting talents to fund raising on behalf of a Guild of Literature and Art. Unlike the Royal Literary Fund, from which Dickens had just resigned, the Guild would not be an eleemosynary society funded by the charitable for the benefit of begging-letter writers. It would be a professional society of authors and artists funded by themselves for their mutual benefit. It was a plan that Lytton and R.H. Horne had advocated in the early 1830s.[52]

It was agreed that Lytton should write a five-act comedy and Dickens and Lemon a one-act farce, both to be performed by the Amateur Company for the benefit of the Guild. Lytton also agreed to donate a site on his Knebworth estate for the building of Guild houses, to be occupied by distinguished and deserving writers and artists. On 5 January 1851 Dickens wrote to Lytton in a state of high excitement, 'I do devoutly believe that this plan carried out will entirely change the status of the Literary man in England, which no government, no power on earth but his own, could effect.' *Not So Bad As We Seem* received its first performance on 16 May 1851 at Devonshire House, courtesy of the sixth Duke. The Queen and Prince Albert presided over a titled audience. For all that it was to be a self-help society the Guild still needed an injection of aristocratic capital. The second performance on 27 May saw the first performance of Dickens's and Lemon's *Mr Nightingale's Diary*. A provincial tour followed this metropolitan success and culminated in a glittering last night at Manchester on 1 September 1852.

Not all writers were impressed. Macaulay confided to his journal 'I utterly abominate it'; to Lytton he wrote 'you will be driven to fill your Guild with, to use the mildest term, second rate writers'.[53] Thackeray was equally derogatory, taking exception to what he regarded as the tasteless spectacle of eminent writers cavorting in fund-raising theatricals. He felt it lowered the dignity of the profession. Thackeray himself had been berated by Forster in the *Examiner* of 5 January 1850 for 'disparaging his fellow-labourers' in the Fleet Street chapters of *Pen-*

dennis. He replied on 12 January 1850 in a letter to the *Morning Chronicle* on 'The Dignity of Literature', claiming that authors had long enjoyed a secure place in high society. He returned to this theme at the Royal Literary Fund dinner on 14 May 1851, two days before the first performance of Lytton's play in aid of the Guild: 'Literary men are not by any means, at this present time, that most unfortunate and most degraded set of people whom they are sometimes represented to be.' He went on to attack 'certain persons' for encouraging the notion that writers were still in the position of the 'miserable old literary hack of the time of George the Second', a reference to a character in Lytton's play. The following day he wrote to the *Morning Chronicle* to clarify his views:

what I intended to say . . . was . . . Mr Dickens, was at that moment engaged heart, hand, and voice, in a work of charity, and that the Queen of the empire and some of the most illustrious people in the country had met to aid his views and do him honour. That we might thence fairly argue that the public was most generously and kindly disposed towards men of letters.

As evidence of this generosity, by the time Lytton had secured an Act of Parliament to incorporate the Guild in June 1854, it was worth £4,184 of which £3,065 had been raised through amateur theatricals, £550 through the auction of the manuscript of *Not So Bad As We Seem*, and the balance through private subscriptions. The subscription list was headed by Victoria and Albert. Henry Hallam, Samuel Rogers and Harriet Martineau were among the sixty or so more modest donors. Lytton was president, Dickens was the sole vice president, and Forster, Lemon, Wilkie Collins, Robert Bell, Charles Eastlake, Augustus Egg and Frank Stone – all of the Amateur Company – were among the twenty-six council members. Charles Knight was honorary treasurer and W.H. Wills, Dickens's factotum at *Household Words*, was honorary secretary.

The objects of the Guild were to provide life and annuity assurance and sickness benefits for professional members and to found and endow a college at Stevenage for the residence of its pensioners. Annual premiums for life assurance were on a sliding scale. A forty year old writer or artist, for example, had to pay £2 11s. 9d a year to earn sick pay of £1 a week after the first six weeks of illness. Most writers clearly thought that these were not particularly attractive terms; they could, after all, apply to the Royal Literary Fund for nothing. Dickens admitted as much in a letter to Alaric Watts who was trying to raise money for the miscellaneous writer Joseph Haydn in May 1854. Although Haydn could join the Guild 'on the easiest terms, still it would not (I apprehend) be able to grant him a sum of money as a gift. If this were its object I cannot imagine that it would have a chance of success, with an *enormously* rich Institution like the Literary Fund already in existence.' How then could the Guild benefit writers? Even the *Athenaeum*, an ally of Dickens in his campaign against the Fund, voiced its doubts:

What we know of the condition of literature and its professors does not seem to us to point the argument in favour of such institutions. There is the Royal Literary Fund Society, for example, with its reserved wealth of somewhere about 45,000l. This wonderful Society, if we are rightly informed, has not been able to dispense its income for the current year in the relief of suffering authors – though seldom rigid in the selection of its objects [25 March 1854].

When the bill incorporating the Guild was published, its uselessness was made even more apparent by the clause which forbade it to grant any pensions for seven years. The result of this parliamentary caution was that by June 1856 the Guild had all but 'disappeared from the Public Eye'.[54] At a meeting on 4 June, Lytton suggested that either the Guild should make a strenuous effort to pay the interest on its funds to a well-known man of letters or transfer the whole fund to the Artists' General Benevolent Institution and the Royal Literary Fund, in spite of the battle between Dickens and the latter. The committee decided to look for a worthy candidate on the assumption that the Act of Parliament did not prohibit them from spending the interest as they thought fit. However, although there were several writers who would have been glad of support, including Lytton's former editor Cyrus Redding and the novelist Julia Pardoe, no further action was taken. The surviving minute books show that there were only four official meetings between September 1856 and June 1861, when the Guild was permitted by law to cease its hibernation.

Even now the Guild moved very slowly. In 1862 a 'select committee' of Dickens, Lytton, Robert Chambers, W.H. Wills and Frederick Ouvry (honorary solicitor) was formed to redefine the Guild's objectives. A year later they agreed to form a building subcommittee to construct the Guild houses. Eventually, in August 1863, 'two acres were chosen in a field close to Stevenage . . . within a short walk of the Railway Station, facing the high road . . . not far from the parish church'. It took the subcommittee another year to agree on builders' estimates, and a terrace of three Gothic houses designed by H.A. Darbishire was finally completed in the spring of 1865. The opening of the Institution of the Guild of Literature and Art, as the rather cramped three-bedroomed houses were called, took place with pomp and ceremony on 29 July. Dickens and the surviving members of the Guild took the train to Stevenage to inspect the property and lunch with a 'large number of the principal families of the county, whom Sir Edward had invited on the occasion'.[55] *The Times* gave a friendly account of the proceedings before expressing its considerable misgivings: 'To the best of our belief and knowledge a decayed actor, or poet or scholar, or man of science would rather have a hundred a year, to live where he liked and with whom he liked, than have it saddled with the condition of occupying a particular house in Hertfordshire.'[56]

At the September meeting of the Guild the hunt for suitable tenants began in earnest. The first candidate, proposed by Lytton, was Robert Folkestone Williams, a former sub-editor of the *New Monthly Magazine* and a biographical writer, who had worked for thirty years as literary adviser to Colburn, and his successors Hurst and Blackett. Lytton told Dickens that the 'selection [of Williams] wd. silence much gabble as to such aid not being wanted by industrious writers'.[57] Unfortunately for Mr Williams, his former employers wrote a damning reference and his application was turned down. He was later awarded two grants by the Royal Literary Fund. At the same time as the Williams application, the Guild heard that Robert Latham, philologist, ethnologist and Civil List pensioner might accept a tenancy. He was considered to be 'a capital tenant', 'a great man; good scholar; a modern Lindley Murray'. But Latham had second thoughts: Stevenage was inconvenient, the district was costly, he would rather live in Bedfordshire. The Guild were no more successful with their third candidate – another long-standing Royal Literary Fund client – the theatre critic, poet and dramatist J.A. Heraud. Heraud declined a house on the entirely reasonable grounds that the last train to Stevenage left too early in the evening for him to be able to pursue his job as a theatre critic. 'The houses were nice enough', recalled J.R. Robinson, a Guild member, 'there was no trouble about *them*. There were pretty gardens, the houses were in an excellent position, and they supplied Lord Lytton with such a happy topic as he rolled by with his friends, on a drive in the neighbourhood of Kneb-worth . . . The distance from London was always a trouble.'[58]

It was not until July 1868 that the Guild made its first grant, of £110, to the dying Peter Cunningham, one of its founder members. A year later the Royal Literary Fund gave his widow £100. Two further grants were made in November 1868, £20 to the widow of the illustrator George Cattermole, and £20 to the sisters of E.H. Wenhert. This was the sum of the committee's achievement by December 1869 when a decision was taken to wind up the Guild after pensioning Heraud, Mrs Cattermole and an artist named Henry Warren. If Heraud ever received his £40 pension he kept it a secret from the Royal Literary Fund, to whom he applied in later years. The decision to give half its assets to the Literary Fund was made with Dickens's consent, although, after his death in June 1870, Frederick Ouvry reported to Charles Dickens junior, the Guild's new secretary, 'I saw Forster yesterday . . . He has the same strong objection that your Father entertained to any portion of the cash going to the Literary Fund.'

It was to take another eighteen years to bury the Guild. An attempt was made to found two Charles Dickens scholarships in literature and art, tenable at London University. Fortunately for the memory of the great believer in the University of Life, this dry tribute to his achievements, like everything else connected with the Guild, came to nothing. The Guild remained technically alive at the offices of *All the Year Round*. J.R. Robinson and John Hollingshead acted as trustees. Mrs Mark Lemon was given £100; R.H. Horne was granted £100 in 1875; Charles Mackay and John Absolom, a founder member, were also given grants. On the death of Charles Dickens junior in 1896 the Guild made his widow a grant of £100 and took the necessary steps to dissolve itself. An Act of Parliament was passed in 1898 and the Guild's assets of £2,114 were, as had long been expected, divided between the Royal Literary Fund and the Artists' General Benevolent Institution.

It has been claimed that 'no project in life inspired Charles Dickens with more practical enthusiasms than the Guild of Literature and Art'.[59] Dickensians write about the 'noble vision' of the Guild – which achieved virtually nothing – while often totally ignoring Dickens's active service on the Royal Literary Fund Committee from 1839 to 1850.[60] Apart from the first few years of play-acting Dickens was remarkably inactive on behalf of the Guild. There were very infrequent committee meetings and these, according to Robinson, were more the shadow than the substance of such occasions. When enough members could be persuaded to attend, the core always consisted of *Household Words*, and later, *All the Year Round* staff: 'voices were high in merriment, and it looked as though the meeting would never begin'. Robinson remembered that Dickens always enjoyed playing the part of chairman, though he did not take the duties of the chair very seriously. Few of Dickens's projects can have been more impractical. For all that he wished to increase the status of literature he quite failed to grasp that to be identified as a broken-down author in a literary almshouse, at the mercy of Lytton and his guests, was anything but dignified. Better by far to apply for a discreet grant from the Royal Literary Fund.

ALTHOUGH no author could be persuaded to occupy a Guild house at Stevenage, in spite of their being 'completed with due regard to the ordinary habits and necessary comforts of gentlemen',[61] a good many were prepared to put up with monastic cells and wear the livery of charity as Poor Brothers of the Charterhouse in the City of London. The Charterhouse was founded in 1611 by Thomas Sutton on the site of a fourteenth-century Carthusian monastery, as a school for poor scholars and a retreat for superannuated soldiers, merchants and servants of the Crown. These elderly retainers, or Poor Brothers, were allowed rent-free room and board plus a small pension. Until the 1840s very few writers were admitted as Poor Brothers without some other qualification; so Elkanah Settle was made a Poor Brother by virtue of his position as City Laureate, and Robert Scott, the military writer, for his service as military prosecutor of the Courts Martial. The governors of the Charterhouse, including the monarch, the Prime Minister and the Archbishops of Canterbury and York, were responsible for appointing the Poor Brothers. Not being particularly interested in literature, they rarely appointed authors and most of the places were filled by their own retired domestics. However, in 1843 Queen Victoria decided to use her nominations to the Charterhouse for the benefit of writers.

Although the Queen had been patron of the Literary Fund since her accession, her constructive interest in the plight of authors coincided with Prince Albert's chairmanship of the anniversary dinner in 1842, his first public engagement as Prince Consort. His speech was a triumph of well-intentioned hyperbole: 'It [the Literary Fund] stands unrivalled in any country, and ought to command our warmest sympathies in providing for the exigencies of those who feeling only the promptings of genius, and forgetting every other consideration, pursue the grand career of the cultivation of the human mind.' The speech clearly commanded his wife's sympathies for on 13 October 1843 her private secretary G.E. Anson wrote to Octavian Blewitt to ask him to present a list of literary candidates for the Charterhouse.

The Queen's initiative had the immediate effect of increasing Blewitt's powers of patronage, as the eligibility of authors for asylum in the Charterhouse rested almost completely on his judgment. His first list of authors were William Moncrieff the dramatist, John Davis the novelist, and William Jones the theologian. Jones had to refuse the offer on grounds of ineligibility: he was a Nonconformist minister and all Poor Brothers were supposed to be bachelors or widowers, over fifty years old and members of the Church of England. The Queen's example of nominating authors was followed by other governors including the Earl of Harrowby and W.E. Gladstone. The Archbishop of York was so moved by Thackeray's description of Colonel Newcome at Greyfriars (the Charterhouse) that, when chairman of the 1865 anniversary dinner, he offered 'to consult the Secretary of this Institution and if he can name to me a person duly qualified as a real literary man . . . appoint him one of the poor brethren of the Charterhouse to succeed Colonel Newcome'. The same description of Greyfriars had been attacked by Dickens as a 'destructive bit of sentiment'.[62] Thackeray's undiluted praise of his old school's rôle as an almshouse was an insult to Guild members with their ambitions for literary lodgings in Stevenage. But Colonel Newcome's successor, civil engineer and railway writer Thomas Baker, had every reason to be grateful to Thackeray and the sentimental archbishop. Before he was appointed a Poor Brother he had been an inmate of the St George's workhouse.

To begin with, the Charterhouse seemed to be a realisation of David Williams's refuge for elderly writers – except that it excluded free-thinkers and women. But the decision to appoint a body of authors as Poor Brothers was not an unqualified success. The facilities were not lavish, consisting of:

a separate apartment [room] with table, chair, bed and bedding kept in repair and clean, fifty-four bushels of coal and 13 lbs of candles yearly, room kept clean, and bed made, and fire lighted by a nurse . . . dinner in the hall when in health, at other times in his room; bread and butter daily for breakfast and supper . . . a cloak once in two years . . . a yearly allowance of twenty-six pounds ten shillings.[63]

In return for this appointment, which was considered by Blewitt and the governors to be an honour, the distinguished but decrepit man of letters had to bow to the disciplines and rules imposed upon a school-boy. A Poor Brother was required to doff his cap in the presence of the Master; was not allowed to visit taverns or ale houses; had to attend chapel twice a day; was required to wear his livery gown at all times, and obey sundry other rules on pain of punishment by forfeits. It could not have been easy for men like Moncrieff, who had been a theatre manager, or the poet and critic J.A. Heraud, or James Logan, Secretary to the Highland Society, to take kindly to such a régime. Moncrieff, who had gone blind in 1843, kept up a barrage of complaints until he was finally invited to the Palace to discuss them with Anson in 1851. His central point was that the conditions and rules of the Charterhouse had not been intended for authors: 'I felt I was totally out of place. . . . the Brotherhood . . . for the major part, were illiterate men – worn out servants, Brokendown journeymen . . . Pauperism in its most degraded sense was strictly incalcated, the main object seemed to be debasement.'

Dickens got to hear of Moncrieff's campaign in 1852. Although Moncrieff had been one of the most persistent plagiarists of Dickens, dramatising his novels with cheerful impunity, this did not prevent Dickens from becoming his staunch ally. Here was a chance to attack yet another hypocritical charity – and one, moreover, which presumed to fulfil one of the principal functions of the newly founded Guild. He promptly commissioned Henry Morley and Moncrieff to collaborate in a public exposure of the Charterhouse in *Household Words* (12 June 1852), in which Moncrieff repeated his charges to Anson, illustrated with anecdotes concerning the outrageous treatment meted out to impoverished gentlemen by the Master.

Dickens had first encountered the Charterhouse through John Poole, who was offered the Queen's nomination by Blewitt in the autumn of 1850. Blewitt's offer was delicately phrased: 'aware that it is far below your reputation and your deserts, but still it is a *provision for life*, and one of the very few which in these times can be accepted by a gentleman'. Poole wrote back from Paris expressing a cautious interest, did Blewitt know what sort of place the Charterhouse really was? Blewitt probably cited Cornelius Webbe as an example of a happy resident. Three years before Webbe had written to Blewitt 'I am thoroughly comfortable. . . . Though I am a moderate feeder, I have been obliged to have the waistcoats I came in with let out; which speaks volumes as to the living here.' Poole was reassured by Blewitt's reply and gratefully accepted a place asking that Dickens and Talfourd should be told of his good fortune. On his arrival in London, Poole checked over his new home. A week later, on 4 November, Blewitt wrote to Queen Victoria's secretary, 'after a personal examination of the Charter House and its regulations Mr Poole cannot reconcile himself to the acceptance of the Poor Brothership'. He was not the only author to decline the privilege. James Elmes, the architect and champion of Keats and Haydon, turned down a place, as did several less distinguished nominees.

At the time of the *Household Words* attack in 1852 there were six literary men in the Charterhouse: Moncrieff; Davis; Webbe; Joseph Snow, the ex-secretary of the Literary Fund; William West, bookseller and anti-quarian; and William Wickenden, farm labourer, sizar of St John's College, Cambridge, curate and author. Wickenden had entered the Charterhouse in March 1852 after a life of penury and hard writing. A year and a half later he resigned: 'I could not possibly have remained longer at the Charter House without encountering the horrors of inevitable madness'.[64] He explained the reasons for his resignation in a well-aimed if vitriolic pamphlet attack on the Master, W.H. Hale. After minutely detailing the conditions of the Charterhouse – 'very indifferent bread', 'tough beef', 'decayed vegetables' – Wickenden accused Hale of greed and corruption, for in addition to his salary as Master of £800 a year, Hale drew a considerable stipend as Rector of St Giles, Cripplegate, and Archdeacon of London:

> Now one would imagine that, having the annual sum of £800 per annum, his board, and a house, worth £350 per annum, rent free, the Master of the Charterhouse would do the requisite duties of his situation himself. This, however, he does not, but employes a subordinate, called a Manciple, to do it for him. Well, at all events, you may exclaim, he pays the Manciple out of his own Magnificent salary. Not so fast, Sir, he does no such thing: his salary is paid out of Charity . . . Is not this a system of vile jobbery?

Apart from the personal attack on Hale, Wickenden's main criticism was that the Charterhouse was an endowed charity, yet the objects of the charity, the Poor Brothers, ate mean food and lived in cramped, spartan conditions while the salaried officials 'were feasting at the expense of Sutton's charity . . . but when did you ever hear of the gullet of a pluralist or an official not wide enough to swallow that?' Such allegations are strikingly similar to the charges levelled against the Rev. Septimus Harding in Trollope's novel *The Warden* (1855).

Hale replied to the charges in an anonymous pamphlet on the history of the Charterhouse in which he challenged the right of the Poor Brothers to regard themselves as gentlemen, drawing up a table to prove that the vast majority of them were tradesmen, servants and lackeys. *Household Words* returned to the attack on 1 December 1855. Morley pitched into Hale for living rent-free in a house with 'thirty-three luxurious apartments' paid for by Sutton's charity while the Poor Brothers lived in dingy cells. And on Founders Day, while the Master and governors feasted in style, their charges were expected to celebrate on double rations of ale in their rooms. There followed further anecdotes concerning Hale's peremptory behaviour towards unfortunate gentlemen.

Hale must have bitterly regretted the Queen's decision to place authors under his care. The Charterhouse assembly books tell their own story. John Dingwall Williams, who took Poole's place in 1850, was a barrister and legal writer and another graduate of St John's. He was the first to attack the running of the charity in a privately printed pamphlet, *Charter House Purity and Probity* (1852), which appeared a few months before *Household Words* aired his and others' grievances before its readership of 40,000. The assembly book for 16 December 1851 reads, 'J.D. Williams expelled for letters insulting to the Governors and to the officers'. In August 1855 'it was ordered that the said William Moncrieff, be deprived of his pension for the last Quarter for profane swearing and abusive language, and for having refused to attend the Master when summoned'. In November 1859 a drunk and disorderly Alfred Addis, BA Trinity, Cantab, was rusticated. In January 1860 Joseph Snow petitioned the governors, complaining that the Charterhouse was neither an 'Asylum of Peace' nor a 'Religious Retreat'. On 24 November 1864 James Logan was rusticated for 'being habitually intoxicated'; he was expelled as an incurable drunk in 1869.

The official version of the Hale years, by G.S. Davies, who was appointed Master in 1908, paints a different picture: 'the changes which most affected the conditions of living for the better were those which took place from the year 1826 to the year 1842 and onwards. These changes were, by common consent, due to the energy and capacity of William Hale.' According to Davies, Hale's most important innovation was the rebuilding of two courts to include 'a house for the Preacher, who hitherto had lived outside, and there is no doubt that this departure . . . very largely affected the well-being of the Hospital [Charterhouse]'.[65] Hale was himself Preacher at the time.

The quality of the governance of the Charterhouse, at least as far as authors were concerned, appears to have improved dramatically with the appointment of G.S. Currey as Master in 1871, in succession to Hale. Like Hale, Currey had been Preacher to the Charterhouse, unlike Hale he was not a pluralist. Blewitt was no longer bombarded with letters from discontented writers. Instead John Sheehan, 'the Irish whiskey drinker' and an old Thackeray crony, wrote to tell Blewitt in 1879 that 'the dinner in hall is excellent; and the extreme kindness from everyone from the Master down to the porter at the gate most remarkable'. The 'old Bohemian' G.M.L. Strauss was appointed to the Charterhouse the same year. His only complaint was that the life was a little too dull for him: 'I would dearly have loved to pass the short balance of my life in its quiet shades. It has been ordained otherwise.'[66] Currey accepted that Strauss missed his beloved Savage Club and awarded him an out-pension – a device which permitted a Poor Brother, on medical grounds, to live outside the Charterhouse yet remain in receipt of a pension of up to 50 guineas a year.

About 50 authors appear to have been among the 300 or so Poor Brothers during the second half of the nineteenth century. They included Heraud, who had refused a Guild house, and – in addition to those already mentioned – W.A. Chatto, Charles Macfarlane, John Madison Morton and Francis Espinasse. In the 1880s the number of Poor Brothers fell from 80 at any one time to 60 'owing to the depreciation of land values',[67] and authors were rarely appointed to fill the vacancies. The governors had learned their lesson: that of all the inmates authors were the most troublesome, and, through their access to the press, the most dangerous. A few authors were humble or grateful enough, like Madison Morton, to refuse to be enlisted 'on the side of the grumblers', but most were unanimous in their complaint that the Charterhouse was a heavyhanded and authoritarian charity which was an affront to their dignity.

The official historian, attempting to excuse the shortcomings of his institution, mixed complacency with condescension:

If any one imagines that all Brothers are at all times satisfied, and that no one ever grumbles, he must also imagine that the Governors of Sutton Hospital have secured a succession of angels rather than of old gentlemen. The Brotherhood of the Charterhouse is not, any more than any other assemblage of similar human beings, free from its percentage of men who estimate their privileges not from the point of view of what has been given to them, but rather of what has not. . . . And here it should be said that the proportion of the unworthy to the worthy is very small.[68]

The inference was that authors, almost to a man, were unworthy. Yet the only men of distinction that G.S. Davies could find among the Brothers to add glory to the history of the Charterhouse were those same authors.

THE AMBITION of all unsuccessful authors was to be awarded a Civil List pension in recognition of their inadequately rewarded services. The Civil List Act of 1782 had been drawn up by Edmund Burke who wished, among other things, to correct the abuses that had led Johnson to define a pension as 'pay given to a State Hireling for treason to his country'. The pension fund came from the hereditary revenues of the Crown, relinquished to the State in return for an allowance to the royal family. To preserve the illusion of royal favour, pensions were conferred in the name of the King and required royal assent, but under Burke's Act it was the First Lord of the Treasury, usually the Prime Minister, who drew up the list and thus exercised the real patronage. Until the 1830s it was quite exceptional for an author to receive a pension. Most Prime Ministers believed, as Macaulay wrote of Pitt, 'that, in general, poetry, history and philosophy ought to be suffered, like calico and cutlery, to find their proper price in the market, and that to teach men of letters to look habitually to the state for their recompense is bad for the state and bad for letters'.[69] Pitt gave no literary pensions. Thomas Campbell received £184 from Lord Grenville, and Southey was pensioned by the Duke of Portland in 1807.

In 1834, on the motion of Lord Althorp, Parliament passed a resolution recommending specific awards for literature, science and art. Harriet Martineau was among those pressed to accept a pension, 'I was told that it was "a great honour". I did *not* refuse out of pride; but still I could not think it an honour, when I saw how Mrs Somerville was paraded, to turn the public attention from some indefensible grants.'[70] This was perhaps a little unfair for as well as Mary Somerville the pension list for 1835 included the Anglo-Saxon scholar Benjamin Thorpe, the historian Sharon Turner, and the poets James Montgomery and Thomas Moore.

In 1837 a select committee was asked to report on the whole operation of the Civil List. Its recommendations were incorporated in the Civil List Act (1837) which provided for an annual sum of £1,200, drawn from the Consolidated Fund, to be spent on new pensions for scientists, artists and public servants as well as authors. Although the Act did not direct that literature should be especially favoured, throughout the nineteenth century authors received the lion's share of the £1,200, taking about £500 worth of pensions a year compared with averages of £333 spent on public servants and £230 on scientists.[71] This was a reflection of the comparative poverty of authors rather than any love of literature in Downing Street.

With only £500 a year to spend on new literary pensions it made little sense to award them to writers of the stature and income of Dickens, Thackeray, Eliot and Trollope. To qualify for a pension in Victorian times a writer had to demonstrate a degree of 'distress' as well as 'desert'. In practice this meant that the majority of writers who received pensions were relatively obscure, for 'first-rate merit is far more generally recognised and rewarded by the public, and it is, as a rule, only second-rate Desert that is sufficiently unremunerated to pass the Distress test'.[72] The only writers who were pensioned as 'first-rate' who were not also in some kind of 'distress', were the Poets Laureate Wordsworth and Tennyson, and Matthew Arnold and John Wilson.

From the first literary pension of £300 awarded to Lady Morgan in March 1838 the list was never less than controversial. Lady Morgan was neither in distress nor particularly distinguished. 'Mere amusement was the end and object of her writings',[73] Elizabeth Barrett wrote in commiseration to Miss Mitford, who had received a more modest pension of £100 under the old Act. Apart from Lady Morgan and Prince Lucien Bonaparte, who was granted a pension of £250 in 1883 for services to lexicography, there were few cases of the pensioning of slight desert combined with no distress. There were, however, several instances of pensioned distress unaccompanied by literary merit. In 1861 Palmerston awarded a £50 pension to John Close, a writer of doggerel patronised by Lord Lonsdale. Questions were asked in the Commons and Palmerston was forced to revoke the pension. The award to Close confirmed Harriet Martineau in her view that 'we want a wholly different system, in which the decisions shall not rest with Prime Ministers who don't read, under a Queen who reads nothing'.[74] There was a similar outcry in 1866 when Derby pensioned Robert Young 'in recognition of his services as an historical and agricultural poet in Ireland'. Disraeli, defending the award, blamed an influentially signed testimonial, 'the moral which this case, as well as the whole experience of my life, teaches me, is to beware of testimonials. Nobody ever acted on a testimonial who had not afterwards cause to regret it.'[75]

It was difficult for governments with no particular literary qualifications, Disraeli excepted, to ignore testimonials when they were signed by eminent authors. The *Saturday Review* attacked a pension of £100 awarded to the 'utterly unknown' Edwin Atherstone in 1858.[76] But Atherstone's memorial had been drafted and presented to Derby by Macaulay and endorsed by Tennyson, H.H. Milman, Sir Charles Wheatstone, Sir Archibald Alison and Thackeray. It would have been perverse for Derby to have ignored Atherstone's claims:

Mr Atherstone's talents are great: his life has been laborious: the tendency of his writings has always been to promote virtue: he is far advanced in years: his health is failing: his means are straightened: he looks forward to the future with natural anxiety. Such are the grounds on which we earnestly recommend him to your Lordship's patronage.

Other pensions attacked by the *Saturday Review* were those granted to

Emma Robinson, supported by Dickens, Thackeray and Blewitt; Leitch Ritchie, supported by Dickens, Thackeray and Tennyson; and Dudley Costello, supported by Dickens, Thackeray and Forster. The Prime Minister could hardly make it a principle to reject every application endorsed by Dickens and Thackeray.

If the question of literary merit had to be trusted to the recommendation of other authors – 'who affix their signatures, in many cases, for no other reason than they are asked to do so'[77] – the business of authenticating distress was a much easier matter. From Sir Robert Peel onwards it was the custom of the wisest Prime Ministers to consult the secretary of the Royal Literary Fund. Octavian Blewitt, secretary from 1839 to 1884, gave his opinion carefully, but without reference to the committee of the Fund. And so, in addition to his powers as secretary and adviser to the Charterhouse governors, Blewitt was chief adviser to the Prime Minister on Civil List pensions. For forty-five years he was the Under Secretary of Literary Patronage, and unsurprisingly the majority of literary pensions were awarded to Royal Literary Fund clients.

An illustration of Blewitt's influence on the Civil List occurred in 1867 when the accident-prone Lord Derby granted Francis Muir, the author of *Income Tax Tables*, a pension of £70. It was a delicate matter; as Sir Frederick Pollock pointed out in a letter to Blewitt, 'it is a pity that the Government should have to be rendered so ridiculous . . . when the Chancellor of the Exchequer is about to preside at the Lit. Fund Dinner'. Blewitt immediately wrote to Lord Stanhope asking him to inform Derby that 'Dr Muir is only 32 years of age, and the grant of a Pension of £70 to a man of that age without any literary pretensions . . . is causing a great deal of dissatisfaction.' The offer of the pension was quickly withdrawn.

The Muir incident demonstrates that when Blewitt was not consulted Prime Ministers were capable of almost any foolishness. When Julia Tilt, an unknown novelist, was awarded a pension of £30 by Lord Palmerston, Blewitt was not asked for his opinion although she had been a client of the Fund. He wrote dryly to Tilt's sponsor in 1870, 'it was felt that she had been more fortunate than many authors of higher literary pretensions, in obtaining . . . a Pension on the Civil List, which though small, has amounted in the last 10 yrs to a sum larger than any Publisher would give for her Copyrights'.

In 1871 Blewitt decided to use his informed position to offer a critique of the pension list in the *Quarterly Review*. He condemned small pensions to poetasters and third-rate writers and recommended a minimum pension of £100. His anonymous article was quite the most constructive attack on the operation of the pension list in the nineteenth century, and was much more to the point than the careless account issued by the Society of Authors in 1889. The civil servant in charge of the list later defended it from Blewitt's strictures: 'It is very easy to produce a list of inferior persons who have received pensions and superior persons who have received less or nothing; but it would be worthless unless it also contained a comparative statement of their income and circumstances. This the critics do not and cannot know.'[78] But Blewitt, of course, knew this even better than Downing Street.

Blewitt and his successor A. Llewelyn Roberts were the only professional literary figures who were regularly consulted, and then usually in cases where the Prime Minister was undecided. Some Prime Ministers were more decided than others. Disraeli thoughtfully pensioned Mrs Falcieri as the widow of Byron's gondolier and only incidentally as the former housekeeper to Isaac D'Israeli. Lord John Russell allowed an Irish bias in his pension list. Palmerston pensioned Cyrus Redding for editorial services to Liberalism, although as the author of *History of Wines* he had genuine and distinctive literary merit.

The acid test of a Prime Minister's concern for literature was the proportion of the annual £1,200 he gave to authors. The most generous Prime Minister was Lord Rosebery who in his sixteen-month premiership gave 80 per cent of the pension fund to authors. His list, however, was undistinguished; his best name was George Augustus Sala. Balfour trailed in second place, spending 48 per cent of £1,200 on authors in his ten years as First Lord of the Treasury (Salisbury was Prime Minister, but chose not to head the treasury). His was a relatively distinguished list of pensioners: W.H. Hudson, Trollope's widow, Rhoda Broughton, Sir James Frazer, Henry Bradley, Gissing's sons, W.E. Henley. His personal interest is clear from the surviving correspondence: 'I think Henley should have £200 or £250 *at least*', he wrote to his private secretary, 'we do not often get the chance of being able to give necessary assistance to really distinguished men of letters'.[79] Henley, who had edited the pro-government *National Observer*, was awarded £225.

Gladstone was probably the most discriminating Prime Minister – at least after reading Blewitt's article. He made a distinction between 'respectable' authorship, which did not have a claim on the Civil List, and 'really distinguished' authorship. In 1872 he told Tennyson, who with Browning and Lord Houghton had signed a not very convincing memorial, 'since assuming my present office I have found that it was

85

necessary, in practice, to recognise loss of health, old age, or calamity as elements in the case for pensions of this class; but I have endeavoured to limit this admission to those cases only where some real service has been rendered by works of intrinsic value to the cause of letters.'[80] He gave pensions to Mrs Oliphant, W.H. Ainsworth, Matthew Arnold, Fanny Keats, F.J. Furnivall and J.A.H. Murray. Murray's 1884 pension of £250 was awarded specifically to assist him to edit the *New English Dictionary*, and was the first time the Civil List had been used to endow research rather than relieve the researcher. Inspite of this achievement, and his policy statements, Gladstone still managed to pension some odd and undeserving writers such as Martin Tupper, author of the banal though bestselling *Proverbial Philosophy*.

Although the critics of the Civil List pensions, notably the *Athenaeum*, the *Saturday Review* and the Society of Authors, heaped ridicule on the selection of so many unworthy candidates, one of their chief objections was not so much the choice of pensioners as the arbitrariness of the value attached to the pension. The value of pensions ranged from the very rare £300 to Wordsworth, Lady Morgan and John Wilson, to the £25 awarded to orphan daughters. Leigh Hunt, Tennyson, Arnold, Henley and Murray received pensions of between £200 and £250, but the majority of literary pensioners, including Mrs Oliphant, Charles Mackay, Sala, R.H. Horne and George MacDonald, received £100. To be offered less than £100 was like a slap in the face to some writers. In 1864 the sixty-four year old Robert Bell, whose industry on behalf of writers, as well as his own literary achievements, entitled him to at least the average pension, was offered a £60 pension by Palmerston. He declined it on the grounds that 'so small a sum would injure his literary career'.[81] But the same year the thirty-eight year old best-selling novelist Dinah Mulock and the forty year old poet William Allingham were pleased to accept Palmerston's offer of the same amount. Allingham's pension was subsequently raised to £100 in 1870. Among the more obvious anomalies were the £150 pension awarded to S.C. Hall, the £600 a year editor of the *Art Journal* and an inspirer of Pecksniff, and the £200 a year to the prolific minor novelist Thomas Adolphus Trollope in 1886.

When the novelist John Saunders failed to qualify for a pension in 1894, his sponsor, R.D. Blackmore, wrote in commiseration 'this simply shows how utterly ignorant those bustling and pushing statesmen are of the Literature of their country'. Behind the statesmen, who may well have had more important matters on their minds, were the civil servants in charge of the administration of the pension list. Most of them were contentedly philistine, capable of frequent and sometimes comic misjudgments. On the death of Gissing in 1904, Edmund Gosse wrote to M.G. Ramsay recommending support for Gissing's orphan sons: 'George Gissing was a pure artist of a very high rank. It is the opinion of the best judges that no one among the younger writers of the day, except Kipling and Barrie, has anything like the chance which G.G. enjoys of being permanently held an ornament to English Literature.'[82] Ignoring this testimony from a distinguished critic who was also Librarian of the House of Lords, Ramsay sent a note to Balfour 'I am rather doubtful whether Gissing is quite big enough'. Balfour had more sense and granted Gissing's sons £74 a year during their minority.

Ramsay's predecessor, F.S. Parry, took the view that 'fiction . . . is only admitted with difficulty, on the ground that the object of novelists is in most cases either personal profit or the mere amusement of the public'.[83] He blocked a pension to Mrs Riddell, a household name in the 1860s but almost entirely forgotten by the turn of the century. Although she had written several novels of considerable literary merit, certainly as good as works by Geraldine Jewsbury or Matilda Betham Edwards, who had slipped through the net before the Parry régime, he took a resolute view: 'On principle, I am not in favour of pensioning any novelist except a classic.' He turned down Francis Thompson for a pension in 1897, 'Thompson I know well by name, but don't possess any of his works. He seems to be a kind of De Quincy [sic] – wanders about the streets destitute, and takes opium.' Clearly, unless the Prime Minister took a personal interest, such cheerfully pig-headed men as Parry and Ramsay wielded considerable power.

Failure to receive a pension did not necessarily mean that the supplicant author came away empty handed. In addition to the Civil List pension fund, the Prime Minister and his civil servants were responsible for the distribution of the Royal Bounty Fund charged to the Civil List.[84] Royal Bounty covered payments to 'females in distress', 'alms', 'privy purse' and 'special services'. Literature and espionage came under the Special Service Fund of £9,000 a year. The amounts awarded were usually between £50 and £300. The criteria for Royal Bounty grants were much the same as for Civil List pensions, except that the standard of literary merit was lower. Occasionally a younger applicant for a Civil List pension would receive a Royal Bounty grant and, on reaching a certain age, achieve a pension. In 1905 the forty-seven year old Conrad was granted £500 from the Royal Bounty Fund by Balfour who 'went off to Scotland, taking with him half a dozen of Conrad's books which so impressed him, that he arranged for a substantial sum to be put at Conrad's disposal'.[85] He was pensioned by Asquith in 1910. More usually Royal Bounty grants were awarded to needy writers whose work was undistinguished though perfectly respectable. The journalist William Blanchard Jerrold received a grant of £250, John Saunders two grants of £250 and £150. A better novelist than Saunders, indeed better than several Civil List pensioners, was Isabella Banks, author of *The Manchester Man* (1876), who received two small grants of £50. Working-class writers rarely merited the dignity of a pension. The Chartist poet Thomas Cooper had to be content with grants of £300 in 1881 and £200 in 1892. The poet Close was granted £100 in compensation for having his pension withdrawn.

Gladstone, when speaking at the Royal Literary Fund dinner of 1872, pointed out that the wealth of the country had increased five times since 1842 but the amount of money disbursed by the Fund had remained at 'the very modest sum of £2,000 a year'. However, although Gladstone had charge of the Civil List for twelve years he made no attempt to increase the £1,200 available for yearly pensions, even to the level of £5,000 that it had been reduced to by Burke's Act of 1782. The inadequacy of the Civil List pensions was admitted in a speech by Gladstone's biographer, John Morley, at the Royal Literary Fund dinner of 1890:

It is commonly supposed that there is an immense fund at the disposal of Her Majesty's Ministers, by which they are able to make easy the last hours, or the hours of privations, of men of letters. I have watched for a good many years the administration of the Civil List pensions, and I venture to say that they are shabby and meagre in amount; that they are so capricious as almost to be grotesque in their application; and that if this country really wishes to do what the Civil List pensions are supposed to do, they must supply – and I cannot see why so wealthy a country as this should not supply – such an amount as will enable a man of letters, leading a thoroughly frugal and homely life, to give most of his time to the great and high interest with which he had charged himself.

Old and new Civil List pensions, combined with Royal Bounty grants, gave the Victorian Prime Minister some £8,500 a year to spend on rewarding literary merit and literary endeavour. Inspite of the 'capriciousness' of the list at the lower end of the scale, there was no case of a deserving eminent writer being refused a Civil List pension and no recorded case of a wealthy eminent writer expecting one. The real failure of the system, a failure shared by the Royal Literary Fund, was its reluctance to move beyond mere alms giving, to – in Harriet Martineau's words – 'a larger system, generous and dignified'[86] which would support literature as well as reward it. But such a system, which would encompass a George Eliot as well as an Isabella Banks, could not be as cheap as £8,500 a year. That sum was too small to embarrass a philistine Parliament, yet large enough to satisfy the consciences of individual cultured Members. It was, and is, a quaint, trivial, though not wholly useless remnant of eighteenth-century patronage.[87]

3

BOHEMIA IN FLEET STREET

During the 1830s the literary hack – from hackney, meaning hired horse – became a literary character; it was an important step in the evolution of authorship. Much of the venomous criticism which had been flung at Leigh Hunt and his 'cockney' school was the result of gentlemanly outrage at the presumption of lower-class writers attempting to rise above hackdom. Authorship was allowed to be the occupation of genius, or the hobby of educated men and women, but everyone else who wrote did so from base commercial motives and were scribblers, hacks and dunces. Robert Southey, who was about the only writer to make a comfortable living from authorship, attempted to protect his unique position by advising his would-be competitors to give up their literary aspirations and accept their allotted rank in life. The young J.A. Heraud cherished a letter from Southey written in 1820 warning him off his chosen profession:

Believe me, when I tell you that of all modes of life, that of the man who trusts to his literary exertions alone for support is the most miserable. And the very end at which he aims in his outset – that of improving and exalting his intellectual faculties – is the most effectually defeated by the means which he pursues. They are worn and jaded by the daily labour to which they must be subjected; and they are inevitably degraded and polluted by the necessity of writing for immediate effect and sale.[1]

Genius and labour are irreconcilable. Coleridge refines the point in *Biographia Literaria* (1817), '*never pursue literature as a trade*', 'be not *merely* a man of letters'.[2]

The problem for the hack, who was nearly always someone of considerable literary ambition unblessed by fortune, was how to avoid the undignified and humble rank of bookseller's employee and become a noble freelance like Southey. This predicament is neatly illustrated by the literary career of George Borrow, who became a hack to the bookseller Sir Richard Phillips in the 1820s, then had a spell in 'regular' employment as agent to the British and Foreign Bible Society, and at last, in the 1840s, was able to set up as an author. For all that it was idiosyncratic, Borrow's twenty-year struggle from hack to the author of

The Bible in Spain (1843) parallels the changing fortunes of the professional writer. After the financial crash of 1826 the stereotype of the rapacious bookseller gave way to the new stereotype of the prudent publisher. This led to large-scale redundancies among hacks and a doubling of applications to the Literary Fund. As some compensation for this loss of employment, advances in printing technology and paper manufacture, combined with the national movement for the spread of 'useful knowledge', led to the steady expansion of the press. By the 1830s journalism had become the chief resource of the erstwhile hack. Those, like Dickens, who had never had money, and those, like Thackeray, who had lost it, became journalists as automatically as Borrow, ten years before, had become a bookseller's drudge. Southey's protégé Heraud was able to abandon his occupation as a law writer's clerk and take up his first literary job as assistant editor of the newly founded *Fraser's Magazine*. After years of accepting humiliating employment the common writer had found a congenial literary occupation. From about 1830 onwards the vast majority of writers – major, minor and insignificant – began their literary careers as journalists.

That the professional writer, as distinct from the genius or amateur, had sloughed off the reputation of hack and scribbler and had, by 1830, acquired a literary character is clear from William Maginn's series in *Fraser's Magazine*, 'A Gallery of Illustrious Literary Characters' (1830–8). Isaac D'Israeli had been the first to draw attention to the existence of a distinctive literary character in *An Essay on the Manner and Genius of Literary Character* (1795), later reworked into a more substantial volume, *Literary Character* (1818). But D'Israeli's interest was in the psychology of great artists, 'men of genius', rather than mere men of letters. And in his other books, notably *Calamities of Authors* (1812), he did much to perpetuate the image of writer as garreteer. Maginn was writing about living authors of the rank of William Jerdan, Theodore Hook, Alaric Watts and D'Israeli himself, as well as 'men of genius' such as Scott, Coleridge and Wordsworth. The tone of the series was set by the first number on Jerdan who, as editor of the *Literary Gazette* from 1817 to 1850, has a good claim to being considered the first professional literary journalist.

Maginn's 'Literary Characters' consisted of eighty-one biographical sketches illustrated with line drawings by Daniel Maclise, and, according to *Fraser's*, aimed to provide 'a record of the countenances of the illustrious obscure who were scribbling away, with more or less repute, in the reign of William IV'. For the first time the reading public, or at least the 8,000 subscribers to *Fraser's* and their families and friends, were presented with physical representations as well as biographical notes of contemporary editors, antiquarians, lady novelists, critics and others who made up the literary corps. Over one hundred 'illustrious obscure' (including three group portraits), of whom not more than a handful were 'Men of Genius', were introduced to the public. Maginn's notices of his contemporaries were quirky, vivid and occasionally libellous, and, taken together, they clarified the activity of authorship and gave flesh to a previously obscure profession. The effect, if not the aim, of the series was to counteract the *Dunciad*'s view of Grub Street by exhibiting its habitués as a self-respecting – if not entirely respectable – Fellowship of the Pen.

It was, however, through his own life and works that Maginn had most influence on the shaping of literary character. For after his death, and after the epithet had gained general acceptance as an appropriate description of the artistic temperament, Maginn and bohemianism were synonymous. Thackeray was probably the first, in *Vanity Fair* (1845), to apply the term to an unconventional way of life, and by the 1850s bohemianism had become a well-defined and much publicised mode of literary life. As the young companion and admirer of Maginn in the 1830s, Thackeray had plenty of opportunity of studying the Bohemian character. And in 1848 when he came to write his autobiographical novel *Pendennis*, Maginn and his equally original colleague Theodore Hook featured as Captain Shandon and Mr Wagg. Thus a Victorian version of the Bohemian of the 1830s was placed before the novel-reading public. The authentic version of the two men's character was considerably more pungent: a vicious wit and joker, a profound though eccentric scholar, a distinguished classicist, a political extremist, a prodigious drinker, an inveterate debtor, a profligate and a boon companion. Few, if any, Victorian Bohemians could lay claim to such a heady combination of virtues and vices, but the model was there to be imitated.

Hook died in 1841 and Maginn in 1842. The moral and cultural anarchy which the pair had come to epitomise was no longer fashionable. The verdict of the Victorian editor of Maginn's 'Literary Characters' on Theodore Hook is a perfect expression of the new spirit:

we are compelled to regard him, as we do his old friend and ally, Maginn, as an illustration of the sententious proposition of Dr Johnson, in allusion to the fate of another literary man about town, – the unfortunate Savage, – that 'those that disregard the common maxims of life will make knowledge useless, wit ridiculous, and genius contemptible'.[3]

Although Maginn's character did not escape Victorian censure much of it was subsequently adapted to serve the needs of the Victorian writer. The common writer might have inched up the social scale but there were still many aspects of the literary profession that went against the grain of Victorian propriety. The most perverse characteristic of writers was their stubborn failure to acquire wealth. The flashy Dickens and his great contemporaries were exceptions, and managed to amass solid Victorian fortunes. But their very success meant that there was less money to share out among the majority of writers, and many of the Dickens circle were in funds one moment and bankrupt the next. Many of these bankruptcies, as noted earlier, were the result of modestly talented writers attempting to maintain the style of the prosperous middle classes. Bohemianism was, therefore, the perfect alibi for indigence. In an age which esteemed sobriety and Mammon, the literary community was bound to feel disadvantaged. However, if the literary character was allowed to be unconventional, then it was not too shameful for a great intellect to remain unencumbered by riches. In 1847, for example, when Henry Mayhew appeared before the bankruptcy court, his counsel, Mr Sturgeon, defended him on the grounds of his genius:

The bankrupt's avocations, those of a literary man, were such as perhaps rendered him too sanguine in his hopes, and somewhat irregular in his accounts, but those failings were almost universal among men of genius, and ought not to be visited with the same severity as would be exercised in the cases of a merchant or broker more fully conversant with the world as respected money transactions.[4]

Once the concept of bohemianism had been established it became possible to flout other aspects of Victorian conventionality. Bohemianism allowed delinquent Victorian writers to crave society's indulgence – Hook and Maginn had been able to suit themselves.

Victorian bohemianism was closely identified with a group of young men, in their twenties in the 1850s, who were followers of Dickens and Thackeray. George Augustus Sala was the most famous member of the Bohemian set, which included Robert and William Brough, Gus and Horace Mayhew, Percy, Bayle and Horace St John, Angus Reach, James Hannay, Henry Sutherland Edwards, Edmund Yates, Blanchard Jerrold, Mortimer Collins, and the publishers Henry Vizetelly and William Tinsley. It is not a list to conjure with. They were precocious, quick-witted and adventurous, but none of them produced a work of more than marginal sociological and historical interest: they were little Dickenses and little Thackerays; they could not compete, they could only imitate. James Hannay, who was regarded as one of the most talented of the young Bohemians, was routinely compared to Thackeray. After a boisterous career as a hard-drinking, scholarly midshipman, which culminated in a court martial, he came to London in 1845, aged eighteen, and, like other young writers before him, became a journalist on the *Morning Chronicle*. Impatient with his reporting chores he left to found his own satirical magazine *Pasquin*, in partnership with another young journalist Sutherland Edwards. This and similar ventures were short lived, and Hannay survived through the 1850s as a freelance journalist and occasional writer of nautical novels. After a spell as editor of the *Edinburgh Courant*, drink and money problems forced him to accept the post of H.M. Consul in Barcelona where he died, probably from alcohol poisoning, in 1873. The *Yorkshire Post*, in an obituary notice, called him 'one of the most brilliant men of letters of his generation'. The *Evening Standard* judged him to be 'almost the parallel of THACKERAY'[5] – but not quite of course.

Hannay was undoubtedly a gifted writer; he and Sala are the only Bohemians to have earned twentieth-century biographies. But by trotting along in the footsteps of their masters, Thackeray and Dickens respectively, they could only break out as their own men through their bohemianism rather than through literature. Indeed the kindly Dickens and the clubbable Thackeray, through their intense enjoyment of discipleship, were at least partly responsible for suffocating the talents of their young admirers. Dickens worked hard, if sometimes ineffectually, on behalf of his profession, but his open-handed generosity did not always have an invigorating effect on literary production. Sala recalled the heady days of the 1850s when Dickens made bohemianism possible:

most of us were about the idlest young dogs that squandered away their time on the pavements of Paris or London. *We would not work.* I declare in all candour and honesty, that, from the year 1852 to the year 1856, both inclusive, the average number of hours per week which I devoted to literary production did not exceed four . . . I usually wrote one article a week for Household Words; and I very rarely contributed to any other publication.[6]

At about six guineas per article Sala enjoyed 'a tolerably certain income'[7] of 300 guineas a year. This patronage had its disadvantages. Dickens could not resist the temptation of rewriting, 'improving', Sala's copy in his own inimitable style which led to Sala being branded a servile Dickensian. The servility of 'Dickens's Young Men' included their devotion to his favourite ink, Stephen's dark blue writing fluid.

Household Words was not the only magazine to sponsor young Bohemia during the 1850s. Other friendly journals included Vizetelly's *Illustrated Times*; the immensely successful *Illustrated London News* owned by Herbert Ingram and edited by Charles Mackay; G.H. Lewes's and Thornton Hunt's *Leader*, and *Punch* under Mark Lemon's editorship. All these journals, including *Household Words*, catered for a growing middle-class readership, a readership that the Bohemians affected to despise. The growth of this contemptible readership was a direct result of the repeal of the remaining taxes on knowledge – the advertising duty (1837), stamp duty (1855) and paper duty (1861) – which enabled newspaper and magazine proprietors to cut prices and increase circulations, always providing their product was neither too offensive nor too clever. The great new cheap newspaper of the 1850s was the penny *Daily Telegraph*. It combined dignified reporting with graphic sensationalism, and, with the help of Bohemian journalists of the quality of Sala, it became as popular with the general public as it was reviled by the intelligentsia.

Because journalism had become such an important source of income to the writers of the 1850s, their work was bound to incline towards the ephemeral. They were not merely born writers with nothing of moral or intellectual significance to say – such an indictment may apply to Sala and Yates but hardly to Hannay and Brough. As lower middle-class writers with neither private incomes nor university educations, they took to bohemianism out of necessity. They could not afford the luxury of writing for the *Quarterly Review*; they relied upon daily and weekly journalism for their income and could only snatch odd moments to work on novels or poems. And, for all that their writings are ephemeral, they still managed to play a prominent part in the literary culture of the 1840s, 50s and 60s.

The main forms of Bohemian literature were 'cockney' journalism, comic writing, burlesques, racy fiction and special correspondence. As an example of high Bohemian achievement Sala's *Twice Round the Clock* (1858) is hard to match. It consists of an hour by hour survey of London life replete with descriptions of Billingsgate, the Queen's Bench Prison, The Fashionable Club, Interior of a Pawnbroker's Shop, A Dancing Academy and Evans' Supper Rooms. True to Victorian bohemianism, Sala took care to describe only those scenes and incidents which 'could be told without offence to good manners and in household language'.[8] The book had a thoroughly Bohemian pedigree. Thackeray had presented Dickens with a copy of *Low Life*, a twenty-four hour guide to eighteenth-century London. Dickens lent the book to Sala who decided to update the idea for a series of articles in the *Welcome Guest*. It would be nice to discover that Maginn had given Thackeray *Low Life* in the first place.

As so much Bohemian literature, including the investigative journalism of Henry Mayhew and Angus Reach, dealt with street life, and as so many of the Bohemian writers were lower class, it was hardly surprising that they should have inclined towards radicalism and, in some cases, outright republicanism. The link between radicalism and bohemianism was not new, it had been forged at least a generation earlier by Godwin, Leigh Hunt, William Hone and others. Although Hunt was still active as a journalist, by the 1840s his politics had grown vague and he was indebted to the government and titled friends for a Civil List pension.

The most radical professional writer of the period was probably the dramatist and humorist Douglas Jerrold, who, like Dickens and Thackeray, was more of an uncle to Bohemia than a Bohemian himself. From 1841 to 1848 he was *Punch*'s chief political writer, when, under Lemon, *Punch* was a liberal paper. *Punch*'s historian has commented:

With his soft heart melting for the poor, and his fiery hatred of oppression warping his better judgment, he was led into that unreasonable attack upon property and authority to which Thackeray deprecatingly alludes. Because the poor are unhappy, according to his philosophy, therefore are the rich, most of them, their direct oppressors, and ruling bodies, tyrants.[9]

It is a fair summary of the radical position and one which was endorsed by the majority of young Bohemians – an exception was Hannay, who, as a disciple of Carlyle, despised the democratic impulse and favoured the leadership of a few wise men. Sala, who was not above trimming his politics to suit the requirements of his journalism, always liked to think of himself as a tribune of the people: 'Vizetelly, Augustus Mayhew, and I were the fiercest of Radicals; and Robert Brough was even more irreconcilable democratic Republican; and not one of us had ever studied at any English public school or university.'[10]

Brough's career is an example of the lower middle-class conquest of the London literary scene. The son of a failed brewer, he began his working life as a clerk in a Manchester office and in 1848, aged twenty, founded and edited a satirical magazine, the *Liverpool Lion*, with his brother William. The same year they collaborated on their first play,

The Enchanted Isle, a burlesque of *The Tempest*, which, after Benjamin Webster had brought it to the Adelphi Theatre, made them the young celebrities of the season. Sala observed:

he leapt at once from provincial obscurity, raw, half-taught, and quite deficient in worldly experience, into a prominent position among the wits and *viveurs* of a bustling time. . . . He had the run of the green-rooms and the literary circles, when it would have done him much more good to have had the run of a decent library, or even a garret.[11]

As Sala implies, Brough was a model Bohemian both in his personal life and in his writings. He was the author of burlesques and comedies, novels and poems and a spoof biography of the Bohemian hero (much admired by Maginn) Sir John Falstaff. As a journalist he contributed to *Household Words*, was co-editor of the *Man in the Moon* and the *Welcome Guest*, was leader writer of the *Atlas* and Brussels correspondent of the *Sunday Times*, as well as writing for every comic magazine of the period. As both a Bohemian and the 'fiercest of Radicals', he had, according to the conservative Edmund Yates, a 'deep vindictive hatred of wealth and rank and respectability'.[12] His politics were most evident in his poetry; his collection *Songs of the Governing Classes* (1855), published by Vizetelly, was openly republican and revolutionary. It was dedicated to his friend E.M. Whitty, 'I believe in the Revolution you have said is coming.' Many of the poems advocated class warfare, such as his spirited diatribe against 'My Lord Tomnoddy' whose congenital idiocy is no obstacle to an Oxbridge education, a commission in the best regiment, a seat in Parliament and membership of the Privy Council:

> Office he'll hold, and patronage sway;
> Fortunes and lives he will vote away –
> And what are his qualifications? – ONE!
> He's the Earl of Fitzdotterel's eldest son.

When applying to the Royal Literary Fund for a grant he omitted to include his poetry among the list of his published works.

Because the Bohemians were identified with radicalism and anti-aristocratic sentiments, and as they were also arrivistes – noisy, swaggering cockneys, sons of tapsters, comedians and clerks – they found themselves attacked by those cultural and political conservatives who wished to preserve the amateur, gentlemanly and classical status of English literature. The most virulent and consistent enemy of the Bohemians was the *Saturday Review*, founded in 1855 by the Conservative MP, landowner and classicist, A.J. Beresford-Hope. From the first number the *Saturday Review* set itself up as the leading intellectual periodical of the day, the *University Review* in fact if not in name. Beresford-Hope hired the ex-editor of the *Morning Chronicle*, John Douglas Cook, as editor with the job of making the magazine a commercial success. Cook, a rough and uncultured professional newspaperman, had no quarrel with the Bohemians, many of whom had served under him on the *Morning Chronicle*; but he recognised the value of controversy and gave his troupe of 'mature puppies',[13] as the *Leader* dubbed his belligerent contributors, full rein to exercise their considerable talent for demolition. The Saturday Reviewers were university teachers, rising politicians, clever young clerics and barristers (chiefly barristers); they were men of education and profession at a time when educational and professional qualifications were designedly expensive. The one thing Henry Maine, G.S. Venables, W. Vernon Harcourt, Fitzjames Stephen and E.A. Freeman were not, was writers by profession.

In 1855, a few months before the first number of the *Saturday Review* was published, Beresford-Hope spoke on behalf of 'the Universities' at the Royal Literary Fund dinner. He remarked on the similarities between the Fund and the universities: 'The same principle that secretly distributes the prizes of this Literary Fund, openly and with all the glory and pomp of a theatre or a senate house, distributes the prizes of our Universities . . . . A University education makes a man.' No doubt it had been most agreeable for Beresford-Hope to win the Cambridge prize for Latin verse, but it must have been most disagreeable for Robert Brough and other impoverished Bohemians to receive the backdoor charity of the Literary Fund. Edmund Yates, no university man, cordially detested the Saturday Reviewers for their persistent denigration of the wage-earning writer:

The gentlemen who just about this time were establishing a new school of critical literature were constantly either savagely ferocious or bitterly sarcastic with professional literary men – persons, that is to say, who lived by the product of their pens, who in most cases had not had the advantage of that University education in which their detractors gloried . . . . And, save that he was endowed with more and finer brains than the average run of humanity, Robert Brough was the exact type of the class thus bitterly reviled.[14]

Brough was in good company as the *Saturday Review*'s fiercest attacks were directed against Dickens, both as a vulgar novelist and as the scourge of the Royal Literary Fund.

The bitter war between the Bohemians and the *Saturday Review* became a truce in the pages of the *Cornhill* (1860) and the *Pall Mall Gazette* (1865), both owned by the publisher George Smith and edited by Frederick Greenwood. The *Cornhill*'s first editor was Thackeray, who had friends in both camps. Albert Smith, Sala and Hannay were among the early contributors, as were Fitzjames Stephen and Matthew Arnold. Greenwood succeeded Thackeray as editor in 1863 and continued his eclectic policy. Although a Tory, Greenwood had been on the fringes of the Bohemian circle in the 1850s, writing for both the *Illustrated Times* and the *Welcome Guest*. In 1865, when Smith appointed him the first editor of the evening paper the *Pall Mall Gazette*, he was happy to employ his old Bohemian acquaintances – at least they were experienced journalists. The *Pall Mall Gazette* had a disappointingly slow start, despite contributions from Fitzjames and Leslie Stephen, R.H. Hutton, Lewes and George Eliot. It took a piece of journalism in the classic Bohemian manner to rescue the paper's circulation. In the spring of 1866 James Greenwood, Frederick's distinctly Bohemian younger brother, contributed a paper 'A Night in a Casual Ward' by 'An Amateur Casual': it was an immediate sensation; exactly the kind of slumming investigative journalism that Mayhew had pioneered in the *Morning Chronicle* and Sala had popularised in *Household Words*.

The success of the *Cornhill* inspired John Maxwell, Mary Braddon's consort and the publisher of the *Welcome Guest*, to found the monthly *Temple Bar* with Sala as editor and Yates as sub-editor. It was a haven for the Sala set, and from the first was attacked by the *Saturday Review* which reserved its most splenetic abuse for Sala and all his works. Among the regular contributors during the 1860s were Blanchard Jerrold, Wiltshire Austin, Sutherland Edwards, Robert Buchanan, Mortimer Collins and Miss Braddon. *Temple Bar* showed the Bohemians, now in their thirties, settling down to solid, middle-range journalism tailor-made for 'the comfortable, literate, but ill-educated middle-class which read magazines for pure entertainment and easy instruction.'[15]

If the 1850s were the heyday of bohemianism, by the 1860s the Bohemian spirit was cracking up. Several of the most talented young Bohemians, including Brough, Reach and E.M. Whitty, had died either from bad luck or dissipation. Jerrold, whose wit was supposed to be peerless, died in 1857. Thackeray, some of whose lustre had rubbed off on Bohemia, died in 1863. In the spring of 1863, Justin McCarthy, reviewing a crop of Bohemian novels in the *Westminster Review*, wrote what amounted to an obituary notice of Bohemia. It was not the death of an English writer that had inspired McCarthy's funereal tone, but the death, a few months earlier, of the French writer Henry Mürger, author of the novel *Scènes de la Vie de Bohème* (1849): 'The era of the recognised distinctive Bohemian is gone: it began with Balzac, and ended with Mürger. Its reign was very brief, and its kingdom very narrow; Paris was its cradle, its home and its grave.'[16] While Balzac, like Dickens, was much more than a Bohemian, Mürger was a thorough Bohemian to whom McCarthy gave credit for artistic sincerity in contrast to the London Bohemian, 'who swaggers through literature more roysteringly and more noisily than his confrère of Paris'. Although Mürger was dead, McCarthy recognised that the literature of French Bohemia would live on (this was some thirty years before Puccini's *La Bohème*), while the literature of the very lively Sala and his friends was in a bad way:

already there are quickly spreading indications that the public have had nearly enough of the fast novel of London life – the dashing article on London haunts, the wearily droll burlesque in which the classic and the Cockney are blended in fantastic *olla podrida*. For, after all, there really is a world outside Fleet Street.

McCarthy's attack on London Bohemia provoked a defence from Mortimer Collins writing in Sala's *Temple Bar*. According to Collins, Mürger was 'a weak and morbid mortal, after all, for whom Bohemia's brilliant atmosphere contained too much oxygen'.[17] The true Bohemian was happy and robust, in short, Falstaffian. Collins singles out Maginn and E.M. Whitty as fine specimens of British bohemianism, and then finds himself forced to admit that, unlike Mürger and de Musset, neither of them wrote anything that had 'a permanent effect on the national literature'. This leads him to concede that they were, in their way, as weak and morbid as Mürger, 'indeed dissipation is sometimes the only resource from the corroding cares against which it has been found vain to struggle'. As self-serving a moral as one could wish for.

Writing some twenty years later, Edmund Yates wisely avoided the whole question of the literary merit of Anglo-French Bohemia. He was interested in bohemianism as a way of life rather than a way for art:

Our British Bohemia . . . differed in many respects from that fanciful territory inhabited by Schaunard [Mürger's hero] and his comrades. It was less picturesque, it was more practical and commonplace, perhaps a trifle more vulgar; but its denizens had this in common with their French prototypes – that they were young, gifted, and reckless; that they worked by fits and starts, and never except under the pressure of necessity . . . and that – greatest item of resemblance – they had a thorough contempt for the dress, usages and manners of ordinary middle-class civilization.[18]

Unfortunately the British Bohemian's contempt for middle-class morality did not result in a British *Les Fleurs du Mal*.

Although the London Bohemians refused to acknowledge the supremacy of Paris in matters Bohemian, nevertheless it was their favourite continental resort. What attracted Sala and his friends to Paris was not so much that it was a city of artistic and moral freedoms – it wasn't – nor was it an urge to pay homage to Mürger and de Musset; rather, as Dickens and Thackeray had found before them, Paris was cheap and made excellent copy. During the French coup d'état of 1851, for example, Paris became the venue for a complete picnic of Bohemian 'special correspondents' including Sala, Shirley Brooks, Sutherland Edwards and Bayle St John.

For all that McCarthy detected a death rattle in the Sala set, he was not unsympathetic to Bohemian character, even if Bohemian literature, Thackeray excepted, was insubstantial, 'In its essence, Bohemia was or is a protest against the subjection of human life to money-making, and of human intellect to conventional rule'. It was a generous assessment, but as an epitaph it was premature. Bohemianism was not dead it had simply entered a period of long decline. Of the original Bohemians, those who did not die young found themselves celebrities and occasionally even rich. They changed from being careless Bohemians into happy hypocrites; members of the Reform or Carlton Clubs. Their legacy, the Bohemian character, was inherited by a generation who seemed to have less literary talent though even more swagger.

The Bohemians of the 1860s and 1870s gravitated towards the Catherine Street offices of the publishers Edward and William Tinsley. Edward had come to London from Hertfordshire in 1854, had met the Broughs and worked on the comic paper *Diogenes*. On discovering that his literary talents were unappreciated, he set up as a publisher in partnership with his older brother William. Their first Bohemian novel was Sala's *The Seven Sons of Mammon* (1861), and other Bohemian writers they attracted to their list included Yates, Blanchard Jerrold, Richard Burton, Andrew Halliday, E.L.L. Blanchard and Mortimer Collins. They did not confine themselves to Bohemians. Their early commercial success was built upon Mary Braddon's *Lady Audley's Secret* (1862), and among their commercial failures were three novels by the young Thomas Hardy.

Edward Tinsley died young and popular in 1866. His brother 'Bill' carried on the business – not very successfully – and died a lonely, garrulous and impoverished old man in 1902. It was under William

Tinsley that Bohemia began to look distinctly shabby. In 1867 he founded the last of the old-style Bohemian magazines, the shilling *Tinsley's Magazine*, and installed Yates as editor. From the beginning it was a failure and confirmed Bohemia's drift towards the third-rate. Yates gave up the editorship in 1869, noting that the 'triumphant success, such as had attended the establishment of *Cornhill* and *Temple Bar*, was no longer to be commanded by the projectors of shilling magazines'.[19] There were simply not enough writers or readers to make a rival to *Temple Bar* viable; especially after George Bentley had bought the magazine in 1867, reorganised its finances, and attracted a galaxy of star writers including Trollope, Wilkie Collins, Turgenev and Mrs Henry Wood. Tinsley, who lacked almost any capital, could not hope to compete. After Yates's departure the magazine was edited 'anyhow' by the firm's accountant, and ran up losses of £300 a year. Tinsley put a brave face on it, 'what cheaper advertisement can I have for £25 a month? It advertises my name and publications and it keeps my authors together.'[20] His authors at this time were hardly household names. Among the regular contributors to *Tinsley's Magazine* were Dick Dowling, Henri Van Laun, and G.L.M. Strauss.

Dr Strauss had been a key Bohemian figure for nearly half a century. An eccentric German chemist, surgeon, author and politician, he settled in London in 1840 and became editor of the *Chemical Times* and the *Grocer*, a crony of Sala and a founder member of the Savage Club. His rambling and charming *Reminiscences of An Old Bohemian*, published by Tinsley in 1882, are a fitting valediction to London Bohemia. Appropriately they were dedicated to Octavian Blewitt, Secretary of the Royal Literary Fund, 'as a feeble mark of the author's heartfelt gratitude'.

THE BOHEMIANS were not earnest. They did not engage in the great debates on sanitary reform, democracy, culture and religion. Except for Jerrold, Vizetelly and Henry Mayhew, who were actively engaged in radical politics, their radicalism was emotional and impractical. Their achievement was to cater for the flip-side of the Victorian coin – an insatiable craving for humour. Above all else a Bohemian was expected to possess a famous sense of humour. This exalting of the joke and the jest was not confined to the club or tavern room, it was expected to permeate the Bohemian's literary work. A few comic masterpieces stand out from the general humorous sludge: *Pickwick Papers*, *Jorrock's Jaunts and Jollities* and *Vanity Fair*. Almost nothing else has survived. But humour and satire are the slaves of fashion and no doubt the satirical magazines and funny satirical novels of our own age will one day be as impenetrable and unfunny as *Man in the Moon, Diogenes* and the novels of forgotten Bohemians.

Pickwick Papers is probably the comic novel of the century. But although Dickens was unrivalled as a comic novelist, the doyen of comic writers and the prince of punsters was Douglas Jerrold. Apart from his reputation in literary circles for spontaneous and even dangerous wit, his public fame rested on his comedies and his comic journalism – both areas in which the Bohemians specialised, if not excelled. Like Sala and Yates, Jerrold was the son of a theatrical family and was educated in the green-room as much as the schoolroom. He began his literary career as a sixteen year old journalist and his first stage play, the farce *More Frightened than Hurt*, was performed in 1821 when he was just eighteen. After several years as a hack playwright turning out farces for £2 or £3 a time, he achieved popular success with the nautical comedy *Black-Ey'd Susan* in 1829. The play made a fortune for the periodically bankrupt actor–manager R.W. Elliston, but earned Jerrold just £70. It did, however, secure his reputation as a popular dramatist and enabled him to graduate to writing for the patent theatres.

The patent theatres, Covent Garden and Drury Lane, were the only two theatres in London that were licensed to stage performances of 'legitimate' drama (Licensing Act 1737), including the plays of Shakespeare. The other theatres were only permitted to stage 'entertainments', where the acting was subordinate to dancing, singing and 'low' comedy. This restrictive practice meant that the majority of playwrights who wished to earn any kind of living were forced to write farces, extravaganzas, burlesques and pantomimes. A would-be Shakespeare, Daniel Boileau, was informed by Elliston in 1822 that his tragedy was unsuitable, 'there can however be little doubt that the author of this drama can succeed . . . if Mr Boileau would attack his mind to a farce'. The challenge proved too much for Mr Boileau who attacked his throat with a razor instead.

In 1843, after a campaign led by Talfourd, Heraud and other writers of dull tragedies, the Licensing Act was repealed. However, accustomed to gaudy and sensational entertainment, the theatre-going public were slow to take advantage of their new-found freedom of choice. In addition, there was a severe shortage of respectable acting talent. When the Lyceum staged *Henry IV* to mark the repeal of the Act, the performance was a disaster and the management swiftly recouped their losses by staging a dramatic version of Dickens's current novel *Martin Chuzzlewit*.

One immediate effect of the repeal was to give a boost to the five-act comedy which was about the highest form of drama that actors and audiences could cope with. The actor–manager Benjamin Webster further strengthened the comic grip on the London stage by offering a £500 prize for the best 'pure and high comedy'. The winner was Mrs Gore's *Quid Pro Quo* selected from ninety-seven entries. Gilbert À Beckett promptly satirised the whole event in *Scenes from the Rejected Comedies* (1844). After the comedy, the favourite vehicle for Bohemian humour was the burlesque, a dramatic form which specialised in parody and allowed full scope for excruciating puns, mild satire, comic songs and special effects. According to Sutherland Edwards the burlesque 'attracted the most original talents'[21] of the age, most notably Robert Brough's.

Until 1860, when Dion Boucicault persuaded Webster to pay him a royalty on box-office receipts which earned him £10,000 for a single play, dramatists were usually payed a lump sum of perhaps £2 a night. Boucicault's pre-1860 income from a five-act comedy was around £300, though the average dramatist would have earned between £50 and £150 – the equivalent of the copyright price for a standard three-volume novel. Against these relatively low payments should be set rapidity of production. It often took a hack playwright no more than a week or two to run up a comedy or burlesque, not least because the plots were nearly always plagiarised from novels or continental drama. À Beckett managed to write at least fifty-five unoriginal comedies during a twenty-year period as a busy journalist, and the Bohemian journalist E.L.L. Blanchard wrote several hundred comedies, pantomimes, farces and burlesques, some at the rate of ten shillings an act.

Quite apart from any hope of financial gain, the pleasures of green-room society were often reward enough for the stage-struck writer. Indeed, the whole ephemeral business of mid-Victorian play-making was essential to the writer who wished to exercise Bohemian freedoms. Jerrold, Dickens, Lemon, Collins, À Beckett, Lewes, Lytton, Brooks, Brough and Taylor were all habitués of the green-room and keen amateur actors not least because theatrical society, unlike club society, encouraged encounters between the sexes. And the less serious the play the more friendly the actress. From the fictional Arthur Pendennis's adolescent obsession with Mrs Haller to Dickens's ardour for Ellen Ternan, the Bohemian and the actress kept close company.

Of more lasting literary and social significance than Victorian comedy, was comic journalism stiffened by a political spine. Until the founding of *Punch* in 1841, comic journalism was a fugitive affair confined to the scurrilous columns of Hook's *John Bull* or Renton Nicholson's *Town*, and to very short-lived comic papers such as Jerrold's *Punch in London* (1833). If *Punch* had a native forerunner it was *Figaro in London* (1832–9), a penny satirical journal illustrated with political cartoons by Robert Seymour and edited by Gilbert À Beckett and Henry Mayhew.

In or around 1837, Jerrold, Laman Blanchard, Thackeray, John Poole, Kenny Meadows, Orrin Smith, Percival Leigh and other founders of bohemianism mooted a London Charivari, modelled on Philipon's *Paris Charivari*, a highly successful satirical daily, illustrated with a full-page political cartoon – the 'large cut'. The new magazine was to be financed by a cooperative of contributors, though, as the cooperators were understandably nervous about each other's solvency, the idea came to nothing. In 1841 the engraver Ebenezer Landells resuscitated the plan, and persuaded the printer Joseph Last to put up the necessary capital. The title and plan of contents was supplied by Mayhew, who became the first editor, assisted by À Beckett, Mark Lemon, Jerrold, Stirling Coyne and W.H. Wills. The new magazine was decent and bourgeois: 'the character of the paper, instead of partaking of that acidulated, sardonic satire which was distinctive of Philipon's journal, on which it was to have been modelled, took its tone from Mayhew's genial temperament, and from the first became, or aimed at becoming, a budget of wit, fun, and kindly humour'.[22]

In its first year *Punch* lost some £600 and published its first obituary – appropriately of William Maginn who had been an occasional contributor of poems and jokes. As an ailing weekly *Punch* was bought by Bradbury and Evans in December 1842, and Mark Lemon was installed as editor in place of the unreliable Mayhew. With one of London's major printing firms behind it, the future of *Punch* was guaranteed. It owed its success (within a few years it had a circulation of 30,000) to a unique combination of sound financing and careful editorship. Like his close friend Dickens, Lemon was a shrewd judge of the new middle-class readership, and was adept at serving up an agreeable blend of topical and family humour. Jokes, quips, puns, pranks, even satire, all had to pass the Lemon test of cleanliness and inoffensiveness. Even the politicians pilloried in the 'large cut' were more flattered than hurt. The Liberal politician G.J. Goschen claimed to have 'attained the highest ambition which a statesman can reach – namely, to have a cartoon in *Punch* all to himself'.[23]

First among the distinguished contributors to *Punch* was Thackeray, who began writing papers for the magazine in 1842 and, with his series *The Snobs of England* (1847–8), became the most popular *Punch* writer. In addition to the founders others who became *Punch* regulars were Gus and Horace Mayhew, Shirley Brooks, Percival Leigh, Tom Taylor and F.C. Burnand, and the graphic artists John Leech, John Tenniel, Kenny Meadows, Phiz and the young George du Maurier. Nearly every comic writer and cartoonist of consequence appeared in *Punch*'s pages except Charles Dickens, who may have shied away from a journal so closely connected with his great rival Thackeray (who in turn never contributed to *Household Words*). Any hope of enlisting Dickens as a contributor was dashed in 1858 when Lemon sensibly refused to print Dickens's open letter on the subject of his marriage difficulties.

By the 1860s *Punch* was a Victorian institution. Lemon, the ex-publican, took pride in his supposition that *Punch* readers were also *Times* readers; '*Punch* keeps up by keeping to the gentlemanly view of things and its being known that Bohemians don't write for it', he is said to have remarked to a *Punch* gathering.[24] This was wishful thinking by a new pillar of the establishment attempting to distance himself from his less successful friends. Bohemians did write for *Punch* from Maginn to Mortimer Collins, though probably the only out-and-out Bohemian appointed to the staff was Gus Mayhew. The *Saturday Review*, which could boast *Times* leader writers among its contributors, sneered: 'In second-class railway carriages, in the lower forms of a public school, amongst the commercial gentlemen at a country inn – wherever there is little education and a good allowance of animal spirits – *Punch* is greedily read.'[25]

The *Punch* regulars earned good salaries, Lemon himself ended up on £1,500 a year – at that time the highest income earned by any weekly editor. This wealth added to *Punch*'s self-importance and inspired a series of imitators and aggressive competitors, particularly during the 1840s and 1850s. *Punch* became a sort of senior common room to which young humorists graduated after working on risky, under-capitalised little magazines of their own founding, such as James Hannay's and Sutherland Edward's *Pasquin* (1847) and *Puppet Show* (1848).

Pasquin was a sharp-edged 'Satirical, Political, Critical, Theatrical, Whimsical, and Quizzical Chronicle',[26] but it lacked both the editorial skills and the funding of its supposed rival *Punch* and ceased publication

after the eighth number. However, Henry Vizetelly had been sufficiently impressed by *Pasquin* to back a successor, *Puppet Show*, edited by
John Valentine Bridgeman with Hannay and Edwards as principal
contributors. *Puppet Show* was hardly a commercial rival to *Punch* though
it proved a quick-witted sparring partner. As well as Hannay and
Edwards, it was packed with young talent – Shirley Brooks, Angus
Reach, Robert Brough and E.L.L. Blanchard – all more than willing to
take a stab at the established reputations of Jerrold, Thackeray, Lemon
and Mayhew. A third comic magazine, *Man in the Moon*, edited by
Albert Smith assisted by Reach and Sala, completed the three-cornered
comic rivalry. This rivalry was intense at an editorial level, and reveals
that the Bohemians were as quarrelsome as they were matey. Hannay
despised Jerrold and Lemon of *Punch* and Smith of *Man in the Moon*;
Lemon despised Smith and disliked Hannay and Sala; Sala and
Hannay disliked each other. None of this was of much consequence, for,
as Burnand recalled, 'their attacks on one another in print were
absolutely unintelligible to the general public',[27] and there were also
those in the other ranks, notably Brough and Reach, who seemed quite
happy writing for all three magazines at the same time.

Inspite of their feuding and infighting, the most striking characteristic of the Bohemian community of comic journalists was their fondness
for each other's company. At the slightest pretext they would form an
exclusive club among their friends. It is sometimes hard to tell which
came first: the members of a Bohemian club deciding to establish yet
another comic paper, or the staff of a comic paper deciding to found yet
another Bohemian club. The staff of *Punch* dined with their publishers
every Wednesday evening fifty times a year. The *Punch* dinner gained a
legendary reputation for exclusivity, so that it became the dearest wish
of the young comic journalist to be allowed to carve his initials on the
famous *Punch* dinner table. The regularity, informality and conviviality
of these occasions is often held up as a principal reason for *Punch*'s
extraordinary success.

The club was the adhesive of Bohemian life. It was more than simply
a haven from family life – or lack of it. It provided writers, who by
definition have to work alone, with an opportunity to meet together. To
have a comfortable rendezvous, close to an oyster tavern and complete
with library and bar, was the Victorian male writer's chief pleasure.
The first formal club designed largely by and for writers was the
Garrick, founded in 1831. For most of the 1830s and 1840s, however, the
small informal dining club was the favourite leisure activity. Jerrold, as

might be expected, was the great founder of such clubs: the Mulberries (1824) which became the Shakespeare Club, the Museum Club, the Wits and Our Club were all small gatherings of Jerrold's good friends. Jerrold was also the founder of a formal club, the Whittington (1847), for clubless young Londoners of the clerkly class. The venture was derided by the smart journals for its presumption in aping the West End. It was further ridiculed for taking the pioneering step of admitting women as members. Women were designed to be kissed or to serve mutton chops, but had no place in the club-room where the conversation was supposed to be both too clever and too coarse for them.

Thackeray, who loved the company of his fellows, was one of the founders of the Fielding Club (1852) which met at Offley's, a tavern in Henrietta Street. The Fielding aimed to provide the livelier members of the Garrick with somewhere to go after midnight, no doubt to indulge in the kind of frank talk that Thackeray, who named the club, associated with the author of *Tom Jones*. Its members included Albert Smith, G.H. Lewes, W.H. Russell, Tom Taylor, Shirley Brooks and Edmund Yates. Another nocturnal club, inevitably called the Sheridan, met at Stone's in Panton Street, and Alfred and Fred Dickens, Gus and Horace Mayhew, Blanchard Jerrold, Richard Burton and Henry Vizetelly were among those who thought it 'the greatest enjoyment in life to prolong the night until an hour or two before sunrise'.[28] All these gatherings were conveniently situated in the middle of a notorious centre for prostitution – a fact which is never referred to in club memoirs.

The most famous and successful of these informal clubs of writers and artists was the Savage, which held its first meetings in 1857 in the Crown, Vinegar Yard, Drury Lane in the room where the *Punch* dinners had been held a decade earlier. The Savage was almost certainly and quite appropriately named after Richard Savage by Robert Brough, who with his brothers and Sala, Strauss and Landells, gave it a distinctive Bohemian character. From the first it was a club of professional writers, including some of those likely to be black-balled by the Garrick and certain to be pilloried in the *Saturday Review*. Most of the original Savages had been contributors to Vizetelly's *Illustrated News*, Yates's *Train*, and *Punch*. For the next twenty years the itinerant Savage Club was the first resort of prominent Bohemians. In time, however, it became almost respectable: barristers became members; Gladstone spoke at the annual dinner, and, in 1881, it abandoned its gentle crawl among the taverns and hotels of the Strand and found an official home in Lancaster House in the Savoy. This marked the demise of old

Bohemia. The following year the Prince of Wales became a life member.[29]

The flavour of club life was captured by Thackeray in his last complete novel, *The Adventures of Philip* (1861–2), in a passage that was often cited as conveying the essence of 50s bohemianism. Thackeray's Bohemia was a pleasant land:

a land over which hangs an endless fog, occasioned by much tobacco; a land of chambers, billiard-rooms, supper-rooms, oysters; a land of song; a land where soda-water flows freely in the morning; a land of tin-dish covers from taverns, and frothing porter; a land of lotos-eating (with lots of cayenne pepper), or pulls on the river, of delicious reading of novels, magazines, and saunterings in many studios; a land where men call each other by their Christian names; where most are poor, where almost all are young, and where, if a few oldsters do enter, it is because they have preserved more tenderly and carefully than other folks their youthful spirits, and the delightful capacity to be idle.[30]

This glows with warmth and fellow feeling; it is touching and finally a little embarrassing. Thackeray liked to think of himself as a boyish oldster, but was not always so kindly regarded by the youngsters. His famous quarrel in 1858 with Edmund Yates, which led to his even more famous rift with Yates's patron Dickens, is evidence of his acute sensitivity to the charge that his lotus-eating was contrived. Yates had sniped at Thackeray in an unpleasant, though not unperceptive, article in the society weekly *Town Talk*: 'No one meeting him could fail to recognise in him a gentleman; his bearing is cold and uninviting, his style of conversation either openly cynical or affectedly good-natured and benevolent; his bonhomie is forced.'[31] Bonhomie was the cement of Bohemia and Thackeray was found wanting. His immediate reaction was to secure Yates's expulsion from the Garrick on the thinnest of pretexts: that Yates's acquaintance with him was entirely derived from their membership of the Garrick, and that Yates had therefore abused the club's unwritten code of conduct. No mention was made of their hearty late-night sessions at Offley's. The episode shows how much he was hurt by the revelation that he was not universally admired by the youngsters. It may also help to explain his valedictory remark in *Philip*, 'I have lost my way to Bohemia now'.

From his early association with Maginn to his quarrel with Yates, Thackeray was never wholly relaxed in Bohemian company. Probably he was too self-conscious and too dignified; he must always have been aware that he was a giant, both physically and intellectually, and that his companions were pygmies by comparison. They might have forgiven him his stature had he not also been a snob: it was alleged that he attended Bohemian gatherings with a dress-suit packed in a bag in case he was called to more exalted company. But, if his position in Bohemia was equivocal, it was generally acknowledged, even by Yates, that no writer had had a greater influence on the creation of the Bohemian identity.

Thackeray was the master of the Bohemian novel – that is, novels with sub-plots set in or around Fleet Street and the Strand. The first whiff of such a novel was Lewes's *Ranthorpe* (1847), the story of a young, vain and silly lawyer's clerk (not unlike Heraud) who sweeps to the top of literary society in the late 1830s and early 1840s. Percy Ranthorpe is more of a middle-class Bulwer Lytton than a Bohemian; indeed he has much in common with Bulwer Lytton's hero Ernest Maltravers. For all that it is a pretentious, even tiresome novel, it gives an account of a young author's struggles and introduces a Bohemian literary world a year before Thackeray's *Pendennis*.

But it was *Pendennis* that gave definition to Victorian bohemianism by refashioning the often sordid world of Maginn and Hook into a romantic 'Corporation of the Goosequill'. The teenage Edmund Yates read *Pendennis* in monthly parts and could not wait 'to get admitted into the ranks of literary men, among whom I might possibly, by industry and perseverance, rise to some position'.[32] A generation later Andrew Lang testified to the novel's potency, 'Marryat never made us wish to run away to sea. . . . But the story of Pen made one wish to run away to literature.'[33] Not, of course, because it could claim the slightest degree of realism; such a novel could hardly have recruited young authors, but because it was a genial caricature that made the whole business of authorship seem gloriously easy; and when it was not easy, this scattering of ink was at least good fun.

Pendennis aimed at far more than the creation of a beckoning literary world. It was Thackeray's grand intention to explore the psychology of an irresolute young man adrift in a pitching society; his choice of authorship as his hero's profession was largely incidental. For Yates and Co., Pendennis's profession was the whole of the novel. Throughout the 1850s the young Bohemians published their versions of the *Pendennis* theme. The result was a string of autobiographical and humorous novels firmly located in Bohemian London: Robert Brough's *Marston Lynch* (1856–7) serialised in Yates's *Train*; Hannay's unfinished *Bagot's Youth* (1857) serialised in his own magazine, the *Idler*; ex-*Leader* journalist E.M. Whitty's *Friends of Bohemia* (1857), dashed off in two weeks; Gus

Mayhew's *Paved with Gold: or, the Romance and Reality of London Streets* (1858). The best of these was Brough's *Marston Lynch* which would never have been written but for Sala's chronic unreliability.

In 1856 following the failure of the *Comic Times*, a magazine edited by Yates and funded by Herbert Ingram in yet another bid to compete with *Punch*, Yates started the *Train* on capital of £120 put up by the contributors. In an attempt to generate a regular readership Sala was engaged to write a serial story for the new monthly. By the time Sala's copy was due he had gone to ground somewhere in Paris. The desperate Yates placed an advertisement in *The Times*, 'Bohemian where art thou',[34] which failed to flush out the intoxicated Sala. Robert Brough was prevailed upon to take his place, and, with so little time to prepare for his first attempt at fiction, launched into a thinly disguised account of his own literary life, *Marston Lynch: His Life and Times; His Friends and Enemies; His Victories and Defeats; His Kicks and Halfpence; A Personal Biography*.

The novel describes the progress of Marston Lynch from teenage editor of the *Longport Flail* (*Liverpool Lion*), a satirical weekly with a circulation of 2,000, through provincial playwright to metropolitan Bohemian. Brough clearly enjoyed himself: the action of the novel is peppered with references to the real Bohemian scene; to the work of Jerrold, Landells, Henry Mayhew, Albert Smith and Kenny Meadows; to the world of comic writers; to his own amateur status as a novelist; to the *Train* for having the courage to serialise his novel in the first place. Unlike *Pendennis*, where Thackeray has remodelled the literary world into a rosy simulacrum, the literary characters and incidents of *Marston Lynch* are raw; quite untouched by art except for the decent masking of proper names. So whereas Thackeray's literary characters are stagy, Brough, faithful to the originals, achieves a triumph of Bohemian characterisation.

For some reason, possibly ill health, Brough failed to complete the novel, and it was left to Sala, as an act of piety, to prepare it for posthumous publication in 1860. In the unfinished version there is a melodramatic sub-plot concerning a secret will in Lynch's favour. The device was hardly original and Brough almost certainly intended it as a burlesque. In the completed posthumous version the will is ignored and with much greater fidelity to the circumstances of Brough's life, Lynch is allowed to achieve success as 'a POPULAR AUTHOR'.

Before Lynch reaches this happy, though possibly unintended conclusion, his 'defeats' afford Brough an opportunity to comment on the vagaries of the literary profession. Among Lynch's defeats is his brief editorship of an unnamed satirical magazine. The chief reason for the magazine's failure was Lynch's suicidal habit of maliciously attacking fellow authors, 'the men of his own thin-skinned order'.[35] Yates and Hannay would have appreciated this analysis. Brough, however, wastes no time in learning his own lessons. The novel contains a four-page attack on the *Athenaeum*, which, as the most influential literary review in terms of sales, was persistently reviled by disappointed novelists, especially under the editorship of the unfortunate Hepworth Dixon who was notorious for puffing his own books. Lynch savages the *Asinaeum* and its editor, 'the flea' Hayporth Dibbs, and his motley editorial crew of 'gangling schoolboys', 'discarded, unjust serving-men, younger sons of younger brothers, revolted tapsters, and ostlers tradefallen'.[36] The *Athenaeum* did not review *Marston Lynch*.

Lynch's major defeat is the failure of his five-act comedy and the subsequent collapse of his health from a 'brain fever' which totally incapacitates him. During his illness he is supported by his friends who undertake his literary commissions as well as their own. This lengthy description of Bohemian esprit de corps is an exact account of the plight of Angus Bethune Reach, who died while Brough was in the middle of the novel.

Reach was one of the best nineteenth-century journalists. He was famous for over-working, and never turned down a commission even if it meant writing eighteen hours a day. He was particularly sought after as a comic journalist, though he is now remembered as a pioneer social reporter – the author of a series of papers in the *Morning Chronicle* on life and labour in northern cities. Charles Mackay considered him the first to turn journalism into a 'fine art':

[He] introduced a style till then [1841] unpractised, except in the editorial articles, by means of which he brought before the reader's mind a vivid picture, such as a novelist would paint, of every occurrence that passed under his eye – rapid, correct, graphic, and full of life and animation . . . picturesque reporting became thenceforward the fashion, and has so remained to this day [1877], when the picturesque threatens to be swallowed up by the sensational.[37]

In 1854, aged thirty-three, Reach fell ill with that common writer's ailment 'brain-fatigue', diagnosed by his doctor as a 'paralytic affection'. As Brough wrote of Marston Lynch, Reach was 'attacked with brain fever, and reduced to the condition of a mechanic with his arms broken, – worse, for mechanics provide against such emergencies by mutual-assistance funds – provisions which literary men never think of, or, if they do, can never agree sufficiently among themselves to put into practice'.[38] (A reference to the failure of the Guild of Literature and Art, and the Dickens, Dilke, Forster campaign against the Royal Literary Fund.)

At first the *Morning Chronicle*, under Cook's editorship, agreed to continue Reach's salary during his illness: but within a few months the paper had changed hands and the new proprietors discontinued the allowance. Shirley Brooks then took it upon himself to write Reach's weekly column in the *Inverness Courier*, handing over the guinea a week income to his sick friend. He also applied to the Royal Literary Fund and the Royal Bounty Fund on Reach's behalf, and obtained £50 and £100 respectively. Other help came from members of the Fielding Club, led by Albert Smith and Edmund Yates, who staged a benefit pantomime in April 1855 in front of a 'liberal' audience including Dickens, Thackeray, Forster and Lemon. On Reach's death in 1856, Thackeray gave a lecture at Edinburgh on 'Humour and Charity' and paid the receipts of £75 to Reach's widow with the advice to invest it in 'a good American security which pays 8 or 9 per cent'. 'What a great good fortune it is that Mrs R did not invest the money as I advised and did my own', he was to write on the collapse of the wonderful American securities in 1857.[39]

Brough's last two years of life were only a fraction less melancholy. His health, never robust, suffered from his relentless bohemianism. In *Marston Lynch* he noted that the vices of the Bohemian included 'improvidence, drink and reckless personal appearance'.[40] He was intimate with them all. Describing the 'Terra Incognita' of Bohemia, he wrote 'I have lived and suffered in Bohemia, and, I thank heaven, have escaped from it so long as to be able to speak of its miseries, which no longer afflict me, without undue bitterness; and of its joys, which no longer tempt me, without a partial fondness'.[41] Brough was only twenty-nine and such an elegaic tone may have been tongue-in-cheek, though both Vizetelly and Yates testify to his bouts of melancholia. In a verse he sent to Yates he struck a more characteristic note:

> I'm twenty-nine! I'm twenty-nine!
> I've drunk too much of beer and wine;
> I've had too much of love and strife;
> I've given a kiss to Johnson's wife,
> And sent a lying note to mine –
> I'm twenty-nine! I'm twenty-nine![42]

At the age of thirty his wine merchant forced him to appear before the

Insolvent Debtors' Court for non-payment of a £13 drinks bill. The court heard that Brough's total debts to sundry creditors amounted to £252, and that he had earned £525 from literature the previous year. Although such events were commonplace in the lives of Bohemian writers, cumulatively they could prove fatal.

In the spring of 1860 Brough contracted 'Neuralgia of the whole trunk of the Body – that he now suffers the most intense debility – amounting to entire prostration of both Physical and Mental Powers'. Brough's wife turned to the Royal Literary Fund, 'Mr Brough has not earned a shilling for more than three months, and, previously to that his health was so precarious that for the last two years his earnings have been insufficient for our necessities'. Brough, the 'popular author', died virtually penniless in June 1860 aged thirty-two. Charles Dickens, as one of the very few authors who knew how to manage money (unlike the speculative Thackeray), was appointed trustee of the Brough Memorial Fund.

IN HIS *Records and Reminiscences* (1904) Sir Francis Burnand, editor of *Punch*, described the Bohemians of the 1860s and 1870s:

These men were of the second or third literary class, who might be included under the heading of 'suppernumeraries'. . . . a convivial fraternity, living from hand (with a glass of spirits and water in it) to mouth, doing odd journalistic jobs, knowing something about everybody; a kindly lot, of little profit to themselves, but of marketable value to newspaper editors. Horace Mayhew, when in funds, would assist several of these impecunious gentry, as would that King of Bohemians, George Augustus Sala, the most brilliant, the most quaint, the wittiest, the kindest, and the most quarrelsome of them all.[43]

It is clear that Burnand regards Mayhew and Sala as Bohemians, if only by association; it is also clear that he does not regard them as second- or third-rate. If there were two dozen well-known Bohemians whose literary work was admitted to possess merit, even distinction, by contemporary reviewers (the *Saturday Review* excepted), there were several hundred undistinguished Bohemians who earned a precarious living from journalism and book making. Indeed, most of the army of very minor writers adopted the Bohemian character as a matter of necessity. In order to distinguish themselves from this rabble the famous Bohemians took to denying their bohemianism or excusing it as the pastime of youth. 'I have lost my way to Bohemia now', Thackeray wrote in *Philip*; 'I was never a real Bohemian', Yates claimed, 'but when my lot was cast among them . . . I had many tastes and pursuits in common with theirs'. 'I have lived and suffered in Bohemia', Brough wrote in *Marston Lynch*, 'and, I thank heaven, have escaped from it'. Even Sala, who admitted to being an 'ultra-Bohemian', was affected by this desire not to offend middle-class propriety and retrospectively referred to his twenties as 'the dark days of the long nightmare of Bohemianism'.[44]

Most writers of Bohemian disposition retained many of their vices into middle and old age, especially where money was concerned. About the only Bohemian who was never hard up was Yates, who had the good fortune to secure a Post Office sinecure at the age of sixteen and end up with an annual income of £600. The others were often on the verge of bankruptcy. When raising a fund for Shirley Brooks's widow in 1874, Sala explained to a prominent London alderman

how sorely difficult it was for a modern English man of letters, even with an income amounting to £2,000 a year [both Brooks and Sala earned this sum in their time], to save anything substantial for those whom he left behind. . . . In addition to his incidental expenses, he is chronically the prey of all the begging letter writers, the secretaries of hospitals, refuges, asylums, and other charitable institutions in London and the provinces.[45]

Poor Sala. In June the previous year he had been forced to apply to the Royal Literary Fund for a grant, following a long and painful illness for which the treatment was regular doses of laudanum and massive shots of morphine. 'Of course', he wrote defensively, 'the worldly wise will say that I should have *saved* money during the period of my validity. I can only say that travelling as I am towards my Fiftieth year I have not been able as yet to *begin* to save.' It was a thoroughly Bohemian vindication of his condition.

Sala's predicament was shared by most professional writers, though to an even greater degree. Until the late 1870s journalism had few salaried posts for writers, as opposed to editors, sub-editors and other technical staff. As Sala, the 'prince of correspondents', explained in his petition to the Royal Literary Fund, 'he is not in receipt of any fixed Salary or Income from any Source: his earnings having always depended upon the amount of contributions he has been able to make to the journal with which he has been connected'. The common writer, the Bohemian of the 'second or third literary class' often survived by becoming a literary odd-job man, accepting almost any non-writing chore as long as it could be performed within the literary world.

George Hodder was such an odd-jobber whose only literary work of importance is his *Memories of My Time* (1870) published by Tinsley.

Hodder is about as obscure an author as it is possible to be without falling into oblivion. His chief claim to attention was a brief stint as Thackeray's secretary, amanuensis and tour manager in 1855, when Thackeray was working on one of his least important and most lucrative projects *The Four Georges*. 'It was my task', the hapless Hodder recalled, 'to write to his dictation, and to make extracts from books, according to his instructions, either at his own house or the British Museum'.[46]

Born in Devon in 1819, Hodder first appears on the literary scene as one of the founders of *Punch*. By his own rather wishful account, he and Henry Mayhew were the original projectors of the magazine. What is certain, is that his career as a literary dogsbody began with his acting as messenger and secretary to Mayhew, Lemon and Landells, while they were planning the first issue of *Punch*. Hodder contributed to *Punch* until 1843 when Douglas Jerrold appointed him sub-editor of the short-lived *Illuminated Magazine* (1843–5). He prospered under Jerrold's patronage, and was clearly a much-loved member of Bohemian gatherings – although he was often the butt of Jerrold's acid humour. Also in 1843 he received his first odd-job post, as acting secretary of the Elton Committee, chaired by Dickens, which raised £2,500 for the family of the actor E.W. Elton. It was the kind of unpaid, unrewarding job that most writers avoided at any cost, but Hodder was easily put upon. Dickens was so impressed with his uncomplaining diligence that he secured him the paid secretaryship of 'The Sanatorium', a private fee-paying hospital for the class who were too poor to afford private nursing yet too genteel to risk treatment in a public hospital. The Sanatorium was one of Dickens's pet projects, but, inspite of Hodder's application and industry, the committee failed to raise enough working capital and Hodder found himself again unemployed and temporarily out of the literary stream. He did not complain; rather he saw the experience as 'an example of that disinterested aid which literary giants [Dickens] are capable of lending to literary dwarfs [Hodder]'.[47]

In 1848 he made the obligatory visit to Paris, where he would have starved to death but for the generosity of a *Morning Chronicle* journalist Thomas Frazer. On his return to England he continued with his journalism, writing more or less trivial articles for *Bentley's Miscellany*, *Leigh Hunt's Journal*, the *United Service Magazine* and the *Welcome Guest*. Dickens never thought well enough of his literary ability to invite him to contribute to *Household Words*. After his work for Thackeray, he became secretary to a William Willatt, a theatrical entrepreneur whose grand 'dramatic and musical Entertainment' did not take Dublin by storm, but left Willatt bankrupt and Hodder penniless. Horace Mayhew lent him money and supported his application to the Royal Literary Fund in June 1861, 'at present, he is dependent on such small bounty as his friends may occasionally spare him – but this is a source, never too bountiful at first, which gradually grows smaller and smaller with every fresh application that is made to it'.

Hodder's chequered and Bohemian career appears to have ended with his working for Sala as he had once worked for Thackeray. 'Dear old George Hodder lived to be my intimate friend, and to do a good deal of useful hack-work for me'.[48] Thus the King of Bohemia kindly remembering the services of one of his subjects. Hodder died in a coach accident in Richmond Park in 1870. His motherless seventeen year old daughter Emily, equipped with small grants from the Newspaper Press Fund and the Royal Literary Fund, embarked on a career as a governess.

THERE WERE a few professional writers who were not part of the Bohemian scene, who were dignified and diligent members of the literary world, yet unattached to university, Inns of Court or civil service department. Such a writer was the little remembered Robert Bell (1800–67). More than many better-known writers Bell deserves the title 'man of letters' – a title synonymous with miscellaneous authorship. For forty years literature was his sole source of income – only a handful of his contemporaries could claim as much. His career is a perfect illustration of the contemporary and posthumous fate of the hard-working, talented, but self-reliant miscellaneous writer. Trollope, a good friend of Bell's, considered him 'one of the eminent literary men of the age',[49] yet was puzzled by his comparative failure:

he never made that mark which his industry and talents would seem to ensure. He was a man well known to literary men, but not known to readers. As a journalist he was useful and conscientious, but his plays and novels never made themselves popular. He wrote a life of Canning, and he brought out an annotated edition of the British poets; but he achieved no great success. I have known no man better read in English literature. . . . Robert Bell certainly never achieved the position in literature which he once aspired to fill, and which he was justified in thinking he could earn for himself. I have frequently discussed these subjects with him, but I never heard from his mouth a word of complaint as to his own literary fate.[50]

Bell's literary fate, as an examination of his career shows, was unfortunately all too predictable. He was a highly skilled hack who refused to abandon his literary pretensions, and a sincere and talented creative writer who was unable to resist the exigencies of the market-place. He was also unfortunate in his timing, for by the time of the great revival in fiction, in the 1840s and 1850s, he was as old as the century and lacked the energy and stamina to sustain a career as a three-decker novelist, let alone compete with younger novelists of the calibre of Dickens, Thackeray and Trollope.

Bell was born in Cork in 1800 the son of a magistrate. His father died while he was still at school and friends of the family secured him a junior civil service post which he soon abandoned in favour of a student career at Trinity College Dublin. At college he was active in university journalism and began writing plays, two of which were performed at Dublin's Theatre Royal. He soon acquired a reputation as a skilful and effective journalist. During Lord Wellesley's administration he was made editor of the pro-Wellesley *Patriot* newspaper and became a vigorous supporter of Catholic emancipation. When Wellesley's anti-Catholic brother Wellington became Prime Minister in January 1828, Wellesley resigned and Bell left Dublin for London.

Bell's twenty-eight years in Ireland were no great impediment to his literary future. Many of the best known literary names in London were Irish, Scots or English provincial, and Bell, with his Dublin education and political experience, was better equipped than most to make his mark. His opportunity came almost immediately when, early in 1828, R.S. Rintoul resigned the editorship of the weekly *Atlas* to start up the more radical *Spectator*, and Bell was offered the vacant editorial chair, a post he was to occupy throughout the 1830s. The *Atlas* had been founded in 1826 as a Benthamite journal; a large-sheet, sixteen-page Sunday paper, it was one of the very first weekly journals to blend news and politics with reviews of literature, art and science. Though not political enough for Rintoul and its original backers, Joseph Hume, Kinnaird and other radicals, under Bell's editorship the *Atlas* stuck to a liberal policy. After only a few months in the job he achieved public fame as an editor of spirit and independence by surviving a libel suit brought against him by the Lord Chancellor, Lord Lyndhurst, and refusing to disclose his sources.

Bell's first book was commissioned by fellow Irishman Dionysius Lardner, a pioneering diffuser of useful knowledge. Lardner was the architect and general editor of the massive *Cabinet Cyclopedia*, a 133 volume work with a range of eminent contributors from Southey to Herschel. For no better reason than the lack of any obvious candidate for the task, Bell undertook a three-volume *History of Russia* (1838) and, more to his taste, a two-volume *Lives of the English Poets* (1839) which Gissing was later to read as background to his novel *New Grub Street*. By the second half of the 1830s Bell was a well-known literary figure on friendly terms with such men as Leigh Hunt, Edward Holmes, R.H. Horne and the young Thackeray among others.[51] He must also have met and impressed Charles Dickens, for in 1839 Dickens wrote to John Murray to recommend Bell as an editor for a projected biographical dictionary.

In 1838 when Lardner and Bulwer Lytton founded the *Monthly Chronicle* as a Whig journal, Bell was drafted in by Lardner as sub-editor, a title that carried with it the duties of deputy editor. Although Bell's position on the *Monthly Chronicle* drew him further into the literary world and away from routine journalism, it had two undesirable effects: it established him as a reliable lieutenant in other men's enterprises, and it cost him money. Bulwer Lytton resigned from the magazine in October 1838 and Lardner became sole editor. However, Lardner's editorial policy, with its emphasis on utility unrelieved by levity, lost readers. In October 1839 Lardner abandoned the magazine and Bell unwisely agreed to take over the editorship. Despite his efforts to make the magazine more lively it continued to lose revenue until it folded in June 1841. Although Bell was the editor and not the owner of the magazine (who, confusingly, was also called Bell) he appears to have contracted responsibility for some of its debts. As late as 1848 he still owed Spottiswoode £154 4s. 2d. for the *Monthly Chronicle* account for printing. Lardner and Bulwer Lytton, however, appear to have avoided financial liability for their offspring.

The immediate effect of Bell's editorship of the *Monthly Chronicle* was his full membership of the higher echelons of the literary world. From 1840 onwards he was a central, almost a key figure; no literary society, club or enterprise was complete without him. He was a founder member of Thomas Campbell's ill-fated Literary Union which became the Clarence Club. In 1842 he was a steward at the Literary Fund anniversary dinner presided over by Prince Albert. His fellow stewards included Campbell, Hallam, Lockhart, Moore and G.P.R. James. In 1843, when other writers were content to simply join the Society of British Authors, Bell served on its policy-making subcommittee along with Carlyle, Dickens, Campbell and Charles Mackay. And when Carlyle, Dickens and Campbell dropped out pleading pressure of work, it was left to Bell to draft a constitution which, though sensible and proficient, was not enough to save the poorly-motivated society. He was elected to the Garrick and Reform Clubs where he made many friends and few enemies. His friendships were nicely balanced: he was a frequent guest and host of both Dickens and Thackeray. In 1850 when Dickens and Bulwer Lytton were contemplating the formation of the Guild of Literature and Art, they invited Bell to join the council of management and to act in Bulwer Lytton's fund-raising comedy *Not So Bad As We Seem*. He was without doubt one of the most popular literary men in London. G.P.R. James, writing privately to the secretary of the Literary Fund in 1843, testified, 'Robert Bell is as kind hearted as he is talented and I do not think it is often that the poor and deserving would quit him unrelieved'. But for all his talent for friendship he found the business of earning a steady literary income a constant anxiety.

His literary work in the 1840s was divided between the stage and non-fiction. Through his friendship with Benjamin Webster, manager of the Haymarket theatre, he wrote three five-act comedies, *Marriage* (Haymarket 1842), *Mothers and Daughters* (Covent Garden 1843) and *Temper* (Haymarket 1847). He was thus part of that brief movement, which included Jerrold and Mrs Gore, that 'failed utterly to revive the comic forms of Sheridan'.[52] At the time, however, his plays were sufficiently well received for him to be honoured by the toast 'Mr Bell and the Dramatists of England' at the Royal Literary Fund dinner of 1850; a toast which previously had been coupled with the names of Talfourd, Kemble and Browning. Bell responded by drawing attention to the difficulty of earning a living as a playwright.

Meanwhile he continued to write well-received though not particu-larly well-remunerated books. His most successful work was a *Life of Canning* (1846) which won him further laurels as an accomplished biographer. However, by 1848 his financial position was clearly shaky; Spottiswoode was pressing him for payment of his long overdue debt and there were domestic difficulties. He was forced to move from the imposing address of the Manor House, Chiswick, to 30 Soho Square. In July he concluded an agreement with Richard Bentley for a series of *Wayside Pictures Through France, Belgium and Holland*, to be published in *Bentley's Miscellany*. Although he was, at this time, one of the top-ranking men of letters his agreement with Bentley shows that he was unable to name his own price. Bentley paid him 12 guineas a sheet (16 pages) at the rate of one sheet per month in return for the copyright.[53] This was the standard rate for monthlies – quarterly magazines could afford from 16 to 20 guineas a sheet. It is clear that Bentley made no allowances for Bell's reputation. Bell received nothing from the volume publication a year later, nor from subsequent reprints of what was obviously a popular travel book.

Despite the poor receipts from *Wayside Pictures*, Bell, pressed for money, was obliged to enter into a second unfavourable contract with Bentley, this time for a novel. Bentley agreed to pay him £200 outright for the copyright of a three-volume novel and to run it in *Bentley's Miscellany* if he 'thinks fit' at £16 3s. 4d. for two sheets monthly.[54] Bell was in no position to bargain. In a stalling letter to Spottiswoode he wrote 'I have suffered severe lapses and disappointments and am struggling against great difficulties'.[55] These difficulties must have been compounded by his contracts with Bentley. Even a little thing like his subscription to the Royal Literary Fund caused him problems. He wrote to the secretary in 1850 to try to defer payment of his arrears but was informed that the books had to balance.

Against this background, aged forty-nine, he began work on his first novel which turned out to be his greatest literary achievement. Appropriately called *The Ladder of Gold*, it was a detailed and imaginative treatment of the Victorian obsession with money. It was a rags to riches story of a miser's clerk, Richard Rawlings, who, through an initial stroke of luck, marries his master's young widow, proves himself a diligent, intelligent and ruthless speculator, amasses a fortune and becomes a power in the City and in Parliament, until that moment when his empire crumbles and he is thrown back on the one resource he has undervalued – the love of his family. It was a very moral tale, but told with skill and subtlety, and – given the opportunity for sensationalism – unusual sobriety. Perhaps its most impressive quality was its unfaltering construction – a rare achievement in a three-decker novel. It was very well received by the reviewers. The *Spectator* gave it a three-page notice: 'In those qualities which conduce to vivacity of effect and to striking situation Mr Bell is not equal to several of his contemporaries. In useful purpose, in elevation of view, in skilfully turning to account a passing event, and in solid strength of composition, he equals or surpasses any of them.'[56] The *Athenaeum* praised his 'more than ordinary force in a style peculiarly smooth and flowing'[57] and his 'power to describe the features of a moral epidemic'. As some measure of the novel's popularity it was reissued in a cheap edition by Routledge in 1856.

There are several remarkable features about *The Ladder of Gold*. It was a mature work; the kind of novel that many an established novelist might envy. Bell, of course, had twenty-five years writing experience behind him and had been an assiduous novel-reviewer; but it remains a surprising achievement for a harrassed middle-aged journalist tackling a new form. His choice of subject, which related to his own concerns, was a piece of inspired opportunism. Throughout the 1840s railway 'mania' had been fuelled by the spectacular success of George Hudson, 'the Railway King', a self-made millionaire, MP and chairman of half a dozen major railway companies. The crash came in 1849 when railway shareholders lost some £80 million. Hudson was held responsible and was sacked from every railway board and, on 17 May 1849, was cut dead by the entire House of Commons. On 22 September, when Bell signed his contract with Bentley, he had a ready made subject, and one which he must have felt particularly competent to handle; he knew only too well the difference between the substance and the illusion of wealth and rank in Victorian society. His portrait of Rawlings/Hudson as a remarkable man with complex weaknesses is completely free from the caricature adopted by Dickens for Merdle in *Little Dorrit* and by Trollope for Melmotte in *The Way We Live Now*, both later versions of George Hudson.

Had *The Ladder of Gold* appeared under the authorship of Dickens or Trollope it would now be in print and highly rated. But with such a huge field to choose from, it was inevitable, though regrettable, that the English literature selectors – critics and bibliographers – would over-look Bell's novel. It is a comfortable assumption that a minor writer's only novel must be a very minor production indeed. In fact, Bell was simply too old to carry on a new career as a novelist. His second work of fiction, a collection of stories, *Hearts and Altars* (1852), marked a return to the domestic themes of his comedies and was a commercial and critical flop. Perhaps with some relief he returned to journalism and non-fiction. In 1854 he began to work on an annotated edition of the English poets, a multi-volume enterprise by which, the *Dictionary of National Biography* falsely predicted, 'Bell will be chiefly remembered'.

In 1851 Bell joined the committee of the Royal Literary Fund having been a subscriber for twelve years. He became one of its most active members, successfully defending it from Dickens's charges of misman-agement. His letters to the Fund's secretary during the 1850s reveal his preoccupation with consolidating his own literary position – a preoccu-pation which often motivated authors to join the committee. At the anniversary dinner for 1856, for example, he asked the secretary 'to place me somewhere in the neighbourhood of Mr Murray as I would be glad to have some conversation with him'. This could not be done and he had to make do with the company of Richard Burton and Professor Owen. At the same dinner he secured the services of D.T. Coulton as a steward, remarking, 'he is important to me in a literary point of view – being the Editor of the Press Newspaper'. And no doubt he wanted to secure Coulton as an ally against Dickens's attacks on the Fund. Ironically a few years later he found himself sponsoring Coulton's widow for a Royal Literary Fund grant. His best dinner placing must have been in 1858 when he sat between Sir Frederick Pollock and Thackeray, opposite Prosper Mérimée and Anthony Panizzi and two places away from Turgenev. He first met Trollope in 1860 at a dinner to launch the *Cornhill*. The two men became firm friends and the following year Bell invited Trollope to join the Fund committee, and in 1862 put him up for election to the Garrick.

Bell remained less than well-off, though not poor enough to accept the £60 Civil List pension offered to him by Palmerston in 1864; it was an affront to his literary reputation when such mediocre contemporaries as Alaric Watts and Eliza Cook were in receipt of £100 a year. Bell's income, including editorships, probably never amounted to much more than £500 or £600 a year. Although this was twice the average literary earnings it was still modest by the standards of his peers. Forster, for example, edited the *Examiner* for 'only £500 a year', and ultimately received a non-literary income of £1,500 as a Lunacy Commissioner which was 'a necessary supplement to his wife's money'.[58]

Bell's perennial problem was how to keep up the appearance of a prosperous man of letters rather than a carriageless common writer, without the support of a private income or public post. That this was a very real problem is clear from a letter he received in 1853 from Bulwer Lytton, in which the wealthy baronet, in the middle of negotiating a £20,000 deal with Routledge for a ten-year lease on the cheap edition of his collected works, advised Bell to write for quarterly rather than monthly magazines: 'you hardly ever find a *Gentilhomme* writes for Magazines – When I undertook the New Monthly I was the first gentleman of birth who had done so more followed my example. I only did it for bread & cheese & soon threw it up convinced how much it lowered me.'[59] Bulwer Lytton's casual assumption that Bell was a writer of independent means who could afford to give up half his literary income in return for enhanced social standing perfectly illustrates the chasm between the amateur and professional writer.

Trollope had no such absurd scruples and knew very well how much it cost Bell to maintain his image. In January 1867 when Trollope accepted the editorship of the monthly *St Paul's Magazine*, he immediately offered the sub-editorship to Bell for £250 a year. This was a fair rate except that Bell had once been a distinguished editor and now, at sixty-seven, was reduced to the minor office to supplement his dwindling earnings (he was also editor of *Home News*, a magazine for the British in India, but it was not a lucrative appointment). As it turned out, Bell was too ill to take up Trollope's offer and died on 12 April. His unpensioned widow was obliged to auction his library of 4,000 volumes. With typical generosity Trollope stepped in and bought the entire collection above the market price. 'We all know' he said, 'the difference in value between buying and selling of books.'[60] He also drafted a memorial for a Civil List pension and got Dickens, Wilkie Collins and John Murray among others to sign it at the offices of the Royal Literary Fund. It was unsuccessful.

During Bell's lifetime his biography had appeared in standard reference works and soon after his death he rated an entry in the ninth edition of the *Encyclopedia Britannica*. Yet few writers of contemporary eminence have vanished so completely. He does not feature in any modern reference book; he does not even manage a place in the *Cambridge Bibliography of English Literature*. But then he was too diffuse. His work did not fall naturally into the simple categories of 'minor fiction', 'minor prose' or even 'other dramatists'. When he does surface, it is as a shadow – a friend of Dickens, Thackeray or Trollope – a mere name. Very occasionally *The Ladder of Gold* is given a brief mention but only in cursory comparison to *Little Dorrit* or *The Way We Live Now*. It is tempting to conclude that, because he did not write Dickens's biography or live with George Eliot, no one bothered to preserve his papers – a simple act that would have secured him a prominent place in literary history.

Bell was aware of his probable fate and, as Trollope noted, did not let it distress him. At the Royal Literary Fund dinner of 1860, Thackeray's old friend G.S. Venables toasted 'the Literature of England, coupled with the name of a person distinguished in more than one department of literature, Mr Robert Bell'. Bell replied:

English Literature is much richer than any of us are very well aware, or even care much to remember. Every age has its clusters of minor writers, just as we have now, who all contributed to promote that intellectual progress, the benefits of which we are now enjoying; men whose light flashed brightly enough in the eyes of their contemporaries, but was too feeble to transmit its rays to us. They had their day, and are now forgotten. We think of the Miltons, and the Spensers, the Fieldings, and the Defoes, but the mighty crowd composed of the Settles, and the Gildons, the Heywoods, Dennises, and Shadwells – the vast rabble of genius that fill up the avenues of our literary history, are entitled to be thought of too, for they, too, contributed to make our literature what it is.

4

THE LABOURING MUSE: WORKING-CLASS
WRITERS AND MIDDLE-CLASS CULTURE

CHAPBOOKS, broadsheets, ballads and penny dreadfuls were the staple printed literature of the working classes until well into the Victorian age. If their authors ever nursed conventional literary aspirations they were soon buried under a shroud of anonymity and the indifference of middle-class critics. In the nineteenth century popular working-class literature made no pretence to become bourgeois art. It was very much a ware to be peddled; it was not reviewed, or handed out as school prizes, or catalogued by librarians, or even remaindered or pulped. The whole concept of authorship, implying intellectual property, copyright and contractual obligations was irrelevant to street literature.

This chapter is concerned with exotic entrants to a middle-class culture: those working-class writers who had conventional literary aspirations; who did not wish to contribute anonymously to popular literature but who hoped to achieve decent reviews and some small literary fame. If, like Ebenezer Elliott, they had written political poems – however bad – they would have met with more posthumous success. But they wanted the approbation of a middle-class readership for whom working-class politics were anathema. If Blacket, Miller, Prince, Ridings, Cooper and Massey are remembered at all it is for their lives rather than their literary works. Their biographies and autobiographies are important social documents but their poems, novels, essays and philosophical speculations are, for the most part, insignificant and remain unread. Even the modest fame they achieved during their lifetime brought them little comfort. The history of these working-class writers is a relatively dismal catalogue of inadequate and cavalier patronage, groundless optimism and commercial failure. Such failure had little to do with lack of talent. Many self-educated writers were as talented as their middle-class colleagues. Yet almost no working-class writer achieved financial independence through the practice of authorship. The literary world had evolved to cater for the tastes of the leisured classes which patently excluded the working man. Scottish literature presents a much more open picture, but the comparatively democratic cultural and educational conditions which nurtured Burns, Hogg and a host of minor writers like Willie Thom and Alexander Smith were unknown south of the border.

In spite of the realities of a literary life there was no shortage of working-class recruits. For many, authorship seemed to be a less arduous way of making a living than by skilled or unskilled labour. And it appeared to have the additional advantage of requiring little or no capital investment. In theory all that the writer needed was writing materials and a degree of intellectual or imaginative skill. Alexander Somerville, an influential working-class writer, showed how easy it was to turn author:

The person to whom I offered my certificate of six months' gratuity for a quire of writing paper and pen and ink to begin to write my narrative of the Legion, would give me nothing for the worthless certificate, but made me a present of several quires of writing paper. I walked out of Glasgow, three or four miles up the Clyde, got into a field of beans nearly ripe, crept out of sight to the middle of the field, lay there three days and nights, writing the first chapters of my narrative, and living on the beans. I sent the farmer a copy of the work afterwards as payment for what I had eaten.[1]

To turn author was one thing but to survive as one was quite another. In practice writers without capital, without some private means of support, were rarely able to give their best to their work. They either had to overproduce as publishers' hacks or abandon their writing for long stretches and return to their former occupations as ploughmen or cobblers, surgeons or solicitor's clerks.

But all authors are sanguine at first and another potent motive that led aspiring Miltons to abandon the plough for the pen was the desire for enhanced social status. Thomas Miller, in his novel *Godfrey Malvern*, suggests that the working man was attracted to authorship because

There is a kind of neutral ground which talented authors will ever occupy; and although they may never become what the world calls 'gentlemen', in the worldly sense of the word, still they will always be received and treated with respect, by those who move in the highest circles of fashionable society.[2]

Of course what this really meant was that the working-class writer was patronised. Patronage however had distinct economic advantages even though it was often humiliating; it provided the writer with a new suit of clothes, with meat and port instead of bread and porter. Inevitably the desire for patronage led to a corresponding desire to please and to an imitative rather than inimitable literature.

Throughout the first half of the nineteenth century poetry was the favourite form of working-class writing, not least because it could be pursued after working hours and attract the same degree of patronage as prose writing for relatively less effort. 'Hech, sir, poetry!' says Sandy Mackaye in Kingsley's novel *Alton Locke*, 'I've been expecting it. I suppose it's the appointed gate o' a workman's intellectual life – that same lust o' versification.'³ Just as the middle-class prose writer was often a poet in adolescence so the working-class writer, whose self-education took much longer, naturally inclined to verse. And the themes of working-class verse kept roughly in step with the inching forwards of social and political reforms. There was a gradual shift away from the rustic musings of Bloomfield's *The Farmer's Boy* (1800) to the radical, Whitmanesque outpourings of Gerald Massey's *Voices of Freedom, Lyrics of Love* (1850). But the writers who wished to keep their patrons toned down their politics to order.

From this 'lust o' versification' came the second important development in working-class writing – the working man's autobiography.⁴ At the beginning of the century no volume of rustic verse was complete without a brief memoir of the ploughman poet, often penned by the local vicar or the lord of the manor anxious to parade a philanthropic part in the nurture of humble genius. Capel Lofft wrote such an introduction to the poems of Bloomfield and was ridiculed for his pains by Byron who dubbed him the 'preface-writer-general to distressed versemen'. Perhaps the most famous of all these memoirs was Robert Southey's 'Introductory Essay on the Lives and Works of our Uneducated Poets', prefixed to the *Attempts in Verse of John Jones, a Servant* (1831), in which Southey discussed the work of earlier 'uneducated poets' including Stephen Duck, John Taylor and Ann Yearsley. The vogue for such memoirs reached its peak in 1833 with the publication of *Sketches of Obscure Poets* with a cast of fourteen including Robert Millhouse, Charles Crocker and Robert Story.

The end of the 1830s saw the serialisation of Samuel Bamford's *Passages in the Life of a Radical*, published in two volumes by Abel Heywood in 1844. Bamford's example was followed by others, notably James Carter's *Memoirs of a Working Man* (1845), Alexander Somerville's *Autobiography of a Working Man* (1848), C.M. Smith's *The Working Man's Way in the World* (1853) and James Burn's *Autobiography of a Beggar Boy* (1855). From the mid-1850s onwards there was a steady stream of autobiographical writing of which the most important, at least from the literary point of view, was *The Life of Thomas Cooper* (1872). In general, although the fictionalising of personal experience may have suited Dickens, Thackeray and Charlotte Brontë, the working man was not prepared to diminish the facts of his hard-won achievements.

From the evidence of these autobiographies it seems that the most potent literary influence on working-class writers was Robert Burns. There were other writers whose work was admired: Defoe, Milton, Thomson and later Shelley and Byron formed a kind of radical syllabus – but Burns was the first writer with whom the working-class intellectual was happy to identify. According to Charles Kingsley:

He first proved that it was possible to become a poet and a cultivated man without deserting his class, either in station or in sympathies; nay, that the healthiest and noblest element of a nobly born mind might be, perhaps certainly must be, the very feelings and thoughts which he brought up with him from below, not those which he received from above in the course of his artificial culture.[5]

If the life of Burns inspired the working-class poet, the poetry of Byron was no less influential. Part of Byron's influence on the writers of the 1830s and 1840s must be attributed to the sheer availability of his poems in cheap second-hand reprints and pirated editions. For example, Byron and Burns were the best-selling poets of William Milner's 1s. Cottage Library, selling six times as many copies as the more radical though less accessible Shelley.[6] In common with Burns, Byron belonged to Carlyle's 'Camp of the Unconverted' and, neither a Tory nor patron, he was believed by many radical working-class writers to embrace their cause. But it was his poems rather than his politics which were revolutionary. Thomas Cooper recalled his fascination on first reading stanzas from *Childe Harold*:

I knew nothing of their noble author's life or reputation; but they seemed to create almost a new sense within me. I wanted more poetry to read from that time; but could get hold of none that thrilled through my nature like Byron's. I had read the 'Paradise Lost;' but it was above my culture and learning, and it did not make me *feel*.[7]

Byron did not reciprocate the admiration of working-class writers. The only poet of humble origins he was prepared to praise was his Cambridge contemporary Henry Kirke White who was a protégé of both Lofft and Southey. All other 'poetasters' were dismissed with lordly disdain. James Burn, another working-class admirer of Byron's poetry, was no admirer of his aristocratic manner, 'he scoffed at the whole family of man from the vantage ground of his great intellect, and treated the highest aspirations of their minds with giant levity'.[8] Several poets, however, whose works justify critical oblivion, owe what tiny literary fame they still possess entirely to Byron's levity. Among the most interesting working-class poets who feature in Byron's poems and letters, is the cobbler Joseph Blacket (1786–1809).

Like many self-educated writers, Blacket wrote a pre-Burnsian poetry; his verse was a careful imitation of seventeenth- and eighteenth-century pastoral. He claimed Shakespeare, Milton, Pope, Young, Beattie and Thomson as his models, and appeared completely ignorant of the poetry of Coleridge and Wordsworth, Burns and Crabbe. The only contemporary poet mentioned in his letters is his fellow labourer Bloomfield. Byron rated Blacket's poems 'as bad as Purgatory',[9] but they were not that bad; in simplicity and sincerity, even in execution, they were often better than those of many of his educated contemporaries. These stanzas, for example, come from 'Midday', one of three poems Blacket wrote on the same day in 1803 when he was just seventeen:

> From the scorching heat of noon
> Panting cattle leave the glade
> Faint the mower sits him down
> At the headland in the shade.
>
> Drooping lags the toiling ox,
> Heedless of the plough-boy's goad,
> Who, delighted, hears the clocks
> Speak the dinner on the road.
>
> In the fields appear the boys,
> Loos'd from school, in frolic gay,
> Echo, at the gladsome noise,
> Seems to share their holiday!
>
> . . .
>
> Now the tender flow'rs decay,
> Wither'd by the scorching heat,
> And the warblers wing their way
> To the thicket's deep retreat.[10]

They are an undeniably simple group of verses with a thin flavour of Thomas Gray, whom Blacket admired. But they are also pleasantly unaffected, even inspired when compared with the blusterings of the Literary Fund poets – the Della Cruscans and W.T. Fitzgerald and Henry Pye – all of whom Byron more fairly attacked. If Blacket failed to soar above the level of a minor Cowper or Bowles it was because his talents were half-starved through lack of learning, and his health undermined by hard work.

The son of a Yorkshire day labourer, he was educated free of charge at the village school, the village schoolmistress having taken a fancy to him. At the age of eleven he was apprenticed to his brother, a master shoemaker in London. While in London he discovered the theatre and began to make his first attempts in verse: 'I assiduously courted the muse of tragedy who continued to claim all the attention I could spare from my business, which I prosecuted with tolerable success.'[11] At eighteen he married a servant-girl in William Boscawen's family, but she died in 1807 leaving him to look after a baby daughter. In 1808, through a friendship with the printer William Marchant, Blacket succeeded in publishing a volume of poems at Marchant's expense. Marchant introduced Blacket to a miscellaneous writer of inflated reputation, Samuel Jackson Pratt. Pratt, the son of a Lord Lieutenant of Huntingdonshire, educated at Felsted and a failed actor, was excited by this unexpected opportunity to lay claim to the discovery of a genuine poetic talent. He befriended Blacket, encouraging him to write greater quantities of poetry – especially epic tragedy at which he supposed, erroneously, the shoemaker would excel. Blacket's first volume was still at press when he began to show symptoms of consumption. Pratt and others rallied to his aid. The publisher Sir Richard Phillips loaned Pratt and Blacket his house in Wales where the climate was supposed to be milder. Then through Blacket's brother-in-law, who was gamekeeper to Sir Ralph Milbanke, he was invited to stay with the Milbankes at Seaham, near Durham.

The Milbankes' physician attended Blacket gratis and Annabella Milbanke read him her poems. 'To Sir Ralph and Lady Milbanke,' wrote their chaplain, Mr Wallis, 'he was peculiarly indebted for kindly and liberally supplying him with every comfort and convenience in their power; and from their amiable and accomplished daughter, who is a favourite of the muses as well as he was himself, he received the most marked and unremitting attention.'[12] And so, according to Byron, the twenty-two year old cobbler fell head over heels in love with the seventeen year old baronet's daughter. He began to write love poetry to his 'Matilda'.

> Say, why has sleep my pillow fled,
> And why within my breast,
> No longer Peace remains a guest?
> And why Content forbears to shed,
> Her pure delights on my bewilder'd head?

Unconscious maid! *thou* know'st not why, –
'Twas friendship fill'd *thy* heart;
Thou dids't not know what painful smart,
Shot from the glances of thy friendly eye,
Which murder'd my repose, and draw *this* heart-felt sigh!

But let me pine, nor once reveal
My love, except at midnight's noon;
To yonder drooping, cheerless moon,
Who listens now with visage pale,
To torments, which thy smiles, alone, can heal!

Poor Blacket, young, lowly and sick, found poetry its own reward. He died in August 1809 a few weeks after leaving Seaham.

Pratt began to busy himself on behalf of his dead friend. He wrote letters to all who had known him; he obtained Blacket's letters to his brother and Miss Milbanke; he collected together the fresh scraps of poetry. This posthumous patronage was ostensibly on behalf of Blacket's orphan daughter. It resulted in a handsomely produced memorial volume, *The Remains of Joseph Blacket*, with a memoir by Pratt and a frontispiece of a well-dressed, handsome, even Byronic Blacket. Subscriptions for the volume were raised by Pratt, Lady Milbanke, Francis Wrangham and the Duchess of Leeds. Between them they collected over £500 from 150 subscribers including half the royal family, a number of bishops, Lady Bessborough, Lords Moira and Erskine, Sir Richard Phillips, Hugh Montgomery, Samuel Romilly and William Wilberforce. Society clearly interested itself in the remains of working-class prodigy. Byron was unimpressed. His 'Epitaph for Joseph Blackett, Late Poet and Shoemaker' began:

> Stranger! behold, interr'd together,
> The Souls of learning and of leather.

It is possible that Byron's unkind satire had something to do with his sense of outrage that a cobbler should presume to woo Miss Milbanke, later Lady Byron. He certainly made little effort to ascertain the facts of Blacket's life. 'You were the ruin of that poor fellow amongst you:', he wrote to his friend Dallas, 'had it not been for his patrons he might now have been in a very good plight, shoe- (not verse-) making: but you have made him immortal with a vengeance. I write this supposing poetry, patronage, and strong waters to have been the death of him.' There is, in this attitude, an implicit belief that the working man should not attempt to become a literary man. 'Cruel Patronage! to ruin a man in his calling', Byron remarks of Blacket in another letter.[13]

Byron's views were shared by most other gentlemen of letters. Working-class writers were always being told to stick to their trade and leave literature to educated professionals and men and women of independent means. This was mostly class snobbery, but it was also a sensible injunction. Few people expected literature to pay. Middle-class writers knew very well how bleak the literary life could be – even for an Oxford or Cambridge man. In contrast, those who fostered working-class aspirations were often amateur men of letters with substantial private incomes. Such patrons were not as Machiavellian as some historians have claimed. Few of them deliberately set out to swamp the revolutionary views of their protégés under a weight of opulence. The reverse was often the case. Capel Lofft, for all his little vanities, was an active radical politician with a genuine admiration for the self-educated writer.

Although Byron was malicious he was also shrewd; poetry, patronage and strong waters ruined many a tailor, cobbler and hatter. Of Bloomfield, Hogg, William Thom, Thomas Miller, Thomas Cooper, J.C. Prince, Elijah Ridings, Robert Millhouse, John Nicholson, Cornelius Webbe, John Clare, Alexander Somerville and Gerald Massey, to list the more important working-class writers, all died on the edge of poverty after various encounters with patronage and the bottle – to which they turned as a consequence of frustrated literary ambition. Probably the only exception to the rule was Ebenezer Elliott who managed, eventually, to make a tolerable success of his business in the iron trade – thanks largely to his wife's money. As well as their financial failure most of them also failed to make a lasting impression on literature: only Hogg and Clare reached the first rank in poetry. All had to struggle for the most rudimentary education and were denied the social and cultural advantages that went with private schooling and university. Consequently in their dealings with publishers, editors and others who made up literary society they were severely disadvantaged. The wonder is that they produced anything worth reading at all.

LITERARY SOCIETY regarded most working-class writers of any merit as entertaining freaks – shoemaking one moment and verse-making the next. They could not hope to compete with educated writers, not least because they were often paid by publishers according to their station rather than their abilities. Thomas Miller was an important exception. He was unique among his fellows for being a miscellaneous writer; combining poetry, novels and non-fiction with a fair degree of literary success. He wrote more prolifically and persistently than any other working-class writer. Between 1833, when he was 26, and his death in 1874 he published about fifty titles. He features in many of the memoirs and biographies of the time, but left no published autobiography. His life illustrates the several themes of working-class authorship: from achieving local celebrity as a poet, through aristocratic patronage and bestsellerdom, to a slow decline as a disappointed hack living on a penny-a-line and charitable hand-outs. Where Miller differed markedly from his contemporaries was in his complete lack of interest in working-class causes from the corn-laws and Chartism to temperance and Christian socialism.

He was born in Gainsborough in Lincolnshire in 1807 and brought up by his mother who had been deserted by her husband. He was educated at the local Free School along with Thomas Cooper who was two years his senior. Cooper was a 'Bluecoat' boy and Miller a 'White Hart' boy; as Cooper explained in his autobiography: 'These were the names of two charities left by deceased Gainsborough gentry, for the education of poor children. Bluecoat boys were allowed a coat and a cap, blue with yellow trimmings, yearly. White Hart boys had simply their education.'[14] Miller was thus accustomed – even conditioned – to charity and patronage at the very start of his intellectual life. Mrs Miller remarried a basket-maker who apprenticed Miller to his own trade. Among the sensible working classes an apprenticeship in a steady trade was considered economically and socially preferable to a grammar-school education which could so easily excite social aspirations without providing the means to achieve them.

Miller married in 1827 and left Gainsborough for Nottingham where he worked as a journeyman basket-maker at ten shillings a week. In his spare time he wrote poetry which was published in the local newspaper. Encouraged by the response to these poems he published his first collection *Songs of the Sea Nymphs* (1832) by subscription and was welcomed into a small literary circle that included Spencer T. Hall, Robert Millhouse and other protégés of William and Mary Howitt, the Quaker druggists and writers. His local fame as a poet briefly helped his basket-making trade. 'There was poetry in his very baskets', Spencer Hall recalled:

the basket maker and his wares well matched each other, as he would take his cigar from his mouth and ask some pretty market-maiden, in his cheeriest tones, as she lingered and looked, if she would not like to purchase. . . . One week we suddenly missed him, and a few weeks afterwards found, by one of the monthly magazines, that he was in London and had literary employment there; and there he has ever since, like a caged thrush, remained, charming the national heart with his outpourings of verse and poetical prose.[15]

Miller's life in London was not as easy and agreeable as Hall makes it sound; from 1833 to 1844 it was a mixture of light and shade, thereafter it was pretty much all shade. His first success was in romantically, if cannily, attracting the attention of Lady Blessington by sending her his poems in a hand-made basket. His good looks, charm and labouring background made him an instant success in the Blessington circle where he worked hard to cultivate the image of a rough diamond. According to Henry Vizetelly, 'Lady Blessington took the uncouth bard under her patronage and, rigging him out in a slop suit, showed him off admiringly at her receptions.'[16] While Miller was dining at Lady Blessington's expense, his wife, his mother and his three children were lodging off St George's Road, Southwark, in anything but splendour.

The main object of Lady Blessington's soirées was to collect writers, editors, publishers, artists and art lovers and introduce them to each other. It seems that Miller met the publisher Henry Colburn at one of Lady Blessington's gatherings, perhaps in 1836. For by March 1837 Miller was writing to C.P. Roney, 'My prospects are now fair, I am drawing 8£ a month of Mr Colburn, living comfortably and paying my way.' The £8 monthly was in exchange for three novels: *Royston Gower* (2 volumes, 1838), *Fair Rosamund* (3 volumes, 1839), and *Lady Jane Grey* (3 volumes, 1840). Presumably Colburn had agreed to pay Miller £100 for the copyright of each novel in monthly instalments. This was four or five times less than he paid writers like Lady Blessington and Benjamin Disraeli: but Colburn fawned on rank and Miller was only a basket-maker; he was paid according to Colburn's estimate of his humble needs. In fact £100 was the going rate for a novel from a professional hack and at least three times as much as Miller was accustomed to earn from making baskets. Another of Lady Blessington's guests was the editor William Jerdan, who gave Miller occasional employment on the *Literary Gazette*. He also began to contribute to the *Athenaeum*, and such casual journalism, together with verse writing for albums like *Friendship's Offering* edited by W.H. Harrison, might have added about £30 a year to his income.

It was, however, very hard work. As early as January 1835 Miller had written to the Literary Fund for a grant complaining that 'without a name or a friend, I was doomed to feed the ever-gaping press. No! Literature is a pleasant Companion, but once take him in to board and lodging, and he will soon eat you up.' At the end of his contract with Colburn in December 1839 he had achieved a degree of fame but little peace of mind: 'I have sat up too long night after night and with depressed spirits driven my mind into its weary task in the hopes of conquering the difficulties that surround me.' His relative fame had led to his being chased by Nottingham creditors in pursuit of old debts, 'whilst my Fame is unfortunately ringing through the country they dream that I must be as rich as Croesus'. Between 1835 and 1839 Miller applied three times to the Literary Fund and was granted £70 to help him pay off his debts.

By 1840, aged thirty-three, after the publication of his third Colburn novel *Lady Jane Grey*, Miller had published three well-reviewed volumes of poetry and three popular historical novels and was, as 'the basket maker poet', a celebrity of almost Burnsian proportions. No other working-class writer of the time had found so much favour in the metropolis. In 1841, like the dénouement of a romance, Samuel Rogers, banker and poet, gave Miller a present of 300 guineas to enable him to buy back his copyrights from Colburn and set up as a bookseller and publisher on his own account. Other than the stipulation that the money should be used to establish a business there were no strings attached. It was the sort of opportunity that every working-class writer dreamt of. Over the next two years Miller wrote and published his two best and most successful novels, *Gideon Giles the Roper* (1842), 'the most popular tale about country life circulating among the lower classes',[17] and *Godfrey Malvern* (1843). He was popular with the upper classes too, and was praised in the *Athenaeum*. G.A. Sala's verdict may be taken as typical of the general view: 'He was a genius of the Bloomfield and Kirk White order, and wrote delightfully about rural life.'[18]

In spite of the commercial success of his novels Miller found himself in increasing financial difficulties. His bookseller's business in Newgate was surrounded by Smithfield butchers who bought neither books nor stationery. His removal to Ludgate Hill at some expense failed to make any difference, and by February 1844 the profits from his novels had been turned into a £50 debt. He wrote again to the Literary Fund begging that his application would be kept a secret, 'I know it would give my kind friend Mr Rogers great pain to have known that after all his kindness I was again reduced so low.' The Fund gave him £50. A year later he declared himself bankrupt. Sir Robert Peel awarded him a Royal Bounty grant to keep him from a debtors' prison and the Literary Fund gave him another £20 after W.H. Harrison reported that 'everything except the clothes on the backs of himself and family had been pawned and even the wedding ring of his wife – a most worthy person – had shared the common fate'. Miller acknowledged his shortcomings, 'Were I made Manager of the Bank of England to-morrow, in a few years the whole firm would become insolvent.' Rogers's generosity, like so many well-meaning acts of patronage, had failed to account for the temperament of the patronised. Vizetelly, himself a publisher, summed up the episode:

Samuel Rogers, after inviting him to his breakfasts, generously set him up in business; not, however as a basket-maker or some kindred craft, at which he might have prospered, but as a bookseller and publisher – of all callings in the world – requiring special training and knowledge, such as a labouring man from the Lincolnshire Wolds would certainly not possess.[19]

Having made a mess of his big chance, Miller did not expect another one: 'my future business will be with my pen. I am fit for no other – but must till the cursed ground of Authorship for bread until the dark angel of death, throws the shadow of his dusky wing over my last page and warns me that my task is ended.' Over the next thirty years Miller applied to the Royal Literary Fund another eleven times. By his death in 1874 he had received £365 in grants, more, at that time, than any other author. He also applied on several occasions for a Civil List pension, but, despite the support of Bulwer Lytton, Rogers, Macaulay and Tennyson, he was unsuccessful. In fact the Civil List secretary had been advised by Octavian Blewitt that Miller was hopelessly improvident.

Mr Miller the 'Basket Maker poet' has been known to our Committee [the Royal Literary Fund] since 1835. In that year Mr Harrison, our Senior Registrar, found him selling his baskets in the streets of Whitechapel, and helped him to emerge from his poverty and pursue his taste for literature.
    I believe Mr Harrison has long felt that he never made a greater mistake, for though Miller must have realized for many years a handsome income from his Books and still more from his writings for Periodicals, he has always been in difficulties which he might have avoided if he had stuck to his trade of a Basketmaker [17 July 1873].

In response to this letter Gladstone awarded Miller £50 from the Royal Bounty Fund but declined to grant him a pension. The money came too late to be of any use as Miller died before he could spend it. The *Bookseller* obituary notice was equally censorious: 'At first he made large sums of money, but he never reserved a copyright nor saved a penny

. . . and thus it was, with almost genius for an inheritance, he was often in want of shillings.'[20] This is only partly fair. In common with most poor authors Miller could not afford the luxury of retaining his copyrights in the hope that they might one day prove an asset. He needed immediate payment to keep his family while writing his books. Also, Miller had his share of common misfortune. During the Crimean war, for example, he lost his job as a leader writer on the *Morning Post*. His wife died suddenly in 1851 and he was left to look after his consumptive unemployed son and his two unmarried daughters. At the beginning of his literary career he was published by Colburn; Smith, Elder and Co.; Chapman and Hall – at the end of his career he was churning out children's stories for Groombridge, J.M. Darton, and the Religious Tract Society – 'the man who is compelled to write for bread' he wrote with feeling in 1869, 'becomes a slave to the Publishers'.

But even allowing for lack of opportunity compounded by misfortune, Miller's failure to develop his talents played a large part in his literary slavery. He wrote to please his patrons: 'The friends and advisers of my younger years were Sharon Turner, Rogers, Moore, Campbell, Mr Harrison, Lady Blessington and Miss Landon and to please them and win their approval I wrote about the green country and the rural life of England which very few care for now [1869].' Like his contemporaries Harrison Ainsworth and G.P.R. James, who found their facility for writing historical novels devalued their critical and financial stock, so Miller discovered that the demand for novels and poems about rural life, at least from his pen, was short lived. However, Ainsworth and James were sons of the prosperous gentry; for Miller, abandoned by his father and brought up by his labouring mother, it was appropriate to claim 'I believe that from my cradle I was doomed to become an Author.'

Miller's novel, *Godfrey Malvern: the Life of an Author*, is the *Pendennis* of working-class literature; the only fictional account by an important working-class writer of a literary career. The novel opens with the hero aged about twenty. Miller shrouds Malvern's background in secrecy. All we know about him, and all he seems to know about himself, is that he has recently been an usher in a small boarding school and has come to a village near the town of Buttervote to bury his father who has been killed in an explosion. After the burial, through the good offices of the vicar, Malvern becomes the village schoolmaster at a salary of £40 a year. Although it is clear that Malvern is no humble, self-educated working man, his career follows the pattern set by such intelligent village boys as Thomas Cooper who became the Gainsborough village schoolmaster aged twenty-two.

Malvern begins his literary career by submitting verses to the county paper – the classic entrance to authorship for the working man. His work is immediately recognised as superior to the run of the mill 'poet's corner' verse, and he is encouraged by the gentlemen of the neighbourhood to publish a volume of poems by subscription. This first venture into publishing is such a success that it earns him 11s. 6d. and the editorship of the local literary monthly, the *Buttervote Magazine*. His fame having spread a dozen or so miles, he begins to dream of greater things: 'To know and be known by such men as Wordsworth, Wilson, Southey, Rogers, Moore and Campbell, and a few others, he considered a higher honour than the praise of millions. He never dreamed of winning wealth by his pen.'[21] With an impulsiveness second only to Miller's, Malvern abandons his school, elopes with the squire's daughter and travels to London in search of Rogers and the rest of them.

Miller's description of Malvern's life as a London author in the 1830s is probably the most complete fictional account we have; certainly it is more accurate in its details than the adventures of Copperfield or Pendennis. It is rooted firmly in Miller's own experience. Once in London Malvern hawks his poetry around the publishers but is told that poetry does not sell, 'Indeed unless it is beautifully illustrated we cannot even get the public to look at it.' He meets a common writer; a man from no discernable class who 'works for the publishers'. This author describes the lower and middle levels of literary society in the London of 1835:

There are, in London, a great number of literary men, whose names are almost unknown to the public. Such are the writers who contribute to cheap periodicals, and now and then, get an article inserted into the magazines, too often without their name being affixed to it. Thus their talents become buried. They have issued no distinct work on which to base their reputation, and consequently can demand no price in the market; yet many of these men are excellent writers.[22]

Malvern finds lodgings for himself on the Surrey side of the Thames, presumably in Southwark. Through his new friend he gets some work as a drama critic on the *Old Monthly Magazine*. From this small beginning he gradually acquires more work until, like Miller, he is hired by a Colburn-type publisher at £10 a month to fill two printed sheets monthly. He also manages to publish his poetry in an illustrated annual. However, all this literary work does not bring him enough money to live in even shabby gentility. Like Mrs Miller, Mrs Malvern is obliged to pawn her jewellery. Like Miller, Malvern discovers the misery of

hard-plodding downright authorship, – that wear and tear of mind, which so many sigh to put into practice, but who have never yet known what it is to write against time – to pile page upon page, until the given gap is filled up, and which, when done, barely 'keeps the wolf from the door'.[23]

In contemplating Malvern's difficulties, Miller launches into an aside on the practice of authorship which includes a delicate reference to the Literary Fund. He declares that authorship is

a sea, whose shores are ever strewn with a thousand wrecks, . . . for not one out of an hundred makes a prosperous voyage. Let anyone who doubts the correctness of the far-fetched image, join the Literary Fund Society, – that little Lighthouse on the gloomy sea of Literature . . . he will there see how many a goodly ship, both name and owner known, and how many a little unknown bark, have steered for it, when there was no other human help on 'this rough dark sea'.[24]

Eventually Malvern's name becomes known; his good looks commented on. He is invited by Lady Smileall to a soirée, described by Miller as a 'literary rat-trap' where 'almost any literary man, who can "show off," may make sure of a supper'. Malvern goes to Lady Smileall's unaccompanied by his wife. At the door he meets a rough, self-educated poet called Tom Grinder, the only unrepentantly working-class writer in the novel. Grinder may be a portrait of the Scottish weaver poet William Thom, who came to London in 1841 and was an instant success at Lady Blessington's. Grinder's first observations on entering Lady Smileall's drawing room are probably identical to Miller's impression of the Blessington soirées, 'Here's some dev'lish pretty lasses among 'em, Godfrey. Dal me, if I won't hev some fun afore I go.' It is never quite clear whether Grinder is an innocent north-countryman out of his depth, or a shrewd publicist, trading, as Miller was alleged to have done, on his exotic labouring background. The scene which follows convincingly, if satirically, shows the fate of a working man exhibited by a countess. Grinder proceeds to call for beer, baccy, bread and cheese in preference to champagne and sandwiches.

He flirted with the young ladies, upset a table while attempting to give one of them a kiss, broke four glasses, and cracked a decanter. . . . Never had the etiquette and ceremony, which was 'iced' to perfection at Lady Smileall's parties, been subject to such shocks of native rudeness before.[25]

Such shocks, however, were the lifeblood of literary gossip and Grinder could be certain to receive a second invitation.

The novel continues with Lady Smileall introducing Malvern to a dark-haired poetess, Maria, a Letitia Landon figure with whom he falls in love. His pregnant wife discovers his new attachment and leaves him to return to her father. Malvern then moves in with Maria and his fame as a writer is secured by the publication of his first three-volume novel for which he is paid £150. Thereafter the story slips into melodrama and throws little light on the literary profession. Maria's child by Malvern is stillborn and she dies herself shortly afterwards, her reputation and honour ruined. Malvern returns to Buttervote where he discovers that he, and not his evil father-in-law, is the rightful squire. Malvern and his wife are reconciled; they go to live in the Manor House and in the fullness of time Malvern represents his county in Parliament. 'He still enacts the part of Author; and now that he is rich, his works seem to attract more attention than they ever did, though there are good judges who say that they are much inferior to his earlier productions.'[26] Miller is prepared to allow Malvern to end his life in wealth and happiness, but he is damned if he will allow him the greater prize of honourable literary achievement.

Miller was unusual among working-class writers: he was completely absorbed into the middle-class publishing world. With the exception of *Gideon Giles* his novels were straightforward attempts to exploit the vogue for history and melodrama in monthly parts. His essays and poems on country life were written for the genteel classes 'who really appreciate the quiet beauties of English scenery and . . . old world lore'.[27] The majority of working-class writers did not live in London, were not published by Henry Colburn, did not attempt to live by their pens and, in Miller's sense, were not professional authors.

IT IS NO ACCIDENT that the most important working-class writers of the 1820s, 30s and 40s lived in the northern industrial towns. The villages of Dorset, Devon and even Yorkshire did not have the mechanics institutes, the libraries, the lectures, the printers and all the other paraphernalia associated with the utilitarian diffusion of useful knowledge. Both the middle-class initiatives of men like Henry Brougham and Charles Knight, which aimed to render the working man decent, moderate and fit for the franchise, and the more radical publishing activities of Richard Carlile, William Cobbett and the 'unstamped' press, led to a huge expansion of the working-class publishing industry.

Manchester was the principal literary city outside London; its

Literary and Philosophical Society had been founded as early as 1781 and by the 1830s it had a mechanics institute, an Athenaeum and the most sophisticated provincial publishing trade. Abel Heywood, a Manchester bookseller and the agent for the *Northern Star* and the *Poor Man's Guardian*, was on his way to becoming the leading provincial and working-class publisher; his list included many Manchester authors, among them Samuel Bamford, Isabella Banks and John Critchley Prince.

To be the subject of a full-length biography is hardly adequate proof of just deserts. The Ayrshire poet James Montgomery, for example, is entombed in a seven-volume biography that is absurdly out of proportion to any merits he may have possessed as a writer. But R.C. Lithgow's stout biography of J.C. Prince, published by Abel Heywood together with a two-volume edition of the poems, is a fair indication of the importance with which Manchester regarded its most famous working-class poet. More recently Louis James has written that Prince 'stands out for the vigour of his imagination. . . . there is no question that Prince wrote sincerely, often powerfully, and was on the mental wavelength of his readers'.[28] Martha Vicinus, who is probably the first person to have subjected Prince's work to textual criticism, concludes that at least he was 'capable of interesting minor lyrics'.[29] In fact Prince is more interesting for the light his career sheds on the status and struggles of the working-class writer than for his intrinsic literary merit. It is enough that for a while he was considered to be the leading Manchester poet of any class.

He was born in Wigan in 1808, the son of a reedmaker – an ancillary trade in the cotton industry. He became an apprentice reedmaker aged nine and often worked a fourteen to sixteen hour day. Inspite of this laborious work, and his father's illiterate scorn, Prince devoured the novels of Defoe, Ann Radcliffe and Monk Lewis. At the age of fourteen his favourite poets were Thomson and Goldsmith; Byron was the only contemporary poet with whom he was at all familiar. At the age of nineteen he married. Three years later, the unemployed father of two children, Prince left his family to the care of the Wigan poorhouse and tramped as far as Paris in search of work. He returned a year later a vagrant and beggar and camped with his family in a Manchester garret – their bed was a bundle of straw. The only work he could find was in his old trade of reedmaking, but he earned less than subsistence wages and his youngest child died.

It was under these conditions, in the early 1830s, that Prince began to write poetry imitating such favourites as Thomson and Spenser. As a release from the hardness of his life he would go for long solitary walks into the soothing countryside. It was not only poets reared in the countryside such as Miller and Clare who were inspired by nature. Nature was, if anything, even more inspiring to the writers surrounded by industrial landscapes. J.G. Lockhart wrote of the Scots poet John Wright, 'he has contrived admidst the severest toils of a cotton manufactory in Glasgow, to embody images of rural scenery and trains of moral reflection'.[30] Perhaps if he had toiled in the fields instead of in the town, nature would have lost some of its charm. But for the industrial worker a day in the country was a glimpse of paradise. James Bradshaw Walker, for example, struggled most of his life in Leeds as a woollen cloth drawer. His poetry, published under such titles as *Wayside Flowers* and *Spring Leaves*, was compared to 'some quiet pellucid brook meandering through some fine English Park, and by some ancient village church, while all around is still and quiet'.[31]

Prince's early poems, composed on his Sunday walks, found favour with the local press. By 1836 he was sufficiently well known among Manchester literati to be invited to join the 'literary twelve', a literary club which met on Sunday afternoons and included among its members J.B. Rogerson, R.W. Procter, G.F. Mandley and occasionally Richard Oastler. In 1841, with no employment available in the cotton industry, Prince took the risk of publishing his poems by subscription, with the encouragement of a wealthy manufacturer J.P. Westhead. To oblige Westhead, Prince agreed to tone down the political content of his verse. Nevertheless the collection included some semi-democratic poems such as 'The Poor Man's Appeal', 'The Slave' and 'A Plea for the Uneducated':

> Ye wealthy magnates of my native land,
> Stretch forth, in pity, an assisting hand;
> Give back a portion of your ample store,
> To purchase wholesome knowledge for the poor.[32]

It was not exactly revolutionary, and it presaged the supplicatory attitude that was to characterise the rest of Prince's literary career.

As a Manchester poet, Prince could hardly ignore the political upheavals of the 1840s. But he liked to regard himself as a moderating influence, checking the 'false doctrines and theories' of Chartism and socialism.[33] Perhaps with an eye to middle-class patronage Prince advocated a personal, spiritual quest. He might almost have taken his text from Charles Kingsley:

Freedom, Equality and Brotherhood are here. Realize them in thine own self, and so alone thou helpest to make them realities for all. Not without, from Charters and Republics, but from within, from the Spirit working in each; not by wrath and haste, but by patience made perfect through suffering.[34]

A great many working-class men shared this view, and those who were writers were, like Prince, enlisted in support of middle-class reformism. Prince summed up his political views in a letter to the Chartist poet Charles Davlin:

I do not deny that they [the Chartists] ask for things for which they have an undoubted natural right, and things in which they stand much in need, but they do not take an elevated and moral line of action; they do not speak like men who have a claim on the fruits and enjoyments of the earth, but like restless and desperate *banditti* who have made up their minds to have something, whether lawfully or otherwise . . . [they] have retarded the cause of reform fifty years at least.[35]

It was a good guess. But the trouble with the working-class writer taking the elevated view and associating with the middle class, was that it exposed him to the patronage of the middle class – to the well-intentioned interference of men like Westhead.

Hours with the Muses was published in 1841 to considerable acclaim. It brought Prince more than local fame. He abandoned reedmaking and set up a more genteel business as a stationer opposite the Sun Inn. The public house soon became the headquarters of the newly established Lancashire Literary Association with Rogerson as president, Prince as secretary and Samuel Bamford, Elijah Ridings and George Falkner among the members. Falkner, the editor of *Bradshaw's Magazine*, became Prince's publisher and Bamford obligingly chose a poem by Prince in *Oddfellow's Magazine*, edited by Rogerson, for a £6 poetry prize. This new-found celebrity was not without its embarrassments. Prince's wife was 'utterly uneducated and prosaic, a good wife to the weaver but no companion to the poet; and, in the meantime, his two daughters were growing up in ignorance as dense as her own'.[36] Prince began to escape his 'cheerless and nearly furnitureless' home by going across the road to the Sun Inn where, according to Falkner 'he found everything congenial and inviting'.[37]

In an attempt to secure Prince's talents from drink and poverty Westhead and others tried to find him a government appointment. Lord Francis Egerton promised to use his influence and at the very least a minor clerkship was expected. But, as so often happens, the patrons misjudged their man. Prince was offered a 15s. a week job as a postman in Southampton. It was an insult to a self-educated artisan. Prince's friends then asked Sir Robert Peel to secure him a librarianship, but as no library appeared anxious to obtain his services he was awarded a £50 consolation prize from the Royal Bounty Fund. The middle classes wanted to help the working-class writer but they were at a loss to know at what level in society such a writer should function. The dilemma was put by J.P. Westhead in a letter to the Literary Fund which clearly demonstrates the perplexity of the patron:

The sudden change in Prince's condition from obscurity to honourable fame as a Poet was attended with results which have been in many respects injurious to him. He was introduced to a new class of society and many who were disposed to befriend him, acted very injudiciously towards him, leading him into traits of habit and expenditure which were baneful to body mind and circumstance. I have already expended upwards of £100 on his behalf and I have used my best influence to find him a suitable situation, but mercantile men, generally, ridicule the idea of employing a poet.

The tone of Westhead's letter is like a headmaster's report on a talented but difficult child. Written in May 1844, a dozen years after the Reform Bill and four years after the founding of the National Charter Association, Westhead's letter concludes with the hope that 'some nobleman [will] place him in a lodge where his wife or children could attend the gate and where Prince might be allowed to be as poets like to be, – idle or active at pleasure'. It appears that noblemen had the same prejudices against tipsy, working-class poets as did mercantile men for no lodge was forthcoming. Instead, and more appropriately, Prince secured the editorship of an obscure local magazine the *Ancient Shepherd's Quarterly* at a fee of £12 a year.

At about this time Prince failed in his stationery business and returned to his trade, setting up as a master reedmaker. This exercise in self-employment was also a failure. Prince stepped one rung down the artisan's ladder and took employment as a journeyman reedmaker, working twelve hours a day for a guinea a week – including the earnings of his wife and daughters. He was soon more than £85 in debt. In September 1846 his Manchester friends organised a public subscription on his behalf, but because no way could be found to prevent Prince from spending it on drink it was withheld by the trustees and used to pay off his smaller debts. Meanwhile Prince applied to the Royal Literary Fund and was granted £40. This was above the average grant of the time and shows that Prince's literary merit was taken seriously; Mary Russell Mitford for example was given £50 at about the same time and Miller's grants had ranged from £15 to £40.

From 1846 onwards Prince's life was a succession of appeals to the Fund against a background of heavy drinking, occasional verse writing and even more occasional employment. In 1847 he was again unemployed owing to the stoppage of the cotton mills in his neighbourhood. His family consisted of his wife, an unmarried daughter, a sick married daughter, her dying husband and their child. In 1854 his father, his unmarried daughter and his grandchild died. Such poverty and suffering combined with an uneconomic literary skill and a distaste for manual labour led, unsurprisingly, to fairly constant inebriation. After the tragedies of 1854 Prince resolved, not very vigorously, to take the pledge. Still unemployed he tramped in search of work and when no work was forthcoming he wrote a steady stream of begging letters, some in verse:

> Poor J.C.P., who has no shoes,
> Nor yet the solace of the Muse,
> But sadly harassed by the 'blues'
>   For want of 'browns'
> Doth hope that you will not refuse
>   Those two half-crowns –
> (That is, if you can spare 'em).[38]

In 1858 his wife died after falling downstairs, apparently in a drunken stupor. Prince remarried in 1862, this time to 'a careful, thrifty and tidy wife',[39] though for all her thrift she could not save what was not earned. Prince's desultory reedmaking came to a complete standstill as a result of the cotton famine caused by the blockade of American ports during the Civil War. He survived by writing rhyming advertisements for a local master tailor. An application to Palmerston for a Civil List pension was unsuccessful, perhaps because Prince was regarded as a hopeless inebriate.

Prince's hard life, for all that it was made harder by a weak character, illustrates the seemingly insurmountable difficulties faced by working-class writers – particularly poets. A 'poet' was understood to be separate from the run of men. Poetry implied refinement, sensitivity, imagination and learning, all qualities which were supposed to be foreign to the masses but were highly valued by cultured middle-class readers. Any working man who read poetry was on the way to self-education and probably to becoming a working-class poet as well. For those, like Prince, who were at the summit of a provincial Parnassus, it was not surprising that they should regard themselves as poets first and working men second. This led them to neglect or abandon their trades which were anyway both exhausting and unprofitable, and, in the absence of anything else, to rely on authorship to provide them with both money and opportunity. In Prince's case it did neither. In his best year while editor of a magazine, the author of a new volume of poetry and occasional contributor to the Manchester press he might have earned as much as £30. Of course literature provided a kind of dole unavailable to other working men. Prince was granted £170 by the Royal Literary Fund, £50 from the Royal Bounty and perhaps as much as £400 from private donations between the publication of his first book of poems in 1841 and his death in 1866. This was the equivalent of £30 a year but it was merely charitable and, for Prince, ultimately degrading. With such hand-outs, his literary earnings and his pittance as a reedmaker Prince could rarely have earned as much as £100 a year, enough to lift him temporarily out of the ranks of the Lancashire weavers but hardly enough to secure him a place in middle-class society.

Another poet of Prince's Manchester circle was an ex-weaver, Elijah Ridings, author of *The Village Muse*. Ridings appears to have had most of Prince's vices though with less compensatory talent. He applied several times to the Royal Literary Fund supported by a galaxy of Manchester luminaries: Samuel Bamford, J.B. Rogerson, Charles Swain, Abel Heywood, Archibald Prentice and Thomas Bazley MP. The Fund, however, although they allowed him grants on four occasions, never awarded him more than £10 a time – a sum that indicates their feeling that his literary merit and social standing barely reached their minimum level. One of his sponsors, J.B. Rogerson, himself a beneficiary of the Fund, found it necessary to testify to Ridings's 'good conduct and sobriety'.

The contrast between Prince and Ridings, two self-educated poets from labouring backgrounds, and two other members of the Sun Inn association, Rogerson and Swain, is instructive. Both Rogerson and Swain came from humble backgrounds but were a notch or two higher in the English class system than Prince and Ridings. Rogerson started working life as an office boy before becoming a bookseller and editor of various local magazines. His clerkly skills combined with his modest literary reputation led to a series of appointments of the kind Prince aspired to but could never obtain: he was successively clerk on Dr Lyon Playfair's public health enquiry; secretary to the Master Builder's Association; and from 1847 onwards registrar of the Manchester General Cemetery at a salary of £80. Apart from his editorships, his literary reputation rested on a few volumes of uninspired poetry, certainly less competent and less original than the poems of Prince. Nevertheless, at the end of his life, when suffering from rheumatism, he was awarded a Civil List pension of £50 'in consideration of his literary merits'.

Charles Swain attended a Unitarian school in Manchester until the age of fifteen and then took a job as a clerk in his uncle's firm. From there he went to work for a lithographer and by dint of tenacity and sobriety bought a controlling share in the firm. In his spare time he wrote popular poetry much of which was set to music. By his middle age he was a leading Manchester citizen with a comfortable detached home and well-married daughters. He was awarded a Civil List pension of £50 in 1856 in recognition of his literary achievements. Dubbed 'the Manchester Tennyson' he was happy to associate with Prince, Ridings and others in the absence of a more illustrious circle.

Both Swain and Rogerson seem to have been steady, sober men, inspite of their poetry, and to have achieved a degree of worldly success. Prince and Ridings may have been inebriates but it is difficult to resist the conclusion that they took to drink to compensate for lack of opportunities rather than lost opportunities. They were the literary equals of Swain or Rogerson, indeed Prince was their superior, but they were hampered by lack of schooling – by being born into the subsistence industry of weaving where basic writing skills amounted to intellectual achievement, rather than into the mobile world of careful-spelling clerks.

EBENEZER ELLIOTT is the first and one of the only outstanding examples of a working-class writer who did not write to please middle-class readers. He wrote an unrepentant political poetry, exhorting the working classes to commit themselves to the struggle against the tyranny of landlords, employers and governments. Unlike most working-class writers, Elliott came from a radical family, his father, 'Devil Elliott', was a Jacobin in politics and worked in the office of a local iron foundry. So although Elliott had an industrial background he was not exactly of the workers even if he was for them. He described himself as from 'one of the lower, little removed above the lowest class'.[40] After leaving school Elliott worked for his father until a fortunate marriage brought him several thousand pounds. He invested his wife's wealth in the Sheffield iron trade and was soon bankrupt. He was rescued by his wife's rich relatives and from 1821 onwards he made a respectable, if precarious, living as the master of his own iron business.

Elliott began to write and publish poetry in the first years of the century. His rather feeble romantic verse in the manner of Thomson led to a flattering correspondence with Robert Southey. It was not, however, until his late forties that he began to write the 'poetry of the poor' that was to earn him national fame. The reform agitation of the late 1820s and Elliott's own experience of the damaging effects of the corn laws led to his conversion to political poetry. In 1829 he published a long poem, *The Village Patriarch*, which gave a vivid portrait of the living conditions of the rural poor and drew immediate comparison with Crabbe's sternest tales of country life. This was followed in 1831 by his most famous collection, the *Corn Law Rhymes*, in which he bitterly attacked the operations and effects of the corn laws:

> Child, what hast thou with sleep to do?
> Awake, and dry thine eyes!
> Thy tiny hands must labour too;
> Our bread is tax'd – arise!
> Arise, and toil long hours twice seven,
> For pennies two or three;
> Thy woes make angels weep in Heaven –
> But England still is free.

The *Edinburgh Review* ran a long and laudatory review by Carlyle, praising Elliott for his 'genuine' feeling, for being free of dilletante patronage, for writing well and accurately about the conditions and experiences of the 'toil-grimmed' working class. As the Anti-Corn Law League was essentially a manufacturer's pressure group it was not surprising that *Corn Law Rhymes* should have proved an instant success with progressive middle-class readers, quite apart from their evident literary merit. Within a year of publication the volume went through three editions. Carlyle's review was followed by an even more enthusiastic notice by W.J. Fox in the *London Review* in 1835: 'God said "Let Elliott be" and there was a poetry of the poor.' Fortunately Elliott was not poor, and as his own paymaster he had no need, like the beggarly Prince, to pander to the views of self-important patrons.

Corn Law Rhymes marked the beginning of a new phase of working-class writing; it gained in self-confidence and expressiveness as much as it lost in delicacy, sensibility and lyricism. Fox declared that a new order had arrived:

It is evidently unnecessary for Societies and Reviewers, and Diffusionists, and Philosophers, and all the rest of us, to talk about enlightening the operatives, and instructing the mass of the population. We may go to sleep, so far as that is concerned. They will not wait for our instructions. They will instruct themselves.

For his part, Elliott continued to work hard for the repeal of the corn laws, giving poetry readings and lectures, though he wrote little more poetry of interest or importance. He joined the National Charter Association and spoke vigorously against the rich: 'I doubt whether there are one hundred men in London, worth twenty thousand pounds each, who do not in their heart hate and fear every working man who is supposed to have a mind of his own.'[41] Such rhetoric however was aimed principally against the corn laws, which Elliott blamed not only for the plight of the poor, but for his own commercial difficulties. Privately he was of a capitalist disposition and was soon out of sympathy with the wider revolutionary aims of the Chartists. But if he was reluctant to endorse the objectives of the Chartists he nonetheless succeeded in demonstrating to them the effectiveness of a politicised literature. Working-class literature had entered the age of Alton Locke.

The 1840s, which saw the repeal of the corn laws and the failure of the Chartist movement, also witnessed an unparalleled interest in working-class literature; both 'cheap' fiction churned out at a penny-a-line by a host of would-be Dickenses, and a more self-conscious, highbrow literature that gave clear evidence of the working-class writer's fitness to aspire to middle-class privileges. In 1845 Thomas Cooper published a long philosophical poem, *The Purgatory of Suicides*, which was regarded as one of the most remarkable literary works of the age, not least because it had been written by a notorious Chartist imprisoned for incitement to riot. It was praised for its 'massive learning and profound thoughts'[42] and was clearly too erudite and metaphysical for most reviewers to comprehend. Working men read and praised Cooper's poem as a working-class achievement. Benjamin Wilson called it 'a work of high standing'.[43] R.G. Gammage in his history of Chartism declared it to be 'a magnificent poem . . . which a large portion of the literary press declared to be equal to any poetical work of modern times'.[44] Probably no one understood the poem and few actually read it from beginning to end but all were overawed by its massive pretensions. In his description of his choice of literary models Cooper reveals the scale of his poetic ambitions:

The remembrance that Byron had shown the stanza of the 'Faery Queene' to be capable of as much grandeur and force as the blank verse of 'Paradise Lost,' while he also demonstrated that it admits the utmost freedom that can be needed for the treatment of a grave theme, determined me to abide by the Spenserean stanza.[45]

Spenser, Milton, Byron, Cooper. *The Purgatory of Suicides* was not supposed to be admired as an astonishing literary feat for a working-class man – it was intended to be a dazzling achievement by any standards; a work that might have been penned by a middle-class genius.

While Cooper was impressing middle-class readers with his learning if not his politics, the publisher Charles Knight was actively seeking working-class intellectuals who would address themselves to their own class; who would preach self-discipline and self-help to the mass of labouring men. Knight was the publisher for the Society for the Diffusion of Useful Knowledge and a pioneer in the field of cheap literature. By 1832 his *Penny Magazine* had achieved a circulation of 200,000. At the end of the 1830s he began to publish a series of trade guides for the use of aspiring apprentices. In 1838 he published James Devlin's *The Shoemaker* and in 1840 *The Tailor* by James Carter. Devlin and Carter were not ambitious to succeed as imaginative writers though Devlin did try his hand at verse: they saw themselves as working men first and only incidentally as authors. Devlin wrote:

I am not an author by profession, but by trade a boot-closer, and with the exception of the money obtained from Mr Knight for the copyright of 'The Shoemaker' I may safely say, that I have never found writing, beyond the pleasure derivable from the thing itself, of any advantage.[46]

Carter echoes this sentiment: 'I am not – nor do I profess to be – a Literary Man; neither do I attempt to procure maintenance by literary employment.' He went so far as to claim, 'I should never have attempted to be an Author, if my ill state of health [he suffered from asthma] had not incapacitated me for manual labor.'[47] Both Devlin and Carter obviously felt that there was something extravagant and presumptuous in a working man attempting to become an author. Knight's object in encouraging them to write is clearly stated in his assessment of Devlin's work:

It has been his aim to raise the moral and intellectual character of his brethren of the 'gentle craft', and to disabuse them of many prejudices which, as he thinks and I believe justly, have operated against their general prosperity. Like many of those in advance of their own class he has from this cause encountered hostility.[48]

Unlike Cooper, Devlin and Carter remained at their trades. They did not aspire to enter the middle class but wished to improve the respectability of their own class. They did not expect to rival Spenser, Milton, Byron or even Mrs Hemans, but aimed to write competently on subjects with which they were familiar, such as the operations of their own trades and the events of their own lives. 'The example of Thomas Carter [sic]', Knight wrote, and of many others who belong to the ranks of self-educated men, is sufficient to prove that if they have talent and good sense, with a reasonable proportion of knowledge, they will want no artificial stimulus to attain some sort of success as public writers upon subjects with which they are really acquainted.[49]

Neither Devlin nor Carter were ambitious writers and for all that their lack of sympathy with the political movements of the day may brand them forelock-tugging flunkeys, their authorship was more genuinely working class than the epics of Cooper or the lyrics of Prince. However, at least one middle-class observer believed that in more favourable circumstances their talents could have earned them literary honour:

I have known . . . Mr Devlin, for a good many years, both as an anxious tradesman whom I believe to be thoroughly honest, and as an author of such considerable natural abilities as I think would have enabled him to distinguish himself in the world had he received the education they merited.

This was written by Leigh Hunt in April 1848, just six days before the fiasco of the Chartist demonstration at Kennington Common which marked an end, for the time being, to all hopes of universal suffrage. 1848 was a victory for the Carters, Devlins and Knights.

After Kennington Common, Charles Kingsley wrote to Thomas Cooper to ask for help: 'I want some one like yourself, intimately acquainted with the minds of the working classes, to give me such an insight into their life and thoughts, as may enable me to consecrate my powers effectively to their service.'[50] Out of this correspondence, which led to friendship, came Kingsley's novel *Alton Locke: Tailor and Poet* (1850), the most famous, if controversial novel about Chartism, and the only novel of substance about the trials of a working-class, self-educated writer. Kingsley chose to make his hero both a poet and an autobiographer, which was an exact observation of the working-class writer in the 1840s. He was also exact in choosing tailoring as his poet's trade, though shoemaking would have done as well. It is unlikely that in researching the background to his novel Kingsley would have overlooked Carter's *Memoirs of a Working Man* concerning the intellectual and labouring life of a tailor.

Whatever the shortcomings of Kingsley's novel as an examination of Chartism, it is a convincing portrait of a working-class author. In his account of Alton Locke's struggle for education, Kingsley perfectly describes the composite experiences of Prince, Cooper, Miller, Carter and other contemporary writers. The young Alton Locke, forbidden all but sectarian literature by his mother, discovers Byron at a second-hand bookstall, 'They fed, those poems, both my health and my diseases

. . . they gave me, little of them as I could understand, a thousand new notions about scenery and man, a sense of poetic melody and luxuriance as yet utterly unknown.'[51] After Byron, Locke discovers the work of John Bethune, a Scottish labourer who had died of consumption in 1839 aged twenty-seven. He then reads Milton, Virgil, Fox's *Book of Martyrs* and other books selected by Mackaye, the bookseller, as suitable for a working man's education. The only time Locke has for reading is at night or early in the morning before his twelve-hour day as a tailor's apprentice.

Look at the picture awhile, ye comfortable folks, who take down from your shelves what books you like best at the moment, and then lie back, amid prints and statuettes, to grow wise in an easy-chair, with a blazing fire and a camphine lamp. The lower classes uneducated! Perhaps you would be so too, if learning cost you the privation which it costs some of them.[52]

Kingsley makes it quite clear that he is writing primarily for middle-class readers, most of whom would have only the vaguest notions of the intellectual activities of the working class. If such readers had heard of Bamford or Elliott they would probably have banned their works from the hearth. The Rev. Charles Kingsley's *Alton Locke*, published by Chapman and Hall, was, inspite of controversial reviews, quite another matter.

After taking so much trouble to read poetry, Locke is soon busy writing it. Sacked from his apprenticeship for complaining about working conditions, Locke tramps to Cambridge to stay with his cousin. Few working men, one supposes, had cousins at Cambridge unless they were of the Kirke White variety. While staying in Cambridge, Locke meets a benevolent young lord and a scientific dean who between them decide that Locke should publish his poems by subscription. While preparing the volume for the press Locke lives with the dean and falls in love with his daughter, as Blacket had fallen in love with Miss Milbanke. And as Prince bowed to the judgment of his patron Mr Westhead, so Locke takes the dean's advice and agrees to excise those political poems that 'were somewhat too strong for the public taste'. He becomes the creature of his patrons.

The serious reviews subject Locke's *Songs of the Highways* to 'searching criticisms' and a 'paternal pat on the shoulder'. The middle-class press hails Locke as it must have hailed Prince and Miller, as a 'voice fresh from the heart of nature', 'another "untutored" songster of the wilderness'.[53] The Chartist press justly attacks Locke for time-serving and submitting to the 'petticoat influence'.

His poems published, Locke turns to full-time authorship: 'It was miserable work, there is no denying it – only not worse than tailoring.'[54] Having led the life of Thomas Miller, Locke is stung by Chartist criticism of his betrayal of their cause. He throws himself wholeheartedly into the Chartist movement and is imprisoned for three years for incitement to riot. Disillusioned with 'physical force' Chartism and the inglorious failure of the Kennington Common demonstration, Locke is converted to Kingsley's Christian Socialism on his release from prison. And, but for his death on an Atlantic crossing, he would no doubt have lived to lecture on the cause until lack of funds drove him to appeal to the Royal Literary Fund and the Prime Minister. Such was the fate of Thomas Cooper.

When Cooper's autobiography was published in 1872 the extent of Kingsley's indebtedness became clear. However, *Alton Locke* not only borrowed Cooper's experiences, it also predicted them, for after its publication Kingsley succeeded in turning Cooper the Chartist into a Christian Socialist who was to devote most of the rest of his life to lecturing on religious subjects. 'I gave up all literary work in 1857', Cooper wrote to the Royal Literary Fund in February 1867, 'and, from a deep conviction of duty, began to address assemblies chiefly of working-men, on the Evidences of Natural and Revealed Religion'. Ironically Cooper's best and lasting work is his autobiography written long after he considered that he had abandoned 'all literary work'. Apart from the autobiography and sundry religious tracts such as *Plain Pulpit Talk* (1872) and the *Verity and Value of the Miracles of Christ* (1876), Cooper's literary career lasted a decade, from *The Purgatory of Suicides* (1845) to the novel *The Family Feud* (1855). During this period he was also the founder and editor of *Cooper's Journal* published by James Watson. Its failure after thirty numbers in 1850 coincided with the end of the era of cheap, didactic fiction.

Unlike Alton Locke or J.C. Prince, Cooper was determined that his first literary work, *The Purgatory of Suicides*, should be commercially published by the best possible firm. He settled on Edward Moxon, publisher of Wordsworth, Shelley, Tennyson and Browning. He managed to obtain an introduction to Moxon through Disraeli, whom he had met through the radical MP T.S. Duncombe. But Moxon, like the publisher in *Godfrey Malvern*, declared, 'I certainly would publish your poem, Mr Cooper, if I saw anything like a chance of selling it; but I repeat to you, that *all* poetry is a perfect drug in the market, at present; and I have made up my mind to publish no new poetry whatever.'[55] It was, of course, a polite brush off. A few months later Robert Browning was writing to Elizabeth Barrett 'I did go . . . to Moxon's. . . . your poems continued to sell "singularly well" – they would "end in bringing in a clear profit". . . . he spoke rather encouragingly of my own prospects.'[56] Disraeli then sent Cooper to his own publisher, Henry Colburn, who asserted, accurately enough, 'we publish no poetry whatever'. Next Cooper sought the advice of John Forster, the most renowned literary agent of the day. Like the dean in *Alton Locke* Forster advised Cooper to banish all taint of Chartism from his text. Eventually, having been shuffled around by London's fashionable authors – Disraeli, Ainsworth, Lytton and Forster, and having been declined by Moxon, Colburn, and Chapman and Hall, Cooper found a publisher more sympathetic to the working-class author. John Cleave, the Chartist and radical publisher who had been imprisoned for blasphemy, introduced Cooper to Douglas Jerrold who took the spurned epic to his own publisher Jeremiah How. The happy outcome was that 'the 500 copies which formed the first edition were sold off before Christmas'.[57]

Cooper's struggle for publication shows that the working-class author was not, as a rule, acceptable to middle-class publishing houses, no matter how good his work might be. It was left to provincial publishers like Heywood, and third-division London publishers like How (the publisher of John Clare's *The Rural Muse*), to take a risk on working-class literature. And without the backing of a Macmillan, Smith or Chapman it is not surprising that the working man made so little from his writing. How's business failed in 1846 and Cooper received nothing for his poem. However it did bring him fame, and the acquaintance of Carlyle, Kingsley, Dickens and of course Lady Blessington. It also paved the way for his gradual integration into the middle-class publishing world. Through his friend Thomas Miller he was paid £25 by Chapman and Hall for a boy's story, *The Triumph of Perseverance*, and the same company reissued *The Purgatory of Suicides* – after its critical success. Routledge then paid a standard £100 each for two novels, *Alderman Ralph* (1853) and *The Family Feud* (1855). Meanwhile, pressed for money, he received occasional donations: Thomas Noon Talfourd, who had prosecuted him for his erstwhile Chartism, was shamed into giving him £25; William Ellis gave him £100 in 1845, and Thomas Chambers paid £50 for the copyright of *The Purgatory of Suicides* and made a present of it to the author.

But for his conversion to muscular Christianity, Cooper was set to follow the downward path of Thomas Miller. Though his conversion outraged his radical friends, it attracted the support of men like Kingsley, Maurice and Thomas Hughes. And having abandoned literature, probably in the nick of time, his new friends secured Cooper a clerkship at the Board of Health – a working man's dream. He resigned the post in May 1858 to pursue his God-given mission as a lecturer. By 1866 he 'had preached 1,169 times and lectured 2,204 times' and all 'in defence of the truth Christianity and in the inculcation of its doctrines and principles among the working classes'.[58] The following year, as a testimony to his labours as a Christian propagandist, his friends raised over £1,300 for the purchase of a £100 annuity. At the behest of W.E. Forster and others, Gladstone awarded the old Chartist £300 from the Royal Bounty Fund in 1881. And just to show that there was no ill feeling he was awarded a further £200 by Lord Salisbury's government in 1892.

The literary career of the youngest Chartist poet spans the second half of the nineteenth century and exemplifies the rise and fall of the Victorian working-class writer. Gerald Massey was only twenty-two in 1850 when Thomas Cooper published his poems in *Cooper's Journal*; when his first collection, *Voices of Freedom, Lyrics of Love*, was published by David Bogue; and when Charles Kingsley secured his services as secretary to the Board of Christian Socialists. The following year Massey was the subject of an appraisal by Samuel Smiles in *Eliza Cook's Journal*. Smiles had been editor of the *Leeds Times* and an activist in many political movements including the Anti-Corn Law League and the Household Suffrage Association. He was, however, firm in his opposition to Chartism. In 1845 he had been appointed secretary to the North Midland Railway company at a time when railways and industrial confidence were synonymous. His first biographical essays were about great engineers and in 1851, although he was a well-known journalist, he had yet to write *Self-Help*, his world famous guide to unctuous entrepreneurship. His essay on Massey was his first extended treatment of a working-class author, though he was later to add such writers as Alexander Murray, John Leyden, John Britton, Samuel Drew and William Gifford to his gallery of exemplary strugglers for whom 'the extremest poverty has been no obstacle'.[59] His introduction to Gerald Massey constitutes an assessment of half a century of working-class authorship:

Give a poor down-trodden man culture, and in nine cases out of ten, you only increase his sensitiveness to pain; you agonize him with the sight of pleasures which are to him forbidden, you quicken his sense of despair at the frightful inequalities of the human lot. . . . And when such a man does find a voice, surely 'rose-water' verses and 'hot-pressed' sonnets are not to be expected of him; such things are not by any means the natural products of a life of desperate struggle with poverty. When the self-risen and self-educated man speaks and writes nowadays, it is of subjects nearest to his heart . . . Hence the most intelligent of working men at this day are intensely political. In former times, when literature was regarded mainly in the light of a rich man's luxury, poets who rose out of the working-class sung as their patrons wished. Bloomfield and Clare sung of the quiet beauty of rural life.

Published in 1851 it might almost have been a review of *Alton Locke*. *Eliza Cook's Journal* had a circulation of at least 50,000 and it may be assumed that Smiles helped to turn Massey into a youthful legend.

Massey was born in 1828 the son of a canal boatman. At eight years old he was sent out to work in a silk manufactory for a wage of 9d. to 1s. 6d. a week. He then went to work as a straw plaiter in the damp and insanitary Hertfordshire marshes. His health was all but ruined by 'country life'. He had to wait until he came to London as a fifteen year old errand boy before he was able to enjoy sufficient health and leisure to catch up with his self-education – Cobbett and Paine were among his early texts. In 1848 he joined the Chartists and edited a revolutionary sheet called *Spirit of Freedom*.

His early life was ideal for the purposes of reformists like Kingsley, Maurice and Smiles. It combined the terrible deprivations of the landless agricultural classes with the passion and fervour of youth. For Smiles, it was the most wonderful proof of 'a spirit working from within', of moral achievement 'made perfect through suffering'. Although Massey himself was attracted both to the gospels of self-help and Christian Socialism, there remained, for his counsellors, the vexed problem of his politics. In his early twenties he had witnessed a European revolution, albeit through the newspaper columns, and he was not yet in the mood to renounce revolutionary verse:

> Fling out the red Banner, O Sons of the morning!
> Young spirits abiding to burst into wings, –
> We stand shadow-crown'd, but sublime is the warning,
> All heaven's grimly husht, and the Bird of Storm sings!
> 'All's Well,' saith the Sentry on Tyranny's tower,
> While Hope by his watch-fire is grey and tear-blind;
> Ay, all's well! Freedom's Altar burns hour by hour,
> Live brands for the fire-damp with which ye are mined.

> Fling out the red Banner! the patriots perish,
> But where their bones whiten the seed striketh root;
> Their blood hath run red the great harvest to cherish;
> Then gather ye, Reapers, and garner the fruit.

> Victory! victory! Tyrants are quaking!
> The Titan of Toil from the blood thrall starts;
> The slaves are awaking – the dawn-light is breaking –
> The foot-fall of Freedom beats quick at our hearts!

If this sort of thing had been published before 1848 Massey might have been imprisoned for incitement to riot or blasphemy. As it was the forces of law and order had so completely triumphed that reviewers felt able to indulge the young man. The only concession Massey made to his new-found friends was to change the title of his book of poems from *Voices of Freedom, Lyrics of Love* to *The Ballad of Babe Christabel, with other Lyrical Poems* in the second edition published in 1854. Hepworth Dixon, editor of the *Athenaeum*, gave the new edition a long and favourable notice. Massey's political views, which would have been dangerous a few years earlier, were treated with magnanimous sympathy:

A first glance down his page is, perhaps, a little startling. Democracy – Socialism, are a few of the words which indicate strong opinions and extreme views. . . . Every line is laden with his sense of social wrongs: and many a line suggests – and many an image vivifies – the idea of a vast social revolution as that which appears to him the natural and inevitable path of issue into a better state [4 February 1854].

Hepworth Dixon goes on to show that he sympathises with the poet's views, that he too is aware of the necessity for social change. He echoes Smiles on the changing concerns of working-class poetry:

What the causes are which drive the more earnest-souled and gifted of the lower orders into poetical politics, – which have changed the pastoral warbling of a Bloomfield and a Clare into the fierce denunciations of an Elliot [sic], a Davis, a Cooper, and a Massey, – would not be far to seek. Society might find these causes out, if it would only try.

But Hepworth Dixon does not wish to alarm his readers or identify his magazine too closely with poetical politics and so he reserves his highest praise for the 'love-verses here intermingled with denunciation and Red Republicanism'. Massey is, despite his republicanism – 'certainly a poet', 'a genuine songster'. Hepworth Dixon unwittingly becomes the reviewer of Alton Locke's *Songs of the Highways*: 'Here we have illustrations won from Nature – images which are sound, beautiful and fresh. . . . It would seem as if the poetic passion – the love of Beauty – the humanizing influence of the elder poetry – had kept our minstrel right.' So Massey is a warbler after all.

On all sides from all quarters it was Massey's love lyrics and nature poetry which received unstinted praise. Landor praised them for their 'exquisite and almost unrivalled beauty'.[60] *The Times* described the love poems as 'unusually sweet and elegant'. The way for Massey was clearly signposted and he was not slow to take the hint. By 1861 the *Examiner* was able to assure its readers, 'there remains now in Mr Massey's verse but little of the old wild reference to what he once considered social wrongs; his muse is soberer, and has not suffered any loss of power'. Massey's critical stock was at its height; a collected edition of his work had been published with an introduction by Smiles and he had even been fêted in New York. His talent for declamatory verse had been turned to such uncontroversial subjects as British military prowess during the Crimean War and the Indian mutiny – 'Some of his verse went round the world like the tap of a British drum'. The most laudatory notice of his collected poems was published in the *London Quarterly Review*:

Mr Massey possesses special qualifications for erotic composition, he has always circled his lyrics of love within the sacred enclosure of home and family life, and has not stooped to be a follower of Moore or Byron, both of whom he could easily have surpassed in breadth of outline and warmth of colouring. To him indeed, we owe the sweetest songs of courtship, the merriest marriage-ditties, and the most touching lays of child-life, that have ever been given to the world [October 1861].

It was a generous assessment.

For all Massey's literary success, money was as hard as ever to come by. He only made £30 by his collected poems. He eked out his poetry earnings by journalism, writing regular poetry reviews for the *Athenaeum*. He was still trapped by his social origins, with no private means and, in a Gissing-like predicament, 'bowed down by that awful calamity a crazy and drunken wife'.[61] Massey's admirers recommended the thirty-three year old poet for a Civil List pension. Tennyson, Browning, Forster, Carlyle, Ruskin, Lytton and Landor were among those who signed the petition which declared, 'The Press, with many voices, has passed one unanimous verdict on his literary merits as a Poet heartily English, and first of all that have, in our time, sprung from the Working Classes.' Ruskin added a personal note:

I rejoice in acknowledging my own debt of gratitude to you for many an encouraging and noble thought, and expression of thought, and my conviction that your poems in the mass, have been a helpful and precious gift to the working classes (I use the term in its widest and highest sense) of the country, and that few 'Civil Services' can be greater than that which you have rendered.

The application was not immediately successful but in 1863 Palmerston awarded Massey a pension of £70 as 'a lyric poet, sprung from the people'. Massey became not only one of the youngest writers to receive a pension but the first and only Chartist, and he was one of the very few working-class writers whose work found favour with Downing Street.

To complete his break with all vestiges of republicanism he secured aristocratic patronage. Until 1862 he had lived at the Coniston home of W.J. Linton, the radical journalist and engraver, but that year an ardent admirer, Lady Marian Alford, offered him a house of his own at Ashridge Park, the estate of her son Lord Brownlow. And he was not even expected to mind the gate. Lady Marian was the daughter of the Marquis of Northampton who had himself dabbled in poetry. She regarded herself as an artist and the patron of artists. In her letter of support for Massey's Civil List pension she had written:

> I am a great admirer of your Poetry, which is thoroughly English in sentiment, strength and patriotic feeling. You may reflect with pride that you have never misled any young imagination from what is honourable, good, and true; and that by your own unassisted genius you have raised yourself from the humble position of picking up the crumbs that fall from the educated man's table to the proud one of being yourself a Teacher and a Poet.

Massey lived on the Ashridge Park estate until 1877 when he moved to London. His relationship with Lady Marian and her son seems not to have been complicated by any feelings of ingratitude. Indeed he became the laureate of the family, composing poems on the occasion of the funeral of the second baron and wedding of the third.

Apart from these occasional poems Massey turned increasingly to prose works in which he allowed his mystical and occult interests free rein. In 1871 he began what he regarded as his greatest work, intended to 'recover and reconstitute the lost origins of the myths and mysteries, types and symbols of religion and language, with Egypt for a mouthpiece and Africa as the birthplace'.[62] With this dotty project Massey entered the last and most melancholy phase of his literary career. Once erroneously thought to be the original Felix Holt, he was now a model for Mr Casaubon. 'Eleven years ago', he wrote in December 1882, 'I began a literary work of great research and enormous labour. Calculating that it would take ten years to complete, I sold the copyright for a small stipend, to be paid annually.' This stipend together with his pension kept his income at around £150 per annum. When the stipend ceased Massey fell back on the Royal Literary Fund. In 1887 Massey's pension was increased to £100. According to James Milne, 'but for his Civil List Pension, he could never have published his six large and expensive volumes on Egyptology'. The money might have been better spent, though Sidney Lee noted in his DNB memoir that 'Massey believed that these copious, rambling and valueless compilations deserved better of posterity than his poetry'. By 1904 Massey was complaining that all his books were out of print. Through self-neglect his poetry had been forgotten and Massey the Egyptologist, mystic and scholar was utterly and deservedly ignored.

Like other self-educated men before him, Massey could not resist the temptation to amass and display vast stores of peripheral knowledge. Lack of formal education was deeply felt and working-class writers often abandoned their youthful muse to satisfy their desire to become 'scholars'; to show those Oxford and Cambridge professors once and for all that a working man might have the intellect of a senior wrangler. Thomas Cooper, with great satisfaction, recalled the achievement of just such a man:

One of the greatest incentives I had to solid study was the reading, in Drew's 'Imperial Magazine,' an account of the life of Dr Samuel Lee, Professor of Hebrew in the University of Cambridge, and a scholar, it was said, in more than a dozen languages. He had been apprenticed to a carpenter at eleven years old.[63]

Cooper almost makes it seem that Lee owed his success to his working-class origins, rather than a unique facility for learning languages. But Lee's career was the stuff of a Smilesian vision – and close to a miracle.

THE ONE AREA of literary culture in which working-class writers managed to achieve a pre-eminent position was dialect writing which had both local appeal and a marketable curiosity value among many middle-class readers. It was a tightrope act where the writer was precariously balanced on the edge of middle-class culture. A flourishing literary genre from the 1860s for almost thirty years, by the 1890s dialect writing had tipped over into the world of the music hall.

Edwin Waugh (1817–90), 'the Lancashire Burns', was a leading dialect writer and literary acrobat. The son of a Rochdale shoemaker he was apprenticed to a printer at the age of fourteen. His literary career did not begin until 1855 when he published a series of Lancashire sketches in the local press. He rocketed to national fame in 1856 with the publication in a Manchester paper of his dialect song 'Come Whoam to Thy Childer An' Me'. Written in an easily understood vernacular style which was nonetheless, as far as the middle-class reader was concerned, gratifyingly picturesque, it told the story of a poor wife's appeal to her ne'er-do-well husband to return to the bosom of his family. It was made much of by the temperance movement and other moral crusaders including Baroness Burdett-Coutts. Printed as a single sheet it 'leapt at once into a popularity unparalleled in the annals of modern song. It was sold literally by the million, not only in Lancashire, but throughout England and in the colonies.'[64] Waugh followed this success with a collection of *Poems and Songs* (1859), many of which he wrote in a self-confessed 'literary English'. From 1860 onwards he became a full-time writer earning the bulk of his income from public readings.

In spite of his popularity among the working classes – Joseph Whitaker called him 'the most popular author in the north of England'[65] – he was swiftly drawn into élitist middle-class schemes for the antiquarian study of dialect. In 1876 ill-health forced him to abandon his public readings and to fall back on his middle-class patrons. A public subscription paid him £200 a year for ten years – 'In order to save his self-respect it was called the Waugh Copyright Fund.'[66] Like other working-class writers his 'self-respect' did not inhibit him from receiving a £100 grant from the Royal Literary Fund in 1882. The same year he was awarded a Civil List pension of £90 after the Prime Minister had received a petition 'signed by several hundreds of Lancashire men of some position in the country, probably the most numerously-signed memorial of the kind ever presented'.[67]

Waugh's schizophrenic literary position is perfectly illustrated by the difference in quality between his dialect poems, which properly belong to the tradition of popular song, and his poems written in 'literary English'. Here is Waugh the songwriter on the merits of porridge:

> Come lads, an' sit down to yo'r porritch;
> I hope it'll help yo' to thrive;
> For nob'dy con live as they should do
> Beawt some'at to keep 'em alive.
>
> . . .
>
> There's mony poor craiters are dainty,
> An' wanten their proven made fine;
> But if it be good, an' there's plenty,
> I'm never so tickle wi' mine.[68]

This sort of thing is untranslatable; there was no place for a porridge song in the gilded world of the Victorian lyric. Waugh derived much of his inspiration from the moorland landscape of his native Lancashire:

> I've worn my bits o' shoon away,
> Wi' rovin' up an' deawn,
> To see yon moorlan' valleys, an'
> Yon little country teawn:

The dule tak' shoon, an' stockin's too!
My heart feels hutchin'-fain;
An', if I trudge it bar-fuut, lads,
I'll see yon teawn again!

. . .

Yon moorlan' hills are bloomin' wild
At th' endin' o' July;
Yon woodlan' cloofs, an' valleys green, –
The sweetest under th' sky;
Yon dainty rindles, dancin' deawn
Fro' th' meawntains into th' plain; –
As soon as th' new moon rises, lads,
I'm off to th' moors again!

Of course there is a danger that any poem in rustic dialect, with a generous scattering of lads and lassies, will bypass critical faculties and appeal directly to sentiment and nostalgia. But Waugh's 'I've worn My Bits O' Shoon Away' has obvious merit, treating a hackneyed subject in an original and lively way (Wordsworth never admitted to wearing out his shoe leather). And we can see the poetry inherent in the dialect in expressions such as 'dainty rindles', which Waugh's editor ponderously glosses as 'pretty rills of singing water'. Waugh's moorland inspirations did not survive translation into 'literary English':

Sing, hey for the moorlands, wild, lonely, and stern,
Where the moss creepeth softly all under the fern;
Where the heather-flower sweetens the lone highland lea,
And the mountain winds whistle so fresh and so free!

He fares no better in less dramatic landscapes:

Now, hamlet urchins roaming,
All the sunny summer day,
From dewy morn till gloaming,
Through the rustling wildwood stray;
There blithely and lithely,
By warbling brook and sylvan grot,
They ramble and gambol,
All the busy world forgot; –
Like birds that wing the sunny air,
And warble in the tangled wild,
Unhaunted by the dreams of care, –
Oh, to be again a child!

This is sub-Blacket. After nearly a century of dogged lyricism and lyric doggerel still the working-class writer strives for a place in *Palgrave's Golden Treasury* and turns his back on the common muse.

163

5

THE FEMALE DRUDGE: WOMEN NOVELISTS AND THEIR PUBLISHERS

THROUGHOUT THE NINETEENTH CENTURY and especially in the Victorian age women writers were distinguished from men not so much by their works as by their sex. Women of such different styles and temperaments as Caroline Norton, Charlotte Yonge and George Eliot were lumped together in the catalogues and literary histories simply because they were women. There were no books or articles on Notable Male Authors of the Day, Silly Male Novelists, the Masculine Lyric, Memoirs of the Literary Gentlemen of England. There is undoubtedly a womanly quality in the best work of women writers which cannot be concealed behind a male pseudonym. Few doubted that Currer Bell, the author of *Jane Eyre*, was a woman, even if only one who, in Lady Eastlake's words, had 'long forfeited the society of her sex'.[1] Conversely, it is often extremely difficult to distinguish the sex of inferior writers: many young men read John Strange Winter's tales of military life, never dreaming that the secrets of the barracks had been penetrated by Mrs Henrietta Stannard.

Discussion of women's literature used to centre around the nature of the feminine imagination; more recently it has moved forward to explore the response of the feminine imagination to the wider social issues of women's rights and rôles. Here male writers begin to play a part, for the 'woman question' grew into a national controversy of such magnitude that men felt obliged to pronounce upon it: Harriet Martineau was succeeded by John Stuart Mill; Meredith, Hardy, Gissing and James were more sympathetic to feminism than a legion of married and unmarried women novelists who insisted that a woman's place was in the home.

Because there was no common ground on the 'woman question' among women writers themselves there was no sisterhood of the pen, no shared commitment to feminist concerns. The point is clearly, if unwittingly, made in a collection of essays on women writers: *Women Novelists of Queen Victoria's Reign* (1897). As far as the literary critic or bibliographer is concerned, Caroline Norton, Charlotte Brontë, Mrs Henry Wood, George Eliot, Lady Georgiana Fullerton, Mrs Ewing, Dinah Mulock, Mrs Gaskell and Hesba Stretton have nothing in common but their sex and the fact of authorship. But if there was no glorious sisterhood of the pen, there was yet a well-established ghetto for women writers; a cramped literary world where women wrote discreetly to each other courtesy of the General Post Office while their male colleagues enjoyed the privileged freedoms of the Garrick Club. The boundaries of this ghetto were well defined, they came into force before the woman writer put pen to paper. Maggie Tulliver's experience in *Mill on the Floss* is typical:

'Mr Stelling,' she said, that same evening when they were in the drawing-room, 'couldn't I do Euclid, and all Tom's lessons, if you were to teach me instead of him?'
 'No; you couldn't,' said Tom, indignantly. 'Girls can't do Euclid: can they, sir?'
 'They can pick up a little of everything, I daresay,' said Mr Stelling. 'They've a great deal of superficial cleverness; but they couldn't go far into anything. They're quick and shallow.'[2]

Middle-class women and the working classes had this in common – an utterly inadequate education. However, it was often harder for a woman with brains to acquire an education than it was for the working man with his evening classes, mechanics institutes and working men's colleges. According to R.D. Altick only twenty per cent of nineteenth-century women writers on whom he was able to collect biographical details had any formal schooling and less than 5 per cent received higher education and then mainly after 1870. In contrast an average of 63 per cent of male writers attended university and only 7 per cent received little or no schooling.[3] A young lady's education fitted her for nothing more than a life of household management inlaid with amateur accomplishments. Women who wanted or were obliged to find work were barred through the lack of appropriate qualifications from all professions save teaching and authorship.

In the middle of the nineteenth century the census returns show that there were 21,373 governesses and 41,888 women schoolteachers. It is hardly surprising, in the face of such competition, that the Brontës failed to establish a school. A step down the shabby, genteel ladder and the desperate young lady could join the half a million women who sewed dresses, made hats, rented out rooms and ran small confectionary businesses. Surprisingly, in the age of Dickens's Mrs Pardiggle, there were almost no paid jobs for women philanthropists. The lists of the 530 London-based charities reveal that apart from matrons nearly all the salaried officers were men, from the secretary of the Royal Society of Female Musicians to the officers of the twenty or so societies established to look after London's thousands of prostitutes. Most women of course were not in paid employment but hoped or expected to be counted among those three million 'persons engaged in the Domestic Offices or Duties of Wives, Mothers, Mistresses of Families, and Widows'. Women had to wait until the late 1880s before career opportunities noticeably improved. The change was recorded by Gissing in his novel *The Odd Woman* (1893), for by 1891 there were 17,859 women engaged in clerical duties.

But throughout the nineteenth century there remained for the bold, the foolish and the talented the open profession of authorship. The foolish were given short shrift by George Eliot: 'The standing apology for women who become writers without any special qualification is, that society shuts them out of other spheres or occupations.'[4] Eliot criticised women of uncultivated minds and no literary abilities who fancied themselves authors, but she could not deny that women of all abilities were very much shut out from making a living. Camilla Toulmin, recalling her literary life between 1820 and 1893, noted that 'if a woman possessed literary ability she might write books and so obtain money, but there was a by-law which made her understand that she did so at the risk of being ridiculed and despised by the other sex'.[5] Their sense of presumption led many women to be self-deprecatory about their work and to claim that they wrote for money, or as a hobby, rather than for laurels. For the majority of women writers money was undoubtedly a powerful incentive. Literary ability could earn a woman, especially a woman with neither private means nor exceptional beauty, a place in the sun. There could hardly have been a single governess or teacher who did not envy Charlotte Brontë her escape from the schoolroom.

Although authorship was more accessible than medicine, the Church or the law, it was not that accessible. The two major obstacles to a successful career in authorship were lack of education and lack of motivation – the latter attributable to the meek acceptance of paternal authority. All the evidence suggests that women formed 20 per cent or less of the literary corps. Walter Houghton states that 14 per cent of contributors to monthly and quarterly magazines have been identified as women, though 'this is undoubtedly too low, since some authors for whom we have only initials and no biographical information . . . are not counted, and some masculine names are surely feminine pseudonyms not yet uncovered'.[6] Women account for 17 per cent of

RLF applicants and 15 per cent of Civil List pensioners. Nearly 20 per cent of writers listed in the *CBEL* (vol. 3) are women. Taking 20 per cent as a probable maximum figure then there were some 4,000 British women writers in the nineteenth century.[7]

With women accounting for 20 per cent of all writers it might be supposed that they account for an equal proportion of major writers – where there is a measure of agreement on what we mean by major. Taking the novel on its own women exceed their allotted proportion. Nearly 30 per cent of the *CBEL*'s 'major' novelists are women and this figure is supported by Edith Batho and Bonamy Dobrée in their thorough trawl of Victorian writers, *The Victorians and After* (1962). However, overall it seems that women have made less of an impact in the top ranks of literature than their numbers would suggest. Of the 423 writers listed by Batho and Dobrée, a figure which includes writers of indeterminate literary status, only 40 (9.5 per cent) are women. In the syllabus-orientated *Pelican Guide to English Literature* (vols. 4 and 5) only 12 out of 111 listed writers are women. This apparent underachievement reflects the almost total exclusion of women from those non-imaginative categories of literature such as history and criticism. Interestingly women writers who do excel in rational, scholarly 'manly' non-fiction such as George Eliot, Mrs Oliphant and Virginia Woolf are invariably listed as novelists – their essays, histories and reviews being considered trivial by comparison. Perhaps this demonstrates the superior nature of feminine genius, for Carlyle and Mill were unable, in their turn, to write decent novels.

It is relatively easy to be precise about the type of authorship women engaged in: their choice of literary activity was governed by their restricted education. Of the women listed in the *CBEL* (counting 'major' and 'minor' writers together) a third are novelists, half are children's writers and 14 per cent are poets. Only 3 per cent of women specialise in other types of literature such as philosophy, history and economics. Men on the other hand appear much more versatile – thanks to their university educations. 25 per cent are poets, 14 per cent are novelists, 14 per cent are 'prose writers' (critics and essayists), 11 per cent write children's stories, 8 per cent are philosophers and the rest are theologians, historians and miscellaneous writers.

Although the Victorian male writer often felt he was being swamped by female competitors, especially in the field of the novel, this was far from the case. Women poets were outnumbered by men by about ten to one. Women only edged ahead in juvenile literature and then they were not often in competition as there were distinct styles of writing for girls and boys. But writing for children has always been considered a minor literary activity (only 6 of Batho and Dobrée's 423 writers are children's writers). The most important area of female authorship from the point of view of the literary critic is the novel. Mackenzie Bell, in his *Half Hours with Representative Novelists of the Nineteenth Century* (1927), lists 370 women out of some 1,100 novelists. Analysis of the *CBEL* shows that 40 per cent of all its listed nineteenth-century novelists were women, though the figures record a decline in numbers from 36 women novelists between 1800 and 1835 to 29 between 1835 and 1870 and 22 between 1870 and 1900. The middle period enjoys the highest percentage of 'major' women novelists. The reasons for such a relatively high proportion of women novelists are not hard to find. According to Camilla Toulmin, herself a contemporary of the great Victorian novelists:

a girl's reading was generally so circumscribed that she had small chance of mental development unless the home library were far more extensive than that which was usually found in a middle-class family. In those days [1820s and 30s] lending libraries seldom supplied anything beyond new novels, and though some of these have survived to become classics, a mental diet composed wholly of fiction, however excellent, is not nourishing.[8]

A diet of novels however, even if only Minerva novels, was the surest way of hatching a novelist.

BY THE END OF THE EIGHTEENTH CENTURY, novel writing was an established commercial activity conducted mainly by women for the entertainment of women – or so it seemed. Much of the credit or blame for this association of women with trashy or light literature must go to William Lane who, in 1770, set up a circulating library which claimed to include among its 10,000 volumes 'every Novel, Romance, Tale, and Adventure in the English Language'.[9] In 1790, to consolidate his reputation as the leading purveyor of Gothic and sentimental fiction, Lane founded the Minerva Press and became the largest employer of hack novelists – particularly women novelists – in the country. In 1798, when Jane Austen was writing her mock Gothic tale *Northanger Abbey*, Lane issued a list of his ten bestselling authors all of whom were women. Jane Austen promptly included two of them, Regina Maria Roche and Eliza Parsons, in Isabella Thorpe's reading list of 'horrid' novels, thus assuring them, in Michael Sadleir's phrase, a 'rueful immortality'. Sadleir shows that Austen's selection of novels for the Thorpe list was 'deliberate rather than random. . . . Chance alone could hardly have achieved so representative a choice.'[10] Fortunately for the literary historian both Mrs Roche and Mrs Parsons (and about 20 other Minerva writers) applied to the Literary Fund – Lane's payments failing to meet their living expenses. The literary career of Mrs Parsons is particularly well documented and she is as good an example as any of a representative woman writer at the turn of the century.

Eliza Phelp was born sometime in the 1740s, the daughter of a prosperous wine merchant. At an early age she married a turpentine manufacturer called Parsons by whom she had a large family. In 1782 a fire broke out in one of Mr Parsons's warehouses and destroyed his entire business. This catastrophe ruined his health and he died shortly afterwards of a 'paralytic affliction'. Mrs Parsons was left, as she was later to write,

under the most deplorable Circumstances with Eight children entirely unprovided for. Born and accustomed to affluence I had no recourse but my Needle and Pen, poor and Insufficient supports for so large a Family. Yet I was compelled to Avail myself of the Fashion of the times and write Novels. . . . Necessity not inclination, nor any Opinion of my Talents induced me to turn Author [17 December 1792].

This is one of the earliest examples of a woman writer disclaiming literary ambition. Certainly there can be little doubt that but for the extreme inflammability of the turpentine trade neither Isabella Thorpe nor Catherine Morland would have had the thrilling pleasure of reading *The Mysterious Warning* and *The Castle of Wolfenbach*.

In both her needlework and her authorship Mrs Parsons was helped along by aristocratic patronage. Just before his death Mr Parsons had obtained a minor appointment in the Lord Chamberlain's department. The Lord Chamberlain's wife, the Marchioness of Salisbury, took it upon herself to make a suitable provision for his widow and children by securing Mrs Parsons the job of Semptress in Ordinary to the Royal Household at £40 a year. To supplement these earnings Mrs Parsons began work on a novel of fashion, *Miss Meredith*, which she dedicated to Lady Salisbury and published by subscription in 1790. Among the subscribers were the Prince of Wales, Mrs Fitzherbert and Horace Walpole.

While Mrs Parsons was stitching the Queen's wardrobe, another more famous novelist 'had the honour of lacing her august mistress's stays, and of putting on the hoop, gown and neckhandkerchief'.[11] Fanny Burney held the office of Second Keeper of the Queen's Robes at £200 a year plus board, a sum that neatly establishes her superior literary as well as social standing to the £40 a year Mrs Parsons. However while

Miss Burney wrote no fiction during her period of slavery at the Palace (and almost died from exhaustion) Mrs Parsons seems to have benefited from being a thimble's length away from royalty – at least to the extent of gaining royal subscribers.

Either her position at court or the intrinsic merits of her novel impressed William Lane who lost no time in signing her up as a Minerva novelist. *Errors in Education* appeared in 1791 and Lane went on to publish ten more of Mrs Parsons's novels including her Gothic tales. He appears to have paid his authors, including Mrs Parsons, slightly above the market rate for such fiction. In 1790 his average payment for copyright was £30; payment varied from £10 for an anonymous story to £40 to his better-known authors. Lane was the Prince of popular fiction and there were plenty of lesser publishers who paid their hacks about £5 or less a novel. Lowndes paid Fanny Burney £20 for the copyright of her first novel *Evelina*, adding a further £10 when the novel became a runaway success. *Camilla* (1796), which she published by subscription, was to earn her the spectacular sum of 3,000 guineas. As one of Lane's top ten authors Mrs Parsons would have received about £40 a novel, which at the rate of one and a half novels a year plus her income from needlework would have given her an annual income of £100 at a time when Coleridge thought he could just manage to live comfortably on as little as £250.

A year after the publication of *Errors in Education* Mrs Parsons broke a leg and was bedridden for six months. In no position to sew or write she was forced to apply to the newly established Literary Fund, naming William Lane as her referee. She was awarded 10 guineas, the largest grant for 1792, and became the second novelist to receive help from the Fund – the first was Charlotte Lennox, the third was another Minerva novelist Maria Hunter. The following year she published two novels for which she must have been relatively well rewarded for she did not apply to the Fund again until July 1796. By then her circumstances were so bad that she was hiding from her creditors in Wandsworth Fields. The main cause of her difficulties was not literature but the failure of the Civil List controllers to pay her for two years work on the Queen's Robes. The fact that she was owed £80 by the King of England did not seem to impress her creditors: 'low minded people cannot be reasoned with and 'tis vain to tell them that I will pay, when I am paid'. She ended her second application to the Fund with a clear statement of the pressures that affected her literary career: 'The public have honoured my Writings with general Approbation Infinitely more than I could hope for, but as Necessity always obliges me to sell the Copyrights, my Advantages are trifling to what the Publisher gains.' (Lane left £17,500 at his death in 1814.) The Literary Fund gave Mrs Parsons a further 10 guineas to enable her to placate her creditors and return to her lodgings in Leicester Square. But she continued to run up debts. In 1798, at the recommendation of Capel Lofft, she was awarded 5 guineas, and in 1799 she had to apply for another 10 guineas. At the same time her rate of composition fell to one novel every two years.

In May 1803 she wrote to the Literary Fund for the last time. Her letter was addressed from the debtors' side of King's Bench prison: 'these two years past I have been a Prisoner, at 62 years of Age I have experienced the loss of liberty and every attendant mortification'. The 10 guineas granted by the Fund was enough to buy her a degree of comfort but the only way she could quit the King's Bench was through authorship. She wrote a four-volume novel under these circumstances and every penny she earned from the sale of the copyright went to her creditors. She did not apply to the Fund again, although she presumably continued to live in uneasy circumstances, perhaps supported by one or other of her children, until her death in 1811.

By the standards of the time Mrs Parsons occupied the middle of the second rank in fiction, perhaps a little below Charlotte Smith and her fellow Minerva novelists Regina Roche and Agnes Maria Bennett. Contemporary reviewers described her as 'a writer of no Inferior talent'[12] and her novels were certainly among the best of those published by William Lane. Michael Sadleir has praised her for possessing 'a sceptical wit and a capacity for trenchant criticism of her age' and 'a gift for downright if astringent character-fiction'.[13] However most estimates of her novels would also agree with him that they are, despite flashes of quality, hastily written, trivial and conceived with that 'cynicism which gives to the public what the public craves'. But she was not only, as Jane Austen could afford to suggest, a popular novelist, she was also a victim to the grind of authorship. The pathetic irony of Mrs Parsons's career as a novelist was that the poverty that released her literary talent was also responsible for her abuse of that talent:

The resources for a well educated [in this context merely a synonym for literate and genteel] female without money are very few, and after several fruitless efforts, I was compelled by dire necessity to become an Author, and in the course of 12 years have written 65 vols of Novels, under every disadvantage of Sickness, Indigence, never ceasing Anxiety and as many repeated misfortunes as human sufference could well support [30 May 1803].

Whereas the possession of money was clearly no guarantee of literary excellence, the lack of it seems to have been an insurmountable obstacle. Of the five women novelists active between 1780 and 1815 whose work is at all well known today – Fanny Burney, Mrs Inchbald, Ann Radcliffe, Maria Edgeworth and Jane Austen – only Mrs Inchbald lacked private means, but she was a beauty, which was nearly as good since it led to a stage career rather than governessing or needlework. Most women simply did not have the leisure to cultivate their talents; they had to dash off fiction at piece rates just to keep a roof over their heads. It is quite clear that during the late Georgian and Regency periods literary women looked upon novel writing as their most likely source of income. It is equally clear that the £2,000 to £3,000 a novel earned by Fanny Burney was exceptional, though the magnificence of such payments was a powerful stimulus to the fortune-seeking writer.

Out of the 100 women authors who applied to the Literary Fund between 1790 and 1830, half were novelists. Over the same period only 25 out of 600 male applicants wrote novels. Between 1790 and 1820 the proportion of women novelists to men was even higher at three to one. By the 1820s men were catching up and by the 1830s they were level-pegging. Of the 50 women novelists 30 described themselves as married, 5 were widows and only 15 were single; 10 admitted to having been schoolteachers or governesses. As well as Charlotte Lennox and Eliza Parsons, their numbers included Elizabeth Helme, Regina Maria Roche, Isabella Kelly, Mary Kentish, Hannah Maria Jones, Louisa Costello and Jane Webb (Mrs Loudon), author of *The Mummy*.

It has been suggested that the novel owed its popularity among women writers to the fact that it 'offered the reward of capital endowment, that lump of money without which middle-class women, whatever their charms, would for long be virtually unmarriagable'.[14] In fact the large numbers of married women who took to novel writing suggests the opposite. The Literary Fund records show that the majority of women began writing to support their families, errant husbands included, or to survive as widows or discarded wives. This was also often true for women who were successful enough not to have to apply to the Fund. Two best-selling novelists of the age were Agnes Maria Bennett and Charlotte Smith. Both of them began writing to support large families, and Charlotte Smith, who had suffered imprisonment with her husband on account of his debts, actually paid him an allowance at their separation.

This glut of minor women novelists during the period 1790 to 1820 coincides with the ascendancy of the Minerva Press. When William Lane retired in 1809 his partner A.K. Newman continued the business until 1820 when he set up as a remainder publisher in his own name. And for every Mrs Bennett, Mrs Parsons and Mrs Roche, who at least enjoyed a certain reputation and some financial reward, there were a host of lesser Minerva novelists hard at work producing light entertainment for Scott and Coleridge, the Austen family and the young Leigh Hunt and Tom Macaulay: Maria Hunter, imprisoned in the Fleet for three years; Eliza Norman, author of *A Child of Woe*, who feigned illness when she could not afford to eat; Emily Clark who in her late teens began writing to support her mother, the granddaughter of the King of Corsica; Anne Burke, widow and governess, forced to sell the clothes off her back to support her child, they had all taken to novel writing in search of the fortune which sadly only their heroes and heroines seemed able to acquire.

If, during the heyday of the Minerva Press, Mrs Parsons found herself a prisoner for debt, the fate of the Minerva novelist who survived into the Victorian age was no less pathetic. One of the last Minerva novelists was Selina Davenport, who has at least scraped into the *CBEL*. And as Mrs Parsons is remembered chiefly for featuring in *Northanger Abbey*, so Selina Davenport has become a footnote in the life of Mrs Gaskell. She was born Selina Wheler, the great-granddaughter of a baronet. In 1800, aged twenty-one, she married an eccentric miscellaneous writer, R.A. Davenport, by whom she had two daughters. The marriage was a disaster and by 1809 the couple were living apart, Mrs Davenport taking charge of the children. In a letter to his friend John Britton written forty years after their separation Davenport fumed against that 'worthless creature whom I have the misfortune to call my wife'. Inspite of his rancour, however, he could not disguise the difficulties his separated wife had faced:

after she opened a school at Greenwich, she continued to run in debt to the tune of £150; she decamped in the night, the moment she had sent my address to all the creditors. Yet this woman and her swindling father I preserved from *absolute starvation*; her father was in jail, and she had not a friend in the world.[15]

It was probably after the failure of her school that she took to novel writing; at first as 'A Lady', but later under her married name. Perhaps through the recommendation of Jane and Anna Maria Porter, with whom she claimed a friendship, her first novel was published by Newman at the Minerva Press in 1813. Over the next twenty years or so she wrote eleven novels in forty-one volumes, many at the rate of £10 each, 'besides smaller publications'.

She seems to have abandoned literature in 1835, or, more likely, no publisher would risk the outlay on her unfashionable work. So she took to selling a little here, sewing a little there, taking in lodgers, writing begging letters to richer relatives. In 1850, when she was living in Knutsford as Mrs Granville, she was 'picked up' by Mrs Gaskell who promptly secured her a £30 grant from the Literary Fund. 'Her sole dependence,' Mrs Gaskell wrote to the secretary on a second occasion in March 1852, 'a very precarious one, is on a small shop . . . and on an annuity of 10£ payable during the pleasure of a relation. Out of her very small earnings she has to support two widowed daughters.' On the subject of Selina Davenport's literary merit Mrs Gaskell was tactful:

about 20 years ago she published a number of novels, which seem to me not without merit, and may in many instances (as I happen to know they have done in some,) have afforded innocent amusement in hours when works of higher pretension, requiring greater exertion of mind, might have failed to do it [3 June 1850].

It was a fair apology for the whole Minerva school. In a letter to another correspondent she was more forthright, 'I saw some of her tales, which were harmless enough, a weak dilution of Miss Porter's in style and plot'.[16]

In 1852 Selina Davenport and her eldest daughter were again 'reduced to very great straits'. Mrs Gaskell wrote, 'these two poor women have tried *many* ways of earning a subsistence; they have had a little shop, taken in plain sewing, kept a temperance coffee-house, opened a dame-school etc'. The Fund awarded her a further £20, and to augment her tiny income of 4s. 6d. a week she accepted dress-making commissions from charitable Knutsford ladies. In November 1852 Mrs Gaskell wrote to her daughter: 'About the night gowns, they are at Knutsford, being made by poor old Mrs Granville, whom it won't do to hurry.'[17] At least Mrs Parsons had stitched for royalty, poor Mrs Davenport was obliged to end her days as Semptress in Ordinary to Mrs Gaskell.

F OR ALL THAT Minerva novels were condemned as trash they were avidly read by middle-class readers and enjoyed a certain affectionate notoriety. By the 1820s and 1830s the homogeneity of the Minerva Press novel was breaking up to be replaced by either sensational penny and sixpenny fiction for the lower classes, or the fashionable novels of the 'silver fork' school which still aimed to bring colour to the cheeks of Bath maidens. Although the new cheap fiction soon acquired the derogatory nickname 'penny-dreadful' much of it was as competent, professional and literate as the ordinary middle-class novel favoured by reviewers. Most of the penny-fiction writers were men: journalists, radicals, out of work actors, gamblers and the occasional young genius like George Borrow at the outset of his literary career. It was a particularly cut-throat world in which women writers, outnumbered by at least twenty to one, had to fight twice as hard as men to avoid being swindled by unscrupulous publishers. Another reason why so few women entered the field of penny fiction was that most of it catered to a male appetite for sex and violence.

The most popular woman writer of penny novels and one of the best writers in the genre of either sex was Hannah Maria Jones, the 'Queen' of cheap fiction.[18] Her most famous novels, *The Gipsey Girl*, *The Gipsey Mother* and *Emily Moreland*, sold 20,000 copies in penny- and sixpenny-issue parts. According to her bibliographer, Montague Summers, her works were enormously popular as attested by 'the plagiarisms, the unauthorized reprints and spurious editions of her work which swarmed even during her lifetime'.[19]

Her background is obscure. She claimed to have begun writing fiction at nineteen years old, and as her first work was published in 1820 she was probably born at the turn of the century. Her literary career began just as changes in the Stamp Act and advances in printing techniques made the publication of cheap fiction a commercial proposition. In her first ten years of authorship she published thirty-three volumes includ-ing three-volume novels published by William Emans and George Virtue and works of non-fiction such as a *Natural History for Youth* published by Thomas Kelly, and a *History of England for Schools* published by Fisher and Co. Her first novel *Gretna Green* (1820) went through several editions, and *Emily Moreland* (1829) sold 20,000 in numbers and was issued in volume form by George Virtue and promptly pirated. The *Athenaeum* described the novel as 'a romance cast after the ancient model, written with a practised pen, and with excellent intentions; and in which, with the exception of the all amiable-hero, the men are libertines and seducers, and the women directly or indirectly the victims of the deceptive arts of the other sex'.[20] It is a better novel than the *Athenaeum* manages to suggest: literate and well paced it foreshadows the more respectable though no less sensational fiction of Wilkie Collins.

Her popularity did not earn Mrs Jones a fortune, nor even a modest living: 'the payment I have received from the publishers into whose hands I unfortunately fell at my outset has been too scanty to enable me to provide for more than the passing day'. The copyright of her works remained the property of her publishers for whom she slaved at the rate of 'fourteen shillings per sheet and that limited to the production of a sheet and a half a week'.[21] As a sheet consisted of sixteen pages Mrs Jones was earning 10½d. a page, considerably less than the penny-a-line usually associated with the meanest literature. In about 1825 George Borrow was earning 1s. a page as the hack compiler of *Celebrated Trials*. In the 1830s E.L.L. Blanchard was paid 5s. a page for his penny-issue life of Jack Sheppard, and Thomas Miller was paid at the same rate, £8 for two sheets monthly, by Henry Colburn. In 1836 Chapman and Hall hired the young Charles Dickens to write *Pickwick Papers* at 9 guineas a sheet or 12s. a page. By the end of her career, in the early 1850s, Mrs Jones was still earning no more than 1s. a page. Her most popular works would have earned her about 30 guineas outright; this may have been more than the payments for a Minerva novel but the average Minerva novel sold 1,000 copies or less where Mrs Jones's novels sold in their tens of thousands. And although the majority of penny-fiction publishers may have been insolvent as often as their authors, Mrs Jones's publishers, Virtue, Kelly, Emans and Lloyd, were the market leaders and died rich men.

When Dickens was writing *Pickwick Papers*, the increasing success of the serial enabled him to demand higher rates. Chapman and Hall paid up, well aware that Dickens was irreplaceable. Mrs Jones was unable to adopt the same tactic because in the world of penny fiction there was no shortage of competent hacks itching to work for a pittance. And although she might have been the best writer available, any of her rivals would have been able to supply an acceptable, if marginally less profitable story. Also, Chapman and Hall had a degree of respect for their authors and a great respect for their own imprint: Emans and Lloyd had little respect for their authors and even less for their imprint – hence their regular excursions into puffing, piracy and plagiarism.

If Mrs Jones put up with appalling rates of pay it was not because she was ignorant of her worth. She was very well aware of her level in the market and was intimately familiar with the parlous state of the bookselling trade as her husband, John Jones, was an out of work compositor. She knew that there was no chance of securing a respectable, moderately generous publisher because, by starting her career with George Virtue and Thomas Kelly, she had branded herself a lower-class writer. The fact that she was one of the most popular lower-class writers of her day brought her no satisfaction; she was as harsh a critic of her own works as a Quarterly Reviewer: 'I disclaim all assumption on the score of their merits. No one can have a lower opinion of them than I have.'[22]

In the 1830s with the publication of her gipsy novels, which set as much as followed a vogue, she was at the height of her fame though still poor enough to qualify for two Literary Fund grants of £10 each, sponsored by Virtue and Edward Bulwer. By the end of the decade her popularity was on the wane. Not that she noticed any material difference for she continued to write for the same rates, living in a single, sparsely furnished room in Rotherhithe for which she paid 1s. 9d. rent a week, and pawning or selling her clothes, books and anything else that could raise a shilling. Her state of mind may be gathered from a poem she wrote in 1844 in imitation of Hood's 'Song of the Shirt':

> With looks bewildered and worn
> And eyelids that weighed like lead
> An authoress sat at her nightly toil
> Spinning her brains for bread
>   Write   write   write
> In poverty, hunger, – and when
> Her trembling fingers failed
> She sang this song of the Pen
>
>   . . .
>
> My head aches as if it were splitting
> I'm worn down to mere skin and bone
> Strange shadows around me are flitting
> Not one is so gaunt as my own
> They are shadows of days long departed
> When bright hopes of fame fill'd my head
> When heedless and young and light hearted
> I dream't not of writing for bread

At about this time she began to live with another Emans' hack, John Lowndes, an ex-dramatic bookseller and author of *Goldsmith's Popular and Modern Geography* and a £20 novel written under the name Amelia Fitzalan. They did not marry, presumably because either Mr Jones or Mrs Lowndes or both were still alive. And so as the disreputable consort of a broken-down old bookseller Mrs Jones became the first woman writer to be discriminated against by the Royal Literary Fund. Applying as Hannah Maria Lowndes in December 1846 she was rejected, not because of insufficient literary merit, but because the secretary,

Octavian Blewitt, through assiduous enquiry, had discovered her guilty secret. As he patiently explained to the poverty-stricken couple:

I need not say that I sympathise with you in the circumstances you mention, but as Mrs Lowndes has already been relieved as Mrs Jones and is known only to the Society under that name, it must be obvious to you that the change of name must be proved in the usual manner [the production of a marriage certificate] before any renewed application can be entertained.

This was pure fantasy on Blewitt's part for although the regulations required that the widow of an author should produce evidence of her marriage there was no similar obligation on a married woman writer. And needless to say no male author was required to show a marriage certificate or prove celibacy before applying to the Fund.

It is clear that Mrs Jones was victimised by Blewitt for being both a woman and a penny novelist. In a note to Lord Stanley advising him not to give Lowndes any private assistance he wrote, 'Mrs Lowndes was never married to him, as she has herself admitted to me. They have been working and writing together for the lowest class of Publishers, and have become well known to the Mendicity Society as Begging Letter writers [1853].' The 'lowest class of publishers' included George Virtue and Alderman Kelly, both stewards and subscribers to the Literary Fund. The only other women writers who had been rejected on moral grounds were Ida St Elme, courtesan and memoirist who wrote as 'La Contemporaine', and Ann Johnston, novelist and, by her own account, 'not the mistress of the Duke of Brunswick'. Mrs Jones, 'my poor creature' as Lowndes called her, was hardly in the same league.

In December 1852 the couple were starving as usual. Their sole income in two years was from an octavo novel by Mrs Jones and Lowndes's completion of a biography of Sir John Franklin by Robert Huish: 'We are now without Bread, without Clothes – the publisher Lloyd having "run us off the Road" his system being to obtain an old work from the Minerva Press rechristen the same and send it forth to the world as a New Work.' At the same time as they made their final unsuccessful appeal to the Fund, Lloyd was advertising the reissue of three 'of the best romances ever written': J.M. Rymer's *Ada the Betrayed*, T.P. Prest's *Ela the Outcast* and H.M. Jones's *The Gipsy Mother* (sic). Rymer was so successful at penny authorship that he was able to take early retirement from Lloyd's list and have £8,000 in hand at his death. Prest died in poverty in 1859 but in his heyday he was the careless star of Lloyd's business, well paid as the anonymous plagiarist of Dickens and in his own right as the 'Prince of Lurid Shockers'. Mrs Jones who was neither a notorious plagiarist nor particularly lurid, but wrote novels of a better quality than either Rymer or Prest at least had her death noticed in *The Times* of 27 January 1854: 'A Sad Fate – Anna Maria Jones, authoress of the *Gipsy* and other popular novels of the day, died on Tuesday at 17, Salisbury-Place, Bermondsey, in the most abject poverty. Her remains await, in all probability, a pauper's funeral.'

HANNAH MARIA JONES was exceptional, the best of only a handful of women who wrote fiction for the lower classes. As a rule, women writers were expected to promote gentility and to remain oblivious of low life. Thackeray noted 'the public likes only the extremes of society and votes mediocrity vulgar. From the Author they will take nothing but Fleet Ditch; from the Authoress, only the finest rose-water.'[23] Rose-water novels, or 'silver-fork' novels as they came to be called, dominated middle-class fiction in the 1830s. They were not the exclusive property of women; Theodore Hook is credited with writing the first silver-fork novel and Bulwer Lytton and Disraeli were the acknowledged masters of the genre. But men were not obliged to write novels of fashion. Lytton, for example, exercised his option to write action-packed histori-cal novels a cut above the Fleet Ditch. The historical novels of the 1830s were nearly all written by men: Lytton, G.P.R. James and Ainsworth were bestsellers. Women were unable to compete; they could not draw on a vast supply of manly knowledge acquired on the playing fields and in the club-rooms and so they found writing about battles and skirmis-hes both difficult and uncongenial. As silver-fork novels and historical romances were the leading publishing commodities, novelists who wished to survive by writing had to produce one or the other. For women there was little choice. An impoverished Mrs Davenport had to hazard her imagination among dukes and duchesses, and a com-paratively impoverished duke's daughter, Lady Charlotte Bury, was forced to trade in royal gossip. That the options for women novelists were so restricted was in part the fault of one man, the publisher Henry Colburn.

Colburn's influence on English fiction was at its height after Con-stable's collapse in 1826. From 1814 to 1826 he laid the foundations for his monopoly of novel publishing which was to last until the mid 1840s. His method of profitable publishing was to create a demand for a wide range of mediocre titles through extensive advertising, which was rumoured to cost him £9,000 a year, and equally extensive news coverage. The latter he achieved through his ownership or part ownership of a number of influential reviews and papers from his *New Monthly Magazine* founded in 1814, through the *Literary Gazette, John Bull,* the *Athenaeum,* the *Court Journal* and the *United Service Magazine,* to his 'considerable interest' in *The Sunday Times.* And when Colburn supplied a paper with regular and lucrative advertising he could usually rely on favourable notices of his books.

For a novel to be newsworthy it had to be brilliant or scandalous or written by a celebrity. In the absence of brilliance Colburn concentrated on creating a list of novels with scandalous or at least gossip-column potential. Theodore Hook, the reprobate editor of the scandal sheet *John Bull* was ideally placed to write such fiction and in 1824 Colburn commissioned him to write *Sayings and Doings,* a barely fictional panorama of London society. The novel was an immediate sensation and together with Robert Plumer Ward's *Tremaine, or the Man of Refinement* (1825) established the fashionable novel as a literary goldmine. M.W. Rosa, the historian of the silver-fork school, observed 'fashionable novels, at least nine-tenths of which bear the imprint of Henry Colburn, are especially susceptible of treatment from the business side, for perhaps more than any other fad in literature, they were the result of a single publisher's enthusiasm'.[24]

In 1825–6, a year of intense financial speculation of all kinds in which no less than seventy-eight banks failed, Colburn was speculating in fashionable fiction with the sureness of Midas. Even as Constable was declared bankrupt and his major author Scott found himself responsible for debts of over £100,000, Colburn was negotiating with the young and unknown Benjamin Disraeli for *Vivian Grey,* inspired by the success of Ward's *Tremaine. Vivian Grey* in turn was the model for Bulwer Lytton's *Pelham* – an even more successful novel published by Colburn in 1828. Between 1826 and 1829 Colburn's income from novel publishing was estimated at £20,000 a year. The respectable publishing houses were not amused. Thomas Cadell wrote to Blackwood in 1827, 'the Trade do not feel disposed to order liberally on account of the very numerous works almost daily emanating from the house of Colburn, which satiate the Public and prevent really good Books experiencing that quick and extensive sale to which they are entitled'.[25] On 17 September 1828 the *Athenaeum* reported that Colburn's seasonal offering consisted of no less than sixty-five new titles including seventy-four volumes of novels and four volumes of poetry.

Colburn's tactic of publishing himself out of the slump largely succeeded, although from 1829 to 1832 he went into partnership with

Richard Bentley to tide him over a rough patch. When the partnership was dissolved authors discovered that Colburn's influence in fiction publishing was stronger than ever for there were now two publishers in the same game, Bentley having adopted many of Colburn's business practices. Colburn was not the kind of publisher to nurture genius. The Colburn–Hook partnership did not have the bracing effect on English Literature of a Constable–Scott or Chapman–Dickens partnership. Colburn was more of a literary pimp casting through the world of letters for writers who could satisfy the public taste, shaped by Colburn himself, in return for relatively generous payments and at least some employment in a period of general depression.

A quintessential Colburn–Bentley authoress was Julia Pardoe (1806–62), who was mocked by Elizabeth Barrett Browning for her relentless attention to the preservation of her youthful charm. Caught in Colburn's net from an early age she was lauded and abused for her intelligent mixture of sugar and spice, sensation and sentiment. Camilla Toulmin's husband attempted a defence:

I am aware that among critics great difference of opinion prevails respecting Miss Pardoe's literary merits. She has been accused of retailing, in her historical works, all the scandalous gossip and tittle-tattle of the age she delineates. . . . She could not make the age better than she found it.[26]

Except that she found it thus at the behest of Richard Bentley who thought a gossipy life of Louis XIV worth £400.

After the publication of some mediocre novels Julia Pardoe achieved something like literary celebrity with the publication in 1837 of *City of the Sultan,* rapidly followed by *Romance of the Harem* and *Beauties of the Bosphorus*. These works of travel were based on a visit to Constantinople with her father. Such accounts by a pure and pretty Englishwoman of her experiences in the territory of a lascivious sultan were the stuff that Colburn's dreams and profits were made of. When her exotic recollections were thoroughly exhausted she 'retired' from authorship for four years until, in her fortieth year, Colburn persuaded her to write a new novel, *Confessions of a Pretty Woman* (1846). It was a stock Colburn title. He paid Pardoe an advance of £150 with the promise of a further £50 when the novel sold 750 copies. According to Pardoe the sales mysteriously stuck at 744 copies and in disgust she went over to Bentley who paid her £200 for a sequel, *The Rival Beauties* (1848). Disillusioned with 'profit-sharing', Pardoe preferred from 1847 onwards to sell her copyrights for a fixed sum. So although Bentley paid her a handsome £400 for *Louis XIV* he made a considerable profit on the second and third editions at a time when she was pressed for money. In 1849 he paid her £300 for the copyright of *Francis I* apologising for the lower payment on the grounds that trade was unusually depressed. By 1850 she was averaging £270 a year from all sources – book writing, compilations and periodical work. At the end of the 1850s, abandoned by Bentley, she was forced to sell her increasingly unfashionable novels to Colburn's successors, Hurst and Blackett, for £50 a time. Lord Palmerston kindly gave her a Civil List pension of £100 'in consideration of 30 years toil in the field of Literature, by which she has contributed both to cultivate the public taste and to support a number of helpless relations'. As late as 1890 the firm of Bentley continued to cultivate the public taste with the reissue of Miss Pardoe's 'tittle-tattle' histories.

In the tradition of William Lane, Colburn's publishing policies directly affected the reputation of women novelists and women writers generally. By 1840 it seemed that the silly lady novelist and the representative woman writer were one and the same. In 1840 Thackeray contributed a satirical sketch of the Fashionable Authoress to Kenny Meadows' anthology, *Heads of the People*, in which he exposed the absurd though insidious literary pretensions of Lady Fanny Flummery:

She has been at this game for fifteen years; during which period she has published forty-five novels, edited twenty-seven new magazines, and I don't know how many annuals, besides publishing poems, plays, desultory thoughts, memoirs, recollections of travel, and pamphlets without number.

Thus Lady Flummery's career neatly fits into the silver-fork era of the house of Colburn – her editor, Gus Timson, is a first draft of Mr Bungay, Thackeray's portrait of Colburn in *Pendennis*. Thackeray is quite clear about the merits of her work, 'her poetry is mere wind; her novels, stark nought; her philosophy, sheer vacancy: how should she do any better than she does? how could she succeed if she *did* do any better? If she did write well, she would not be Lady Flummery.' In elaborating on Lady Flummery's pretensions it becomes clear that Thackeray is most infuriated by her exploitation of her rank and sex to bribe male editors and reviewers to puff her work, a technique not generally available to male authors, with the possible exception of Disraeli. The sketch continues in Thackeray's most heavily sarcastic manner until all women writers stand condemned:

she [Lady F] does not know her own language; but in revenge has a smattering of half-a-dozen others. . . . Are authoresses to be bound by the rules of grammar? The supposition is absurd. We don't expect them to know their own language; we prefer rather the little graceful pranks and liberties they take with it.

M.W. Rosa has identified the principal model for Lady Flummery as Lady Charlotte Bury. Lady Flummery is the author of *Heavenly Chords: A Collection of Sacred Strains*, Lady Bury was the author of *Suspirum Sanctorum: A Collection of Prayers*. The daughter of the Duke of Argyll, she had a bluestocking upbringing in Edinburgh, followed by two marriages and eleven children. On becoming a widow for the second time she was appointed lady-in-waiting to the Princess of Wales, later Queen Caroline. Her recollections of scandal at court were later squeezed out of her by Colburn when she was living in less than ducal circumstances. According to Rosa, 'comparative poverty . . . and frequent childbearing, were the principal elements in turning this charming and witty fine lady into the shallow and rather silly writer of bad novels'. Although Colburn paid her around £200 a novel she never earned enough to retire even in the face of increasingly hostile reviews: 'For a woman of birth and social position there must have been something positively revolting in being forced to write hackwork like *The History of a Flirt* when she was sixty-five, or a cook book at sixty-nine.'[27]

If Lady Flummery owes something to Lady Bury she owes more to Lady Blessington. Thackeray was a regular visitor to Lady Blessington's ménage at Gore House and, despite Lady Flummery, was to become one of her most loyal friends. Lady Blessington was born in the village of Knockbrit, near Cashel in 1789; Lady Flummery was also born in Ireland at Kilbrash Castle in 1789 or 1790. There are other parallels including Lady Flummery's marriage to a simple young aristocrat and inveterate gambler. Like Lady Flummery, and unlike Lady Bury, Lady Blessington edited the principal annual of the day, *The Book of Beauty*, and was a major contributor to other annuals, particularly *Portraits of the Children of the Nobility*, *Flowers of Loveliness* and *Gems of Beauty*. For her part Lady Flummery wrote scores of 'Lyrics of Loveliness', 'Beams of Beauty', 'Pearls of the Peerage' and 'Beauties of the Baronetage'. Lady Flummery was a ubiquitous author, writing 'desultory thoughts, memoirs, recollections of travel' as well as novels and poems. Lady Blessington's *Desultory Thoughts and Reflections* were published by Longman in 1839. And, importantly for Thackeray's argument, Lady Blessington, a noted and notorious beauty, was much more expert in wooing editors than the elderly Lady Bury. Thackeray ends his sketch by looking forward to an age when flunkeyism is dead and 'the Fashionable Authoress is no more! Blessed, blessed thought!'.

Thackeray's attack was on the fashionable authoress rather than the author of fashionable novels. Mrs Gore, for example, achieved

183

uncontroversial literary eminence in the genre and Thackeray himself, with *Vanity Fair*, wrote the pre-eminent fashionable novel. However, Lady Bury and Lady Blessington could hardly be blamed for turning to authorship as a means of earning a living without losing too much caste. Their work was certainly no worse than the work of the majority of their untitled contemporaries. If Lady Blessington was sniped at it was because she was paid in proportion to her rank and notoriety rather than her literary merit – but that was the fault of her publishers. An American admirer of Lady Blessington, Nathaniel Parker Willis, reported in 1835 on her literary earnings:

Her novels sell for a hundred pounds more than any other author's except Bulwer's. Bulwer gets fifteen hundred pounds, Lady B. *four* hundred, Honourable Mrs Norton *two* hundred and fifty, Lady Charlotte Bury *two* hundred, Grattan three hundred, and most others below this.[28]

Camilla Toulmin recalled that on her first meeting with Richard Bentley at Gore House he spoke 'chiefly about Lady Blessington and her books, dilating on the eagerness with which her works were read'.[29]

Charlotte Brontë and her sisters were among those women authors whose confidence was undermined by the ridicule heaped on Lady Flummery. When, in 1845, the Brontës published their poems under the names of Acton, Currer and Ellis Bell they did so because 'we did not like to declare ourselves women . . . we had a vague impression that authoresses are liable to be looked on with prejudice'.[30] George Eliot, as her unambiguously male name suggests, was less vague about the status of women writers. Through her literary eminence she was instrumental in exorcising the spirit of Flummery; consciously, however, she sided with male critics. Her aggressive attack on 'Silly Novels by Lady Novelists' in the *Westminster Review* (October 1856) must have helped to sustain the general prejudice against women writers even though the specific objects of the attack, Lady Bury, Lady Chatterton and Lady Scott, were dead or dying:

We had imagined that destitute women turned novelists, as they turned governesses, because they had no other 'lady-like' means of getting their bread. On this supposition, vacillating syntax and improbable incident had a certain pathos for us. . . . We felt the commodity to be a nuisance, but were glad to think that the money went to relieve the necessitous, and we pictured to ourselves lonely women struggling for a maintenance, or wives and daughters devoting themselves to the production of 'copy' out of pure heroism, – perhaps to pay their husband's debts, or to purchase luxuries for a sick father. Under these circumstances we shrank from criticising a lady's novel. . . . This theory of ours, like many other pretty theories, has had to give way before observation. Women's silly novels, we are now convinced, are written under totally different circumstances. . . . It is clear that they write in elegant boudoirs, with violet-coloured ink and a ruby pen; that they must be entirely indifferent to publishers accounts, and inexperienced in every form of poverty except poverty of brains.

Once again a specific attack on the fashionable authoress (who was far from indifferent to publishers' accounts) has turned into a campaign against a larger group of women writers; for the silly novel encompasses not only the silver-fork school but also the domestic novel, the evangelical novel, the exotic novel and the sensation novel. Eliot must have known that her original supposition concerning the authorship of silly novels was all too accurate. For every Lady Flummery there were a dozen Jane Eyres struggling 'for a maintenance'. That Eliot chose to pummel the shrinking reputations of a handful of titled ladies shows how the work of the fashionable authoress had come to epitomise the general level of women's literary achievement. Indeed as far as male novelists were concerned, it had become almost impossible to represent a woman writer as other than an avatar of Lady Flummery. The temptation to create fictional equivalents of Charlotte Brontë, Mrs Gaskell or George Eliot was resisted. In *The Way We Live Now* (1875) for example, Trollope draws a portrait of Lady Carbury, the author of *Criminal Queens*, who relies upon sex appeal rather than literary brilliance to secure kind reviews from impressionable male editors:

She did work hard at what she wrote, – hard enough at any rate to cover her pages quickly; and was, by nature, a clever woman. She could write after a glib, commonplace, sprightly fashion, and had already acquired the knack of spreading all she knew very thin, so that it might cover a vast surface. She had no ambition to write a good book, but was painfully anxious to write a book that the critics should say was good.[31]

And the critics were painfully anxious to please her. In his collection of stories, *An Editor's Tales* (1870), Trollope gives what we may take as his own experienced view: 'Young women are very nice; pretty young women are especially nice; and of all pretty young women, clever young women who write novels are perhaps as nice as any; – but to an editor they are dangerous.'[32]

It seems that whenever a man wrote about women writers he could not help sounding like Mr Stelling lecturing Maggie Tulliver on the flimsiness of the feminine intellect. Women, particularly women writers and especially pretty women writers, are 'clever' – that is shallow in comparison with the rugged, trundling profundity of men. Even Henry

James, not noted for his insensitive portraits of women, did not escape the Stelling syndrome. The heroine of his story, 'Greville Fane' (1892), is his most detailed portrait of a woman novelist. Mrs Stormer, 'Greville Fane', has no title of her own but has acquired one for her stony-hearted daughter. She is an 'industrious widow' writing fashionable novels to provide, like Lady Carbury, for her dissolute son:

She was not a belated producer of the old fashionable novel, she had a cleverness and a modernness of her own, she had freshened up the fly-blown tinsel. She turned off plots by the hundred and – so far as her flying quill could convey her – was perpetually going abroad. . . . She had a shrewd perception that form, in prose at least, never recommended any one to the public we were condemned to address, and therefore she lost nothing (putting her private humiliation aside) by not having any. . . . With no more prejudices than an old sausage mill, she would give forth again with patient punctuality any poor verbal scrap that had been dropped into her.[33]

In his notebooks, James refers to Greville Fane's 'natural penchant to license à la Ouida'.[34] He obviously felt that his female colleagues were inferior writers. In all his stories concerned with the literary world, his male novelists tend to be distinguished artists while his female writers – 'Guy Walsingham' (based on George Egerton), Mrs Highmore and Minnie Meadows are dismissed as prolific, or precious or merely popular. It seems that because the fashionable authoress was so easy to caricature her image survived the eclipse of the fashionable novel. She was useful ammunition to male novelists intent on discrediting the female opposition inspite of the fact that the opposition declined as the century progressed.

No sooner had fiction writing become the most profitable form of literary activity, in the 1840s, than men began to outnumber women in the fiction publisher's lists. But by public demand, or publishers' edict, the subject matter of fiction seemed to have become more feminine. The new themes were 'anti-romantic, un-aristocratic, home and family centred'.[35] According to the nation's largest purchaser of fiction, C.E. Mudie, a novel should be suitable for reading aloud in a respectable middle-class home. Ironically the vision of the younger daughter blushing at, or worse, imitating the ways of the world seems to have inhibited male writers much more than female writers. Thackeray, in his preface to *Pendennis*, lamented that a man could no longer write with frankness of the escapades of Tom Jones – a view echoed by Dickens, Collins, Reade and Meredith. Charlotte Brontë, Mrs Gaskell and George Eliot, on the other hand, had far less qualms about disturbing the public taste, perhaps because they had fewer illusions about the susceptibilities of seventeen year old girls. And the sensation novels of the 1860s, which derived their enormous popularity from the shocking behaviour of their good-looking heroes and heroines, were nearly all written by women writers. It seems that having been diagnosed as incapable of profound literary endeavour, many women novelists became much more relaxed than their male colleagues; less pompous and prudish and less concerned with the dignity of their profession. The contrast between the two sexes is well illustrated by the gulf between Greville Fane and the solemn narrator of her story: 'she scorned me when I spoke of difficulty – it was the only thing that made her angry. If I hinted that a work of art required a tremendous licking into shape she thought it a pretension and a *pose*'.[36]

Even aristocratic families have domestic concerns. The home of a gambling duke may be as anxious a place as the home of an out-of-work clerk, and the fashionable novels of the 1830s were not without affairs of the hearth as well as the heart. But the bourgeois domestic novel dates from the 1840s and its most flourishing period lies somewhere between Dickens's *Nicholas Nickleby* (1839) and Trollope's *Autobiography* (1883) which, while not a work of fiction, is a glorification not only of the art of the bourgeois novel, but the life of the bourgeois novelist. Trollope, unlike Thackeray, was untroubled by the thought of tailoring his fiction 'for the amusement of the young of both sexes'. Even when writing about the life of a prostitute in *Vicar of Bullhampton* (1870) he was careful not to endanger 'the sweet young hearts of those whose delicacy and cleanliness of thought is a matter of pride to so many of us'.[37]

In so far as it was a publisher's commodity, the golden age of the domestic novel began in 1846 when an enterprising Belfast publishing house, Simms and McIntyre, published fourteen popular novels at 2s. each. Until that date, although there had been many schemes to publish cheap middle-class fiction, the only series of any note was Bentley's Standard Novels which were priced at 6s. a novel. In 1847, following the success of the Parlour Novelist, Simms and McIntyre dropped the price to 1s. for a one-volume reprint in boards and 1s. 6d. in cloth, and changed the name of the series to the Parlour Library. Between 1847 and 1863 the Parlour Library grew to 279 volumes of new and reprinted fiction. According to Sadleir, 'its immediate and overwhelming popularity transformed it in a few weeks from a local Irish speculation into an international property of great value'.[38] Other publishers were keen to share in the profits. Bentley reduced the price of a Standard

Novel to 3s. 6d. Routledge began his famous 1s. Railway Library and Blackwood started a London Library. However even at the low price of 1s. such novels remained luxuries to the working class and were aimed at a middle- and lower middle-class readership.

The two major series were the Parlour Library and Routledge's Railway Library. Between 1847 and 1860 they accounted for some 340 novels by over 100 British authors.[39] All the main categories of fiction were represented: the nautical novels of Marryat and Howard; the fashionable novels of Mrs Gore and T.C. Grattan; the historical novels of Ainsworth and G.P.R. James; and the Irish novels of William Carleton and Charles Lever. By far the largest category, appropriately enough for the aptly named Parlour Library, was domestic fiction whose leading author was Mrs Anne Marsh. Sixteen of Mrs Marsh's eighteen novels were published in the Parlour and Railway Libraries. As far as the publishers were concerned she was the most popular female novelist of her day. Of the top fifteen novelists in the two series she ranked third; Lytton had nineteen titles in print and G.P.R. James a staggering forty-seven titles (because Simms and McIntyre had bought his entire copyright in a job lot). Mrs Gore was represented by ten novels, Mrs Trollope by seven and Jane Austen and Emma Robinson by six each. The majority of the ninety or so other authors had only one or two novels published in either series.

Mrs Marsh, hugely successful and an heiress in middle-life, is hardly a representative domestic novelist, nor even a representative woman writer. Her novels were intended entirely for the edification of Mudie's innocent daughters. Harriette Maria Smythies, née Gordon, variously known as Mrs Gordon Smythies and Mrs Yorick Smythies, is an utterly representative domestic novelist of the mid-Victorian period. Between 1840 and 1865 she wrote twenty-two novels and two books of verse. Her publishers included Colburn, Bentley, Newby, Saunders and Otley, Hurst and Blackett, and William Tinsley. Six of her novels were reprinted in the Parlour Library and she was also published by Blackwood's London Library and in the Library of Popular Authors.

She was born in Margate in 1813, of, as Bulwer Lytton phrased it, 'an antient family'.[40] Both she and her brother had literary ambitions and in 1835 she published a long poem, the *Bride of Siena*, a romance based on the story of La Pia in Dante's *Divine Comedy*. To aspire to take up where Dante left off was perhaps a little rash. In the publishing double talk of the day the poem 'did not answer', nor presumably did her first novel, *Fitzherbert* (1838), for her publishers, Saunders and Otley, did not do well enough by either book to take any further risks on her work. Her mood at this time may have been similar to that of Geraldine Brown, the poor but literary heroine of her subsequent novel *The Jilt* (1844): 'There are no publishers now-a-days, enterprising enough to purchase a poem: a poem by a young lady too, unknown, unrecommended! But Geraldine had all this to learn; she thought of Byron's profits, and her heart beat high.'[41] Bentley, however, thought well enough of Miss Gordon to publish her second novel, *Cousin Geoffrey*, in 1840. And Theodore Hook was prevailed upon to attach a story of his own to make up for a shortfall in the third volume. It was moderately successful for several of her subsequent works were attributed to 'the author of *Cousin Geoffrey*' and it was reprinted nineteen years later in the Parlour Library. Her career as a reliable domestic novelist seemed assured.

In 1842 she married the Rev. William Yorick Smythies and in the next eight years bore five children, four of whom survived infancy, and wrote six three-volume novels for which she would have received between £100 and £150 each. In 1844, probably as a result of Bentley's financial difficulties, Mrs Smythies changed publishers. Between 1844 and 1851 her novels were published by T.C. Newby, who both socially and economically was sub-Colburn. It is extraordinary that at the same time as Newby was publishing Mrs Smythies's *Warning to Wives* (1848) he should have brought out *Wuthering Heights*, though rather less extraordinary that posterity should revile him for rewarding Emily Brontë with a niggardly £50. The author of *Warning to Wives* however was both more experienced and better known than Emily Brontë or the young Anthony Trollope (also published by Newby), and would have received more generous terms, though probably never much more, under the half-profits system, than £100. Still, it was a useful addition to a slender clerical income.

As early as 1842 on the publication of her fourth novel, Thomas Campbell was supposed to have dubbed Mrs Smythies 'The Queen of the Domestic Novel',[42] but it was not until the 1850s that she profited much from her reputation. In 1857 she began to write serial fiction for *Cassell's Family Magazine*, the *London Journal* and the *Ladies Treasury*. These stories were subsequently published by Hurst and Blackett who, as the middle of the road, unadventurous successors to Colburn, were well established as the first resort of second-division authors. The combination of a popular serial story followed by volume publication was lucrative: 'I had the privilege of selling the copyrights of the novels which I wrote for the London Journal as three-volume novels, and ultimately as Railway reprints.'[43] At the rate of one and a half novels a year Mrs Smythies might have been earning an annual income of £500. There were snags, however, of the kind that gave authors nightmares. During 1860 and 1861 the *London Journal*, with a circulation of around 350,000, published Mrs Smythies's serial story *Our Mary*. In 1862 she began another serial story for which she was paid at the rate of 8 guineas a week. But

the bankruptcy of Mr Stiff (proprietor of that paper) . . . has suddenly deprived me of my weekly income (on which so many depend) and of the sums I had relied on for the Copyright. The present proprietors of the London Journal would gladly engage me to finish the novel in question but that Mr Stiff (who valued it highly and who did not like his successors to start (under the new management) with it, has distributed the types, destroyed the blocks and secreted the M.S! The present proprietor cannot engage me to finish a tale of which two thirds are missing . . . and so I lose my income and my copyright [5 May 1862].

The extent of Mrs Smythies's talents can be judged by the narrow range of her novel titles which were nicely calculated to assure her readers that they were getting more of the same. All her plots revolved around the perils and little victories of courtship, marriage and family life: *Matchmaker* (1842), *Breach of Promise* (1845), *A Warning to Wives* (1848), *Bride Elect* (1852), *Courtship and Wedlock* (1853), *Married for Love* (1857), *A Lover's Quarrel* (1858), *True to the Last* (1862), *Guilty or Not Guilty* (1864), *Faithful Woman* (1865), and so on through twenty-two novels. Such novels, with their constant attention to the complications of marital and pre-marital relationships, usually from the woman's point of view, did not endear themselves to reviewers. The *Athenaeum* dismissed them as 'Minerva-press progeny', the *Spectator* took a sterner line and criticised their 'disagreeable worldliness' and 'inflated sentimentalism'. Mrs Smythies's *The Daily Governess* (1858) was even honoured by an attack in the *Quarterly Review* along with twenty-three other sensation novels including works by M.E. Braddon, Mrs Henry Wood and Wilkie Collins – it was one of eight bigamy stories.[44]

For all her crude melodrama, absurdity of plot and sentimentality, vices common to most Victorian novels, Mrs Smythies had a keen eye for the motives and manners of her characters and the often pathetic details of their struggles to keep up appearances. The Victorian family in their parlour clearly appreciated her skill and no doubt enjoyed the illicit activities of characters who might be their neighbours. Righteous parents could always justify their addiction to such fiction on the grounds that it offered an object lesson to their sons and daughters.

Lytton, one of Mrs Smythies's most stalwart admirers, wrote in 1864 'her works are generally published in popular journals, and are always characterised by the moral and religious tone which may be expected from the wife of a clergyman', and on another occasion he praised her novels for 'their *considerable* merit in the department of letters she has chosen and with *much wit* and knowledge of life have combined excellent tendency and object'.[45] Among her other upper-class admirers were Lord Brougham and the society hostess Mrs Milner Gibson: 'her writing bears the stamp of the woman of intellect who tries by her pen to advance the cause of justice and right in all classes'.[46] All of which amounts to a fairly thorough defence of the bigamy novel.

Most of Mrs Smythies's readers however were the young ladies hooked on 'the popular journals'. 'Who are the young ladies who read stories of this character?', Thomas Frost asks in his *Reminiscences*:

Apparently, not work-girls and domestic servants, as some persons seem to suppose; for a very large proportion of the answers given in the correspondence columns relate to questions of etiquette and precedence, presentations at Court, wedding breakfasts, and like matters of interest for young women in the higher grades of the middle class.[47]

As evidence of Mrs Smythies's authority in this field the *Ladies Treasury* entrusted her with a series of papers entitled 'Conduct and Carriage; or Rules to Guide a Young Lady on Her Entrance into Society' (1857–8). For those who profited from a study of her rules she wrote a sequel, 'Advice to Young Wives' (1859–60).

Behind such authorship lurked the inevitable ironies. Her own domestic circumstances were far from comfortable. Her husband proved to be a complete failure: he was an invalid; he had no Church preferment; he took over the management of his church farms and promptly lost their income; he ruined himself in litigation. At about the time Mrs Smythies completed her advice to young wives she left her husband and moved to lodgings in London with her children and mother. Their support cost her more than she could earn by writing novels. After the failure of her serial in the *London Journal* she struggled on at the rate of a novel a year, with some intermittent help from the Royal Literary Fund. Her principal expenses were medical fees for her consumptive daughter. It was probably her daughter's painful illness that inspired her to publish a poem, *Incurable* (1863), in aid of the Royal Hospital for Incurables. In the decade after her daughter's death in 1866 she lost 'every brother and sister and all my children save one son'. Her own death in 1883 went unnoticed.

Mrs Smythies's novel-writing career spanned forty years of Victorian fiction. She began to write when the fashionable novel was still marketable and her last novel was published in 1880, the same year as Gissing's first novel, *Workers in the Dawn*. Patricia Thomson has referred to Mrs Smythies's 'very subaltern position in the monstrous regiment of minor fiction'.[48] However, at least by the standards of the editors of the Parlour Library she was one of the regimental commanders, and her novels were an important part of the reading of Victorian families – a yardstick by which they could measure the achievement of great contemporaries such as George Eliot. Her work, viewed as a whole, can be seen as mainstream domestic fiction, and it accurately reflects mid-Victorian preoccupations. In 1858, for example, she wrote a serial story *Hope Evermore* 'to promote the interests of the temperance movement and the ragged schools'; predictably it was much admired by Lord Brougham. In the early 1860s she tried her hand at sensation fiction. In 1870 William Tinsley published her novel *Acquitted*, at the same time he was negotiating with Thomas Hardy for *Desperate Remedies* – at least the titles were well matched. Her complete immersion in the vital concerns of her age is best demonstrated by the publication of two volumes of verse in one auspicious year – 1854: *Sebastopol* and *Prince and People*, a spirited defence of the conduct of Prince Albert.

At first Mrs Smythies wrote out of a burning desire to achieve literary fame; later she wrote to supplement the family income. In the end her writing was quite simply a matter of life and death as she spent her energies and her income in a vain attempt to prolong the lives of her children. In this, as in much else, she was not untypical. She was neither strikingly talented like George Eliot, nor fortunately married like Mrs Gaskell. Both George Eliot and Mrs Gaskell, though they eventually earned large literary incomes, did not have to do so in order to survive. They were able to write against or ahead of the public taste when aesthetic or moral considerations demanded, and this in turn strengthened their work and contributed to its survival. The quality of Mrs Smythies's best fiction suggests that she could have written works of more than ephemeral interest if her career had not, out of necessity, slotted so firmly into a commercial rut.

One of the more striking examples of original female talent falling victim to commercial and family pressures is the literary career of Mrs Isabella Banks. Isabella Varley was a Manchester bluestocking, poetess and youthful schoolmistress. The daughter of a well-to-do small-ware manufacturer and amateur artist, she was a full participant in the unique cultural and political life of Manchester in the 1830s and 40s. She joined the Mechanics Institute in the late 1830s and served on the Ladies Committee of the Anti-Corn Law League. Her neighbours, luckily for her, included the publishers John Cassell and Abel Heywood. As well as writing a volume of well-received poems *Ivy Leaves* (1844) she was the author of the *Lace-Knitters Intelligible Guide*, a self-help manual published in 1847, the year of Mrs Gaskell's first Manchester novel *Mary Barton*. In 1846 Isabella married George Linnaeus Banks, a provincial journalist and miscellaneous writer. For the next twenty years, out of deference to her husband's inferior literary abilities, she abandoned her own literary aspirations. Her friend Mrs Fenwick Miller was later to write:

not till she was forty-three did Mrs Banks resume her pen and then it was rather because her circumstances compelled her to try to help find food and education for her brood than because she desired a literary position. Her life had many troubles: ill-health of an almost incessant character and sorrows and trials of no slight severity – including the deaths, at different periods, of five of her children – had worn on her spirits, but left a deep residuum of feeling and thought on which to draw for her writings.[49]

Mrs Miller tactfully made no reference to Mr Banks's mental illness. By 1865 he was incapable of earning a living; his most frequent delusion was that he was the second Christ. Mrs Banks became the sole support of her family and responded to the challenge in the only way open to her – by writing books. Her husband survived under her care for another fifteen years, 'fatally addicted to drink and in fact a madman, whose chief pleasure is to threaten and persecute his unhappy wife'.[50]

Her domestic worries inevitably left their mark on her fiction. In the words of her biographer, 'Mrs Banks was rather humourless and it is difficult to find much evidence of any joyful – as distinct from cynical and bitter humour in her works. This was perhaps part of her character but was also due, no doubt, to the sadness of her life in general.'[51] Nevertheless her works attracted decent reviews and a fair readership. Her first novel, *God's Providence House* (1865), published by Richard Bentley, went into three editions and her most famous novel, *The Manchester Man* (1879), was reissued at least five times and has been published as a twentieth-century reprint edited by Q.D. Leavis. In 1881, as a tribute to her reputation as a Manchester novelist, Abel Heywood launched a uniform edition of her works on a royalty basis.

Inspite of this modest popularity she never earned a great deal from her novels. In her best year she earned £300, more often she earned about £150. And with what labour:

I have been gradually freeing myself and family from the incubus of debt, incurred in bygone efforts to keep home together. *But* – to accomplish this, and maintain ourselves respectably I accepted literary engagements beyond my physical strength. A strong man could scarcely have achieved more than I have done; viz, kept a weekly journal and a monthly magazine supplied with a separate serial story at one and the same time not a chapter being ready in advance. – How I have done it is proved by the success of my 'Manchester Man' in *Cassell's Family Magazine*. . . . Since last October I have been working unremittingly until 3.4.5.6 in a morning. Have had my household cares in the day and a fearful load of domestic anxieties. – Have lost my aged mother by sudden death, have seen my eldest daughter fading day by day, and to crown all have had my husband come home half-killed, to need constant tendance for six weeks, and during that time was myself suffering from a painful disease joined to the consciousness that I was '*breaking down*'. – I wrote my last monthly installment for Cassell's with vinegar to my head and ice to my throat; with the close railway trains whizzing and shrieking past the study window every 5 minutes [1 July 1875].

This must be one of the most graphic accounts of the terrible pressures of literary composition that exists outside fiction.

THERE WERE no novels about literary life by women to compare with *Pendennis* and *New Grub Street*. And although many male novelists wrote at least one novel about the business of literature the major work on the subject by a woman is non-fiction – Mrs Gaskell's *Life of Charlotte Brontë*. *Jane Eyre* comes quite close to describing the making of a novelist though in the end Charlotte Brontë makes her governess heroine an artist rather than a writer. By the late Victorian period, however, women writers seem to have overcome their reluctance to write about their literary experience and there are good novels on the subject by Mrs Oliphant, Mrs Riddell, Rhoda Broughton and Mary Cholmondeley.

Charlotte Riddell's autobiographical *A Struggle for Fame* (1883), a title which says it all, is quite the most detailed novel by a woman on the theme of authorship. Mrs Riddell's career began in 1855 when she came to London a dispossessed Irish girl with a sick mother and an unpublished Irish novel. Her second novel, *Zuriel's Grandchild*, was set in Lancashire and eventually found a publisher in the ever ready Newby. There were no profits. Her second published novel, *The Moors and the Fens* by 'F.G. Trafford', met with more success. Smith, Elder and Co. paid her £20 for it. The following year she married J.H. Riddell, a civil engineer and City businessman; after her marriage many of her novels dealt with the very unfeminine world of business and commerce. Her most successful work, *George Geith* (1864), was a sensation novel with a City background and earned her £800 from William Tinsley, the principal purveyor of sensation fiction. It was later adapted for the stage.

Following the publication of *George Geith*, Mrs Riddell enjoyed several years of literary celebrity and in 1867 became part proprietor and editor of the *St James' Magazine* in succession to Mrs S.C. Hall. For much of the 1860s and 1870s she was one of the dozen most popular women novelists, and if she never earned as much as Mrs Oliphant, Mrs Ward and Mary Braddon she was, for a time, regarded as their equal. But Mrs Riddell, in common with so many of her colleagues, had her share of family problems. Her husband proved an inept businessman and shortly after her marriage she became the principal wage earner. And although she was under no legal obligation to do so, she struggled to pay off her husband's debts to his family after his death in 1880. In all she wrote fifty-six works of fiction between 1855 and 1902. However, by the time she wrote *A Struggle for Fame* in 1883 her day was already over.

Because the plot of *A Struggle for Fame* is based on Mrs Riddell's light and dark moments of authorship it is less woeful than *New Grub Street* and a great deal more realistic than most other novels in the genre, where, as in novels by Walter Besant and James Payn for example, the heroes and heroines ascend to fame rather than struggle for it. Glen Westley is a dreamy Irish girl who comes to London in 1854 with her bankrupt father. Like many other young ladies 'she was fairly educated, but she did not know enough to teach',[52] so she hawks a manuscript tale around the publishers but is told, quite truthfully, that 'Irish stories are quite gone out'.[53] She makes friends with a kindly publisher, Mr Vassett (Charles J. Skeet), who becomes her literary adviser and introduces her to some of his authors: Lady Hilda Hicks, the ubiquitous fashionable authoress, whose several novels about the transgressions of her ex-husband (à la Caroline Lamb, Caroline Norton and Rosina Lytton) are beginning to bore the public; Miss Yarlow, the author of *Six French Actresses* and *Nine Poems by V*; and Will Dawson, an actor–journalist of the Bohemian school. In a sub-plot Dawson befriends a young Irishman, Bernard Kelly, whose calculated infiltration into the world of literary journalism in search of a snug little editorship at £300 a year anticipates the self-seeking philosophy of Gissing's Jasper Milvain.

While nursing her father and her own literary ambitions, Glen meets and is courted by Mr Lacere, a City accountant. His attitude to her authorship is indulgent but dismissive:

There never yet lived a wise man who wished women to turn artists, or actresses, or authors; and Mr Lacere, theoretically at least, was a wise man. By some subtle intuition he knew Glen would be far happier if she never gained a hearing – if she laid aside her manuscripts as a child lays aside its toys which have pleased it a while, and betook herself to the business of life, as such business usually presents itself to her sex, taking her pleasure while she could, mixing with other young people, going to places of amusement; then being loved and loving; then marrying and ruling her husband's household.[54]

Such sentiments, though attributed to a pompous young accountant, nevertheless probably reflected Mrs Riddell's ambivalent feelings towards her position as a working woman. There must have been occasions when she longed for a prosperous husband whose liquidity would have enabled her to take a rest from authorship, or to write better books. Like her heroine she began to write to give vent to her romantic imagination. She then became an apprentice author in the hope of providing for her dying mother. Finally she became a professional author, shackled to her desk, writing a stream of three-volume novels to support her husband and pay his debts. Of course, like Mrs Oliphant, she wrote because writing gave her pleasure, 'because it was like talking or breathing'.[55] But both women's first thoughts were to earn a good living for their families in the absence of male breadwinners, rather than to write a masterpiece. When Glen marries Lacere he tells her, 'Remember, dear, that I never wished you to think of publishing except for your own pleasure. Do not trouble yourself now about money or money-making; leave all that to me.'[56] But Lacere fails to become that dream of the Victorian woman novelist, the husband patron. Instead he loses all his money through the speculations of a partner and Glen becomes the provider.

Glen's first novel, *Tyrrel's Son (Zuriel's Granddaughter)*, is published by Pedland (Newby), whose firm is compared to the Minerva Press. The novel is slaughtered by the reviews and earns her £20. Her second novel is a philosophical treatise on the creative impulse, as manifested by a broody stained-glass maker. She finds intellectual subjects are unpopular with readers: 'It is a morbid, unhealthy book . . . why did you not give us a story calculated to make us all happier and brighter and better – a womanly sort of tale about flowers and children and happy lovers?'[57] She takes this advice and begins to write novels about 'lovely women'. She soon realises that 'ladies and boys were then the audience to whom all authors, who wished either for "praise or pudding" or both, felt it wise to appeal. . . . Where, for example, George Eliot counted her thousands, the *Family Herald* counts its tens of thousands.'[58] Her literary earnings begin to rise from £150 to £250 a novel. Her increasing success attracts the attention of the speculative publishers Felton and Laplash who offer her £800 for her next novel. She reaches her top price, presumably in the mid-1860s, with *Heron's Nest*, for which Felton and Laplash pay £1,000. It is the sensation of the season and its author becomes the toast of literary London, 'Even in dreams was no warning vouchsafed of the hour . . . when she should know in all its bitterness what it is to be forgotten.'[59]

Glen's puffed reputation steadily deflates. Felton and Laplash have no capital invested in their business but run it in advance of their author's assumed earnings. Glen's receipts from her novels begin to decline from £800 after *Heron's Nest* to £500 and less. Laplash tells her:

Novel-writing's not a gold mine, and, if it were, you're not the woman to dig out the gold. I can see very plainly what the result of your career will be. You'll have to apply to the Royal Literary Fund, and then you'll see whether you like their terms better than mine.[60]

A threat indeed. Just seven years after the success of *Heron's Nest*, she is completely unknown. '"I don't remember your name," said one editor to her. "What have you done?".'[61]

In April 1900 when J.M. Barrie secured a Royal Literary Fund grant for Mrs Riddell, 'a novelist of considerable distinction', he wrote to the secretary; 'Tho' once a popular writer there is now little demand for her work'. As if to demonstrate the haziness of her reputation he reminds the Fund of her two most famous works, *George Geith* and *The Junior Partner*. His memory was at fault – she was the author of *The Senior Partner*. Mrs Riddell, like her heroine, lived long enough to witness her complete eclipse. 'The lady's story is not cheerful;' the *Athenaeum* commented in a review of *A Struggle for Fame*, 'but if it serves to deter persons of no aptitude from writing novels it will have done good.'[62] But Mrs Riddell, and presumably Mrs Lacere, had a considerable aptitude. They shared an unfulfilled desire to write a first-rate novel of ideas. Unfortunately their families demanded a steady flow of dependable pot-boilers. As Mrs Oliphant writes, somewhat desperately, in her posthumously published *Autobiography*:

I pay the penalty in that I shall not leave anything behind me that will live. What does it matter? Nothing at all now – never anything to speak of. At my most ambitious of times I would rather my children remembered me as their mother than in any other way, and my friends as their friend. I never cared for anything else. And now that there are no children to whom to leave any memory, and the friends drop day by day, what is the reputation of a circulating library to me? Nothing, and less than nothing. . . . An infinitude of pains and labour, and all to disappear like the stubble and the hay.[63]

No doubt one reason Mrs Riddell wrote *A Struggle for Fame* was to inform her loyal readers of the enormous effort it cost her to keep them entertained. The popular image of the popular author bordered on envy, such as Henry James's narrator feels for Greville Fane, or Gissing felt when he heard that Mrs Humphry Ward's *David Grieve* had earned her £20,000. Perhaps the fictional Laplash turns out to be the shrewdest judge of literary fame. Of Mrs Oliphant's and Mrs Riddell's well-known contemporaries a large number ended up with Civil List pensions or Royal Literary Fund grants, including Katherine Macquoid, Mrs Alexander, 'Holme Lee', Emma Marshall, Amelia Edwards, Agnes Strickland, Rhoda Broughton, Matilda Betham Edwards, Elizabeth Missing Sewell, Mrs Cashel Hoey, 'John Strange Winter', 'Ouida', Helen Mathers, 'Maxwell Gray', 'Lucas Malet' and 'Rita'. 'Rita', or Mrs Desmond Humphreys, the founder of the Writers Club for Women, succinctly stated the nature of her predicament: 'My husband is alive – but has no profession or income (He is Irish).'[64]

Perhaps the most striking example of the identity crisis that faced the late Victorian woman novelist can be seen in the work of Henrietta Stannard (1856–1911). As John Strange Winter she wrote militaristic novels which, according to her eminent fan John Ruskin, gave 'the most finished and faithful rendering . . . of the character of the British Soldier'.[65] Her stories of gallantry no doubt helped to propel the boys of the 1890s into the trenches of 1914. Her novel *Bootle's Baby: a Story of the Scarlet Lancers* (1885) sold over two million copies in ten years. But John Strange Winter was more than a recruiting sergeant, she was also 'an excellent wife and mother, a kind friend, and a philanthropic member of society'.[66] Among her causes were dumb animals and women journalists, of whose society she became president. Nothing better illustrates the perfect confusion of her literary career and its abiding concern with the profit motive, than her exploitation of her fame as a soldierly novelist to serve the interests of the cosmetics business:

her publishers went bankrupt, and she found herself heavily in debt and an unsecured creditor for a very large amount. From a merely business point of view she should then have sought the relief of bankruptcy. Instead, she faced the heavy task of endeavouring to work off her losses and to her eternal honour did so to a great extent through her toilet preparations.[67]

ALTHOUGH IT IS TEMPTING to pass over the overwhelming contribution of women writers to juvenile literature, it would result in a very partial account of women's authorship. Half the women writers listed in the *CBEL* wrote children's books. Only 10 per cent of male authors were similarly engaged. Unlike most other literary genres the market for children's books steadily increased during the nineteenth century in response to both the developing school system and the Victorian concern for a moral education. It was inevitable that middle-class women, who had so little experience of the work-a-day world outside their homes, should provide the bulk of this well-intentioned literature. It is also inevitable that those women who had the least literary talent should choose the least demanding literary form (at that time) as a way of earning money. Men who wrote for children were exercising a choice. For the averagely educated but uninspired and inexperienced literary woman there was no choice. To write even second-rate fashionable novels required a degree of familiarity with the beau monde, to write a sensation novel required at least knowledge of, and probably imaginative sympathy with, sexual and social deviance. But to write a children's book required only a modest literacy and experience of childhood. Percy Muir, in his *English Children's Books 1600–1900*, observes with some justice: 'The long line of women writers for girls, from Agnes Strickland to Mrs Molesworth and from Mary Elliot to Juliana Horatia Ewing and Mrs Marshall, are all inferior . . . to their male counterparts'.[68]

The greatest patron of inferior children's writers was the Church, and the influence of religious publishing houses rubbed off on secular firms such as Blackie, Dean and Munday, and J.M. Darton. The one talent in a children's author prized above all else was religious conformity – a 'sound moral tendency'. For example, Eliza Meteyard's first book for children, the autobiographical *Doctor's Little Daughter* (1850), was denounced by an irate reader, in a letter to her publishers Hall and Virtue, as 'papistical'. As the whole of Anglican Britain was up in arms against the Pope's appointment of Nicholas Wiseman to be the first Archbishop of Westminster and an English cardinal, Hall and Virtue took fright and advised their young author to find 'a more suitable publisher . . . than themselves' for her future work.[69]

The pressures on children's writers to display their orthodoxy were immense. By the 1870s and 80s little religious tales swamped the juvenile market. Gissing's Jasper Milvain, no slouch at identifying commercial opportunities, advised his sisters to write religious stories because they would be sure of a 'tremendous sale':

'In your place, I'd make a speciality of Sunday-school prize-books; you know the kind of thing I mean. They sell like hot cakes. And there's so deuced little enterprise in the business. If you'd give your mind to it, you might make hundreds a year.'

'Better say "abandon your mind to it."'

'Why, there you are! You're a sharp enough girl. You can quote as well as anyone I know.'

'And please, why am I to take up an inferior kind of work?'

'Inferior? Oh, if you can be a George Eliot, begin at the earliest opportunity. I merely suggested what seemed practicable.'[70]

Milvain's assumption that such books earned their authors 'hundreds a year' was rather less accurate than his observation that hundreds of people were writing such books. The religious publishing houses were notoriously mean. The most sophisticated and indeed the sharpest of these firms was the Church of England's Society for the Propagation of Christian Knowledge, whose annual profits exceeded £7,000 in the 1890s. Walter Besant delivered a scathing attack on the SPCK, the 'literary handmaid of the church', for paying its authors as little as £10 for the copyright of their stories, and he dubbed it a 'Society of sweaters for the greater glory of Christ'.[71] These sweaters were mostly women and many of them applied to the Royal Literary Fund only to discover that to publish moral tales with the SPCK was insufficient proof of literary merit. Commenting on the application of Annie Armstrong, whose sister Jessie also applied to the Fund, Besant wrote in October 1892:

Miss Armstrong is one of those women who, I fear, besiege your doors in daily increasing numbers. They have considerable merit – but there are too many of them . . . For my part I do everything that I possibly can to dissuade women from trying to live by literature.

However, probably more than in any other branch of literature, women who wrote children's books did so to make money. Although it was home work for piece rates it required neither genius nor learning, only patience and necessity. Here is Mary Howitt's portrait of the struggling young children's writer:

Miss Eliza Meteyard ('Silverpen') is with us. She is now a sufficiently old friend of ours for us all to feel perfectly at ease with one another. She has her work as well as we. Poor dear soul! She is sitting by me at this moment with her lips compressed, a look of abstraction in her clever but singular face, and her hair pushed back from her forehead, while she is busy over a story about a Bronze Inkstand, which she hopes to make a very fine one. A good creature is she! She has just published a most interesting juvenile book, called 'The Doctor's Little Daughter'. It is her own early life. Out of the money thus obtained, she has provided for and sent out a younger brother to Australia; while for another she is striving in another way. Indeed she is both father and mother to her family – yet she is only seven-and-twenty, and a fragile and delicate woman, who in ordinary circumstances would require brothers and friends to help her. How many instances one sees almost daily of the marvellous energy and high principle and self-sacrifice of woman! I am always thankful to see it, for it is in this way that women will emancipate themselves.[72]

High principle and self-sacrifice were common themes in Sunday-school literature and most children's stories were calculated to preserve the traditional rôles of men and women, Church and State. Miss Meteyard might have achieved a measure of emancipation for herself but she did not peddle such radical causes among her young readers. Beauty, duty and piety were the three qualities most acceptable in the little heroes and heroines of children's books. It was possible to write about sinners but only if they were killed off or otherwise punished. Such consideration for youthful susceptibilities influenced adult literature, most obviously in the Old Testament endings of sensation novels. Even George Eliot felt obliged to drown the restless and too passionate Maggie Tulliver.

In 1886 Edward Salmon reported in *Nineteenth Century* on 'What Girls Read'. He was cautious about the results and suggested that the sample of 1,000 girls aged from eleven to nineteen gave answers that they thought would win adult approval. Dickens was judged the safest bet and received 330 votes. Charlotte Yonge came second with 91 votes and Mrs Henry Wood third with 51 votes. In all 1,000 girls chose 48 authors. Near the bottom of the poll were Mrs Gaskell, Charlotte Brontë and Emma Marshall with 5 votes each. Emma Marshall was just the kind of writer one would expect to find in such company. Her speciality was historical fiction, often with a clerical setting, and her novels made ideal Sunday-school prizes. The Dean of Salisbury regarded her as 'a true daughter of the Anglican Church' and praised her efforts 'to add something to literature which can attract and elevate the young'.[73] Her status as an influential children's writer was recognised by Hurst and Blackett when they asked her to contribute an essay on Mrs Ewing to their *Women Novelists of Queen Victoria's Reign*. Other contributors included Mrs Oliphant on the Brontës and Eliza Lynn Linton on George Eliot.

Emma Martin was born into a Norfolk banking family with Quaker connections and in 1854 married Hugh Marshall, a director of the West of England Bank. She spent the rest of her life in west-country cathedral towns making friends with bishops, deans and canons, the Arnolds and the Kingsleys, and, by correspondence, with Longfellow. She began writing fiction to amuse and instruct her own children and the children of friends. Her daughter Beatrice Marshall recalled her attitude to her authorship:

She must have been often writing, but I have no recollection of her then as I have of her in later years, seated in the midst of us with her pen gliding rapidly over sheet after sheet of foolscap. Never did a mother who was a writer of books make less fuss about the business of writing them. The children came first, the books second.[74]

In 1878 her husband's bank failed leaving him with heavy liabilities and for the next twenty years she became the principal wage earner writing a total of nearly two hundred volumes. By the 1880s her literary earnings were running at a respectable £300 to £500 a year. In addition she had a legacy worth £300 a year and, eventually, her husband earned £100 a year as secretary to the Clifton Suspension Bridge, a post he owed largely to his wife's influence. With this income of between £700 and £900 she was able to equip her five sons for the army and Singapore, the Bank of England, Oxford and the Church and the medical profession.

While her books were usually well reviewed and gave her the reputation of a popular author, they did not earn her as much as she felt she deserved:

There is a general impression – I know – that my books so widely circulated *must* be the source of a very considerable income.

It is not so. – I am receiving from my publisher precisely the same amount for *Penshurst Castle* as I received eighteen years ago for a story of modern life. – *Penshurst Castle* reached a 4000 very quickly and I have 30£ on every thousand. But this is scarcely what many imagine are my profits. The sale of editions of course is most important and I am bound to say my chief publisher Mr Richmond Seeley is prompt in his half yearly settlement and rigourously *just* in regard to former books on which I hold the copyright. But compared with the modern Society novel or the sensational novel my earnings are in proportion to labour – but small [31 March 1894].

Her most popular book, *Life's Aftermath* (1876), reached 13,000, followed by *Under Salisbury Spire* (1869) at 12,000. Most of her stories were exhausted at 5,000. This was respectable though hardly spectacular and she was consumed by envy for the success of, in her view, markedly inferior work. When Hall Caine's *The Christian* (1897) achieved a print run of 70,000 she found it 'sickening' that a man who wrote such 'slipshod English' could be so popular: 'There is not a word of reality in it, and all the materials got up from hearsay, not experience. Yet I hear people say they have been enthralled by it.'[75]

Mrs Marshall could not grasp the self-evident fact that to write best-selling fiction involved pandering to the public taste. 'There surely is a very degenerate taste abroad. Even a harmless story by Margaret Deland, "Philip's Wife", must make a married man love another woman. This phase of society I cannot touch.'[76] Nor, of course, could hundreds of other writers for children who were unable to take advantage of the relaxing of the adult public taste. On 17 December 1898, six months before her death, she wrote a sad and bemused letter to her publisher:

The Queen has a very nice notice of 'The Dome of St Paul's'. I wonder why it is they say these books are for children? Certainly I do not think they are intended for children. The fact is, that unless novels or stories have some incident arising from a man loving the wrong woman, and the woman loving the wrong man after marriage, the taste of the great majority of story-readers is not satisfied. *This*, from principle and the knowledge that it is too common in life as in fiction, is a theme I will never introduce into my books.[77]

In both her avowedly juvenile tales and her 'historical stories' as she liked to call them, Mrs Marshall modelled herself on her favourite author Charlotte Yonge, and constructed simple, innocent stories. It pleased the Sunday schools, the Church and pious parents – it did not altogether please the young: 'I tried reading "The Heir of Redcliffe" to some girls not long ago. They seemed glad when I stopped!'[78] While entirely proper from the moral point of view – such works were undoubtedly a major influence on young behaviour – Mrs Marshall's attitude to literature helps to explain the inferior quality of most children's books written by Victorian women. In the war between the Mrs Marshalls and the Marie Corellis the latter won all the worldly prizes: wealth, fame and a flickering literary reputation. For all her bishops and deans Mrs Marshall's reputation is utterly extinguished.

Lack of education, lack of opportunity, lack of status and lack of property all combined to narrow the literary horizons of women and to make it that much harder for them to achieve artistic distinction. This reality of female authorship has too often been obscured by the achievements of Jane Austen, Charlotte Brontë, Mrs Gaskell and George Eliot. These four exceptional novelists have cast the work of the majority of women writers into the deepest shade.

6

GISSING'S NEW GRUB STREET, 1880–1900

GEORGE GISSING'S *New Grub Street* is the first major novel to place authorship at the centre of the plot rather than as an incidental achievement of the hero or heroine. Dickens and Thackeray, in their autobiographical novels *David Copperfield* and *Pendennis*, present a genial view of literary life. The runaway success of *Pickwick Papers* enabled Dickens to leapfrog the apprentice years of literary struggle. Thackeray had enough self- and class-confidence to squander a private income and a Cambridge education in pursuit of agreeable literary fellowship. There are no hardships in his Grub Street, not even in debtors' prisons. The whole of his prospect of Fleet Street has been tinted by his nostalgia for his student journalist days.

New Grub Street was criticised on its publication in 1891 for ignoring the happy side of literature: the world of large incomes, social engagements and comfortable London clubs. Such a world is glimpsed. Disappointed hacks malign successful novelists, one is even visited in his West End home, but the starry version of literary life does not dominate the novel any more than it reflects reality. In attempting to write about a whole literary system Gissing naturally chooses the Grub Street perspective, the view from the base of a literary pyramid whose summit is in the clouds. The result is a painstaking and painful examination of the unglamorous machinery of literature. It was even more of a blow to the legend of literary creativity than Trollope's *Autobiography*.

That *New Grub Street* is the most powerful and detailed novel about the literary world is partly because it was written at a time when social and economic changes had a more dramatic effect on the conditions of authorship than at any time since Gutenberg. Ostensibly the novel covers the years 1882 to 1885, but, written in 1890, it encapsulates Gissing's literary experience throughout the 1880s and anticipates the death of the three-volume novel in 1895 – a date which conveniently marks the end of nineteenth-century publishing methods. Between 1880 and 1895 the world of publishing and journalism underwent a radical transformation: the introduction of syndication, the expansion of the popular press, the founding of the Society of Authors, the rise of the literary agent, the relaxing of mid-Victorian pruderies in fiction, the triumph of the adventure story and of the gossip column – all led to the climate of change and controversy that pervades *New Grub Street*. Literature, especially fiction, became a battleground between 'tradesmen', as Gissing called them, writers such as Walter Besant, Anthony Hope, and Andrew Lang, and 'artists' such as Henry James, George Meredith and Gissing himself, who had little confidence in the market-place but some confidence in posterity. Both sides emerged victorious, even strengthened by their conflict. The authors of *King Solomon's Mines* and *The Prisoner of Zenda* were to meet posterity in the cinema and on television. The authors of *The Egoist* and *The Odd Woman* were to achieve a modest popularity in their lifetime and classic status after their deaths. The losers were the characters of *New Grub Street* and their living counterparts. As John Morley noted in a widely reported speech at a Royal Literary Fund dinner in May 1890, 'there is no mercy, I will not say for mediocrity, but for unmarketable mediocrity'.

The literary market-place amounts to the number of people able and willing to read. By the 1890s there was a general belief that the 1870 Education Act (which extended state education at primary level) had trebled the reading population and created a monstrous half-educated audience avid for new, lighter, cheaper reading matter. According to Walter Besant, the Board schools had instilled a love of reading into millions of boys and girls who in previous generations would have had no access to books at all: 'The favourite amusement of these young people is reading. It is, of course, nonsense to suppose they read for study: they read for amusement: and it is, or should be, a more desirable and more innocent form of amusement than the billiard-room and the music hall and the tavern bar.'[1] He went on to assert that, far from being dangerous, such dedication to light reading would lead to intellectual development; to 'a stage out of which the stronger and the keener mind will presently emerge'. Frederic Harrison, the positivist and Gissing's first patron, forcefully expressed the opposite view, condemning light literature as a 'debilitating waste of brain in aimless, promiscuous, vapid reading, or even, it may be, in the poisonous inhalation of mere literary garbage and bad men's worst thoughts'.[2] Besant, himself a popular writer, saw this growth of the young reading public as a wonderful challenge as well as money in the bank. His enthusiasm was boundless. He guessed that, largely as a result of British colonial policies, the readership of the English speaking world had expanded from 50,000 in 1830 to 120 million by the late 1890s.

There is still some controversy about the impact of the Board schools on the number and tastes of new readers. Apart from leading to a greatly expanded textbook market, one major effect was the provision of equal educational opportunities for girls. After 1870 the literacy rate, which was a measure of basic writing skill rather than reading ability, increased from 80.6 per cent of men and 73.2 per cent of women in 1871 to 93.6 per cent of men and 92.7 per cent of women by 1891. As important as the increase in adult literates, which probably had a greater impact on the growth of popular journalism than on book production, was the increase in disposable incomes. Between 1850 and 1880 the number of families with incomes of between £150 and £400, the nucleus of the book-reading public, rose to 285,100, a threefold increase.[3] While incomes rose book prices fell, though less steeply. Although the three-volume novel remained an exorbitant 31s. 6d., by the 1860s 6s. reprints were increasingly common and by the 1870s it was virtually standard practice for a moderately subscribed new novel to be reissued within a year or two as a one-volume reprint at 6s. or even less. Throughout the 1870s publishers vied with each other to produce quicker and cheaper reprints of new books, as distinct from the 1s. reprints of out of copyright works and old favourites. In the early 1870s Tinsley was issuing reprints at 2s. and 2s. 6d. and in 1876 Chatto and Windus, one of the leading publishers of new fiction, published 2s. reprints of novels by Wilkie Collins, James Payn and Walter Besant, and in 1880 reduced the price of their 6s. Piccadilly Library to 3s. 6d.[4]

It is difficult to generalise about the volume of books produced as so much depended upon the reputation of the individual authors. In *The Pen and the Book* (1899) Besant calculated that a novelist had to sell 600 copies of a one-volume novel before making a profit and 2,000 copies to make a profit of £200. He estimated that of the 1,300 novelists whose works were stocked by W.H. Smith, at least 1,000 earned less than £200 from their novels. It is clear that the print run of the average novel rarely exceeded 2,000 copies and was much more often set at 1,000 or less. This was not much of an advance on the days of the Minerva Press. The dramatic increase was not in individual sales, except for the rare bestseller, but in the number of new titles. Gissing's first novel *Workers in the Dawn* was one of 380 new novels published in 1880; by 1891 *New Grub Street* was competing for attention with 896 new novels and by 1895 there were 1,315 new novels.[5]

This increase in the production of novels was partly due to the gradual shrinking of the novel form from the standard three volumes to one- or two-volume works. A diligent manufacturer of fiction could write at least two short novels in the time it took to write a three-decker. The three-decker had dominated fiction publishing since the 1820s and by the end of the 1880s it was an anachronism, kept alive by a cartel of publishers and circulating libraries who depended on its high price for their stable profit margins. It was quite possible for the established publisher to realise £100 on a sale of 500 after paying the novelist a standard £100 for the copyright. Even third-rate novels published by Newby or Tinsley could pay their way without too much difficulty. Indeed the system encouraged the third-rate, for publishers could sell a small but remunerative quantity of almost any novel provided it filled three volumes and was inoffensive. Even a £10 profit was worthwhile for the publisher when added to a similar profit on fifty other novels. The novelist, of course, could not survive on £10 or £20 and many gave up altogether. However there was no shortage of aspirants who were more than willing to help the publisher keep up his quota, and not all of them were victims. The practised three-decker hack could manage one and a half to two novels a year, and by selling the copyright could earn a steady income of between £200 and £300.

Because the three-decker cost 31s. 6d. in the shop it was far too expensive for the average reader to buy. And if the circulating libraries refused to stock it readers could not borrow it and publishers would not reissue it as a cheap reprint. Thus the libraries, particularly the giant firm of Mudie's, were highly effective literary censors. George Moore launched a fierce attack on Mudie for refusing to circulate his novel *A Modern Lover* (1883) after 'two ladies from the country' objected to the working-class bible-reading heroine modelling as Venus for the artist hero.[b] But by the mid-1880s Mudie's power, as well as his once sound commercial judgment, was waning. The reading public was ready and even eager for franker fiction, and while the market for expensive library editions continued to shrink the market for cheap quick-issue reprints was rapidly expanding. The logical outcome of this trend was the cheap one-volume novel. An increasing number of writers began to publish first edition one-volume novels at the reprint price of 6s., including such popular novelists as Rider Haggard, Hall Caine and R.D. Blackmore. Gissing's friend Morley Roberts, whose writing career began in 1887, baulked the three-volume system altogether. Gissing commented enviously in 1892, 'Roberts . . . [has] disposed of *five* books in *half a year.*[7] The bulky, costly three-decker could not compete and when Mary Braddon reluctantly abandoned the form in 1895 it was pronounced dead. One immediate result was a reduction in earnings for mediocre novelists, for the patron was no longer the mean though predictable Mudie but the fickle, book-buying public.

If the price of books was falling and the print run remained the same then writers had to look to sources other than volume rights to sustain or increase their income. Novelists had been earning reasonable sums from magazine serials since the 1860s, but in the late 1870s the development of newspaper syndication by the Bolton firm of Tillotsons opened up a much wider market than that offered by the magazines.[8] Writers who would never have gained admittance to the pages of respectable magazines like *Macmillan's* and the *Cornhill* and who depended on the far from rich *Tinsley's* and *Belgravia*, were suddenly offered quite large sums for the privilege of running their novels through a chain of provincial newspapers.

Tillotsons began by serialising new fiction in their own newspaper, the *Bolton Journal*. By 1873 W.F. Tillotson, the manager of the family firm and brother-in-law to W.H. Lever, later Lord Leverhulme, had established the Tillotson Newspaper Syndicate which bought fiction for the firm's own chain of north-country newspapers and, by the 1880s, acted as an agency for the supply of fiction to the newspaper trade in general. The first novel to be widely and successfully syndicated was Mary Braddon's *Lucy Davoran* (1873), followed by *Taken at the Flood* (1874), which she dedicated to Tillotson as a testimony to his innovative publishing skills. It needed someone as popular as Miss Braddon to demonstrate the potential of syndication. Many authors believed that they would lose considerable caste by publishing in newspapers rather than in magazines. Gissing wrote to his friend Eduard Bertz in 1889: 'Of course I should never dream of writing a *story* for a newspaper syndicate; the kind of stuff they publish, and the way they advertise it, is too ignoble.' It was an untenable position for in the same letter he admitted 'I cannot stand obscurity'.[9] In the end, Tillotson was able to attract the work of the most self-conscious authors with princely syndication fees which did not affect their earnings from volume rights. A Tinsley author, Dick Dowling, received £100 for the syndication of a 'half three volume length' novel while the best-selling Conan Doyle was paid £2,500 for the syndication rights of a 60,000 word novel.

In tandem with the newspaper publication of novels was a surge in demand for short stories. The principal publisher of Gissing's short stories was Clement Shorter, who in 1890, on the strength of a freelance gossip column in T.P. O'Connor's *Star*, was plucked from a clerkship at Somerset House to become editor of the *Illustrated London News*. Shorter's philosophy of journalism was simple and profitable:

Very early in my journalistic life I discovered the greater attraction of the picture as against the best possible writing matter. I saw how little attention was paid to the literary contributions in the illustrated newspapers of the early 'nineties compared with the demand for illustration. A royal wedding or a royal funeral added thousands to our sales, whereas the most exciting story or the most eloquent article left our subscribers cold.[10]

In spite of this Shorter made every effort to secure copy from the best possible writers, even if it was nowhere near their best work. Gissing wrote a number of stories for Shorter, acutely aware that they were, by his standards, trash. However he was glad enough for the 2 guineas a thousand words that Shorter paid him – it was more than twice as much as he could earn from novel writing. He even managed to swallow his pride and contribute to Shorter's *Sketch*, an illustrated sixpenny-weekly aimed at the music-hall public.

The growth of the illustrated press was only one aspect of the changing character of journalism. Daily and weekly papers were increasingly adopting the transatlantic techniques of the interview, the gossip column, the campaign and the sensational news story. This change was most obvious in the *Pall Mall Gazette* when, in 1883, W.T. Stead succeeded John Morley as editor. Stead, a Tynesider and an ardent Congregationalist, was the pioneer of what his detractors dubbed 'yellow journalism' and he called 'new journalism'. Stead first used the phrase 'new journalism' in a *Contemporary Review* article 'The Future of Journalism' published in November 1886. The press, he maintained, was an 'engine of social reform . . . for the service, for the education, and for the guidance of the people'. And the editorial chair was nothing less than 'a seat of far-extended influence and world-shaping power'. To further his aim of 'government by journalism' Stead founded the monthly *Review of Reviews* in 1890 on capital supplied by George Newnes of *Tit-Bits* fame. A resounding success, it made a profit of £4,200 a year and provided the reading public with its first experience of a literary and political digest: 'condensed culture, the swiftest, deftest and most complete achievement of sub-editing ever seen'.[11] Stead next applied the digest principle to the publication of classic novels; his 'penny Steadfuls' included works by Dickens, Thackeray and Trollope condensed into eighty pages. In all his entrepreneurial and editorial activities he was a passionate believer in the value of educating and influencing the mass of readers.

The new audience of this new journalism required a constant supply of short, racy copy. For those writers who could oblige the rewards were high. Gissing came close to doubling his income from the sale of short stories and he noted that Morley Roberts 'by short stories alone . . . is now [1893] making some £500 or £600 a year'.[12] For the adaptable non-fiction writer there was a wide range of outlets: gossip columns, interviews, bookish anecdotes, snippets of information, jokes, comment, thoughts for the day. And by the end of the 1880s the favourite standby of the would-be writer – book reviewing – had become, for many, a full-time occupation. Walter Besant, recalling the Grub Street of the 1870s, thought that 'there were many more seedy literary men, because in those days the great doors of journalism were neither so wide nor so wide open as they are now',[13] a claim supported by the investment figures for the newspaper industry. In 1875 the called capital of newspaper companies was £13.7 million, ten years later the figure was £205.6 million, of which a significant fraction found its way into the writer's pocket.[14]

Quite apart from the new markets provided by journalism, the marketing of a literary work was further extended by the signing of the Berne Convention on copyright in 1886 and the Chace Act in the United States in 1891, both of which gave some degree of protection from piracy to the author attempting to sell overseas rights. After 1891 authors had to keep track of an increasingly complicated list of potential rights: volume rights which could be disposed of in a number of ways including outright sale, sale on commission and half-profits and royalty agreements; serial rights; translations rights; US rights; representation rights – all of which were protected by law subject to careful drafting of contracts. It was hardly surprising that this accumulation of rights, for which authors had been fighting since the days of Dickens, Lytton and Talfourd, led directly to the rise of the literary agent and the founding of the Society of Authors. The outstandingly successful writer had always relied on a business manager; Dickens was managed by John Forster, George Eliot by G.H. Lewes, and Mary Braddon by her publisher husband John Maxwell. Less successful authors were obliged to trust their publishers. But by the 1890s book publishers were in competition with newspaper syndicates and magazine publishers. The older firms like Bentley and Cassell were losing their commercial flair and buckling under ever more complex innovations, while go-ahead young publishers like William Heinemann, John Lane and J.M. Dent were regarded with suspicion. Authors had to look elsewhere for 'independent' advice.

A.P. Watt was the first agent of any reputation.[15] He started in publishing as assistant and later partner to his brother-in-law Alexander Strahan, the publisher of Tennyson's *Idylls of the King*. By 1881 he was acting as a 'literary agent'. His first clients were George MacDonald and Wilkie Collins and over the next ten years or so he acted for Besant, Conan Doyle, Rider Haggard, Kipling, Hardy and Gissing. Besant found him 'dirt cheap at ten percent'.[16]

Watt's first rival was William Morris Colles, a barrister and occasional journalist who ran the Society of Authors 'Authors' Syndicate' during the 1890s. Heinemann considered the 'hot-tempered' Colles the best literary agent in London.[17] Gissing switched from Watt to Colles in 1893 and found him satisfactory but they were never on cordial terms and in 1897 he employed the likeable and dedicated J.B. Pinker as his literary agent. Watt, Colles and Pinker handled nearly all the famous names of the 1890s and Pinker was prepared to work for lesser-known authors including the unknown Joseph Conrad.

As well as established literary agents there was a host of fringe literary figures – failed novelists, canvassers, bookseller's clerks, briefless barristers – who were more than willing to act on behalf of authors, particularly novice authors. This advertisement appeared in several literary papers in May 1880 and is typical of its kind:

To Authors: The Advertiser, a Journalist, Critic and an Author of repute, undertakes the revision of MSS., reads same, and gives opinion thereon, and when so requested submits MSS (of which he approves) to suitable PUBLISHERS. FEES – One Guinea for reading and opinion; Two Guineas for submitting MSS, to a Publisher, payable only on the Author signing agreement with said PUBLISHER for its publication. Critic, 13, Warwick Court, Holborn.

In addition to such hazardous freelance advice there were a range of guide books to the literary world, most of them cheap and useful. The most popular was Percy Russell's *The Literary Manual* (1886), recast as the *Authors' Manual* in 1891, which gave a detailed account of the mechanics of publishing and journalism. Such books were aimed at the Board school entrants to the literary profession for whom a sub-editorial job or the publication of a technical book was the height of their literary ambition. While the university-educated writer might scorn Russell's guide it was the kind of work that undoubtedly raised the general standard of journeyman authorship.

The single most important event in the literary 1880s was the founding of the Society of Authors in 1884.[18] The Society owed its existence to the energy and perseverance of Walter Besant, popular novelist, middle-brow critic, amateur antiquary and indefatigable controversialist. As W. Robertson Nicoll put it 'He had a most singular reluctance to admit that he had made a mistake, and that he made many mistakes in fighting the battle of the author against the publisher no unprejudiced person with a knowledge of the facts could possibly deny.'[19] Despite his mistakes Besant did much to create a climate of constructive debate ranging over almost every aspect of literature. Even Gissing, who blamed Besant for 'the extent to which novelists are becoming *mere* men of business', had to 'cheerfully admit that much is owing to him for his efforts to improve the payment of authorship'.[20] This view was shared, though from a different perspective, by Heinemann, who wrote to the *Athenaeum* in 1892 to protest at the effectiveness of Besant's Society:

a trades union more complete, more dangerous to the employer, more definite in its object, and more determined in its demands than any of the other unions – conducted, besides, with intelligence, with foresight, with purity of purpose, but unquestionably and avowedly against the publisher . . . royalties are actually being paid which, with the increase in the cost of production, leave the publisher barely his working expenses [3 December 1892].

Heinemann left £33,000 at his death.

Literary agents may have offered more practical help to busy authors than the belligerent Society of Authors, but the Society, directed by Besant, kept up a constant pressure on the publishing fraternity. Through its campaigns, jamborees and reports on publishing villainy it placed the whole issue of the value and status of literary culture at the centre of late-Victorian debate.

IN 1890 the young H.G. Wells cheerfully embarked on a literary career secure in the knowledge that the dead weight of the nineteenth century was behind him:

The last decade of the nineteenth century was an extraordinarily favourable time for new writers and my individual good luck was set in the luck of a whole generation of aspirants. Quite a lot of us from nowhere were 'getting on'. The predominance of Dickens and Thackeray and the successors and imitators they had inspired was passing. In a way they had exhausted the soil for the type of novel they had brought to a culmination. . . . For a generation the prestige of the great Victorians remained like the shadow of vast trees in a forest, but now that it was lifting, every weed and sapling had its chance, provided only that it was of a different species from its predecessors.[21]

Not everyone shared Wells's relief at the passing of the Victorian giants, and while it was a matter of rejoicing for most young writers a whole tribe of Jeremiahs, including Gissing, saw only crumbling standards and literary decay. The speakers at the Royal Literary Fund dinners issued regular warnings of the approaching literary deluge. The murmurings began in 1883 after the death of Trollope and reached a climax in 1893 after the death of Tennyson. At the dinner of 1883 G.S. Venables, barrister and Saturday Reviewer, mused on the future of post-Trollopian literature and reached a pessimistic conclusion – 'I do not think there are any new great novelists arising'. At the same dinner J. Cotter Morison, another Saturday Reviewer, took a more optimistic view but noted that 'literature of the present day has got two very serious rivals, namely science and politics'. The historian W.E.H. Lecky elaborated on this theme in 1888 as part of his oration on the deaths of Matthew Arnold and Sir Henry Maine:

A Literature which has very recently been adorned by such names as these ought not to be spoken of in any tone of despondency. It is true, however, that in the present day it is exposed to great and unusual competition. Politics on the one hand, and Science on the other, have drawn away many fine intellects that in other ages would have pursued it. Not a few men in our day have deliberately turned from the paths of Literature, for which they had shown an eminent aptitude, and devoted themselves to the noisier career of politics; and, perhaps, Literature loses still more by the large amount of literary talent which is devoted to what cannot be properly called Literature – which is pulverised and absorbed in the daily or weekly Press. I suppose there has never been a country or an age in which so large an amount of excellent literary talent has been devoted to writings which are at once anonymous and ephemeral.

Coming from a distinguished historian who was also very much involved in the profession of authorship this is important testimony.

All who spoke at the Fund dinners were aware that the dignity of literature had been called into question and many were on the defensive. The unconvincing optimism of Rabbi Hermann Adler was typical: 'can it be said that all originality is dead when such novelists as the one of whom our noble Chairman has spoken [Walter Besant], when such men as Mr Stevenson and Mr Rider Haggard are forming, or, at least, reviving, and not unsuccessfully, the romance of adventure' (1889). In all the speeches of the 1890s no one even alluded to the work of Meredith, Hardy, Gissing, James and Conrad. The most prominent attack on the decadence of literature was made by the chairman of the 1893 dinner, A.J. Balfour, then leader of the government in the Commons. It was the first dinner since the death of Tennyson, and Balfour was in a negative mood:

We have all felt that the great names which rendered illustrious the early years of the great Victorian epoch are, one by one, dropping away, and now, perhaps, but few are left. I do not know that any of us can see around us the men springing up who are to occupy the thrones thus left vacant. I should not venture to say – and, indeed, I do not think – that we live in an age barren of Literature. But none of us, I fear, can deny that, at all events at the present moment, we do not see a rising generation of men of letters likely to rival those of old times. (Hear, hear.) . . . we do not at present see among us their successors. (Hear, hear.) It is a most interesting situation, because I am prepared to admit that we live in an age which bears upon it the marks of decadence. (Hear, hear.)

Among those listening to Balfour's speech was Thomas Hardy. He was unimpressed and noted in his diary: 'A great lack of tact in A.J.B. who was in the chair at the Royal Literary Fund dinner which I attended last night . . . he dwelt with much emphasis on the decline of the literary art, and on his opinion that there were no writers of high rank living in these days. We hid our diminished heads and buttoned our pockets.'[22]

Men like Venables, Lecky and Balfour represented the orthodox, élitist view of literature; that it should be commemorated in Westminster Abbey and engage the upper ten thousand. Their keyword 'decadence' referred to all novels written after the death of George Eliot, all poetry after the death of Tennyson and all prose after the death of Arnold and the madness of Ruskin.

The decadence of the 1890s is usually associated with the *Yellow Book* era. Arthur Symons summed up his view of his age in *Harper's New Monthly Magazine* in November 1893: 'it has all the qualities that mark the end of great periods, the qualities that we find in the Greek, the Latin, decadence; an intense self-consciousness, a restless curiosity in research, an over-subtilising refinement upon refinement, a spiritual and moral perversity'. This description suits the literature of Oscar Wilde, of Ernest Dowson, of Enoch Soames, but it has little in common with the literature of Rider Haggard, Conan Doyle, Marie Corelli or even Gissing and Hardy. Holbrook Jackson in his influential *The Eighteen Nineties* is more even-handed although he devotes separate chapters to such minor poets as Francis Thompson and John Davidson while treating the work of Gissing, Hardy and H.G. Wells in a few lines:

The Eighteen Nineties were to no small extent the battleground of these two types of culture – the one represented by *The Yellow Book*, the other by the Yellow Press. The one was unique, individual, a little weird, often exotic, demanding the right to *be* – in its own way even to waywardness; but this was really an abnormal minority, and in no sense national. The other was broad, general, popular; it was the majority the man-in-the-street awaiting a new medium of expression. In the great fight the latter won.[23]

In fact there was no fight between the Yellow Press and the *Yellow Book* – except perhaps at the time of the trial of Oscar Wilde. They were two uncompetitive facets of decadence. The great cultural debate was not about Beardsley's decorative phalli, Dowson's absinthe-soaked verse, Hubert Crackanthorpe's tremendously slight short stories or even Oscar Wilde's wit and homosexuality; it was about art in the market-place. The aesthetes were above the market-place: they were, for the most part, poets, illustrators, essayists and short-story writers. They were not novelists. And from the Prime Minister to the pupils of the Board schools, the novel remained the dominant literary form. H.D. Traill, editor of *Literature*, the forerunner of the *TLS*, and an outspoken cultural critic of the day, was in no doubt where the greatest danger to cultural standards lay:

The number of novels the publishers issue every year is not only startling but appalling. The enormous torrent of novels seems to submerge and sweep away every other kind of literary product, and it is only dimly and with difficulty that one discerns after a time a few volumes of biography, here and there, an historic study, or volume of travel and adventure floating on the surface of the flood.[24]

'Who in heaven's name buys all the books that come forth?', Gissing asked in 1892, 'day by day new publishing firms appear and the weekly issue of books is appalling'.[25]

The metaphor of a literary deluge carried with it the implication of divine anger and retribution. Those who were on the side of God included those writers who felt that their work was unjustly ignored by an undiscerning public. They could not understand why the public had apparently shifted its allegiance from the great Victorians to the likes of Hall Caine and Marie Corelli, and they blamed the Board schools. Gissing was keenly aware of the effect of this shift on literary incomes, 'it is not always a Dickens who gets satisfactorily paid; the richest authors, today, are generally the least important, as everyone knows'.[26] R.W. Buchanan, who had no reason to complain of any lack of public interest in his long-winded and discursive narrative poems and dramas, was probably the most quarrelsome author of the day. He raged against decadence like an Old Testament prophet:

The great newspapers, with their monstrous machinery, swallow up men of talent by the dozen. If here and there a tricksy spirit escapes, it is to degenerate into a fashionable author or a fourth-rate politician. If by chance a solitary writer attempts to be original and to think for himself, he reaps the privileges of literary martyrdom. Meanwhile if we look quietly round in the world of life and literature, what do we see? The great waters of Democracy arising to swallow up and cover the last landmarks of individualism; a few isolated figures standing on ever-narrowing islets, and crying like Canute to the flood; bogus reputations going down into the angry living tide, volcanic notorieties springing up for a moment and disappearing . . . After the School Board has come the Deluge.[27]

For all that it is a passionate diatribe, Buchanan's attack, written in 1886, anticipates Lecky's more dispassionate after-dinner analysis. And Buchanan is perhaps more honest than Lecky and Balfour for he is not afraid to identify the enemy as democracy and the growth of the reading public.

Many writers who were anti-democratic were, like Max Beerbohm's character Enoch Soames, envious, embittered third-raters; others, like Gissing and James, were genuine artists. For Gissing and James it was axiomatic that the writer had a duty to lead the public taste, or, if the public taste would not be led, to ignore it altogether. The popular writers, by definition, believed the reading public had infallible, if unsophisticated taste. And to justify the financial advantages of such a belief they argued that by amusing their readers with good value entertainment they could slip in, almost unnoticed, a package of good moral values. This distinction between the popular and the profound had been almost unknown to mid-Victorian writers. Serious literature, brimming with moral and social issues, had made no apology for its popularity. No one suggested that Dickens's *Oliver Twist*, Tennyson's *In Memoriam* and George Eliot's *Middlemarch* were not literature because they contained ideas which found a wide and receptive audience. But in the 1880s changes in the price and distribution of books allowed readers to exercise a much more direct choice over their reading matter. This gradual shift of power from paternalist libraries to childish readers helped to alter and relax public taste to the point where readers became increasingly impatient with anything that smacked of old-fashioned didacticism. Hence the stealth with which the popular writer set about instruction. By the mid-1880s an irrevocable schism had occurred in the bourgeois literary world. Where there had been literature there was now middle-brow and high-brow literature. The two antagonistic positions were clearly marked out in an exchange of essays between Walter Besant and Henry James on the Art of Fiction.

Besant's *Art of Fiction* (1884), a lecture delivered at the Royal Institution, was less about the art of fiction and rather more of a blueprint for popular novel writing. Modern fiction, Besant argued in self-justification, 'almost always starts with a conscious moral purpose'. Without using the term he claimed that the popular 'middle-brow' novelist was the true heir of the great Victorian tradition. By implication the high-brow novelist, the art for art's sake advocate, failed to strike a responsive chord in the average reader and so failed in an artist's chief duty – to entertain: 'in story-telling, as in almsgiving, a cheerful countenance works wonders, and a hearty manner greatly helps the teller and pleases the listener'. However crass such a view may seem it had been tried and tested in the market-place. Besant's bluff heartiness won him thousands of readers and thousands of pounds and it helped to make his unexceptional 'moral purpose' palatable.

Besant's cardinal rule of fiction was utterly uncompromising – 'everything in Fiction which is invented and is not the result of personal experience and observation is worthless'. This is absurd and Besant unwittingly exposed the weakness of his rule by substituting for 'fiction' the word 'romance'. In the new romances of Rider Haggard and Anthony Hope there was a great deal of colourful imagination, stereotyped characterisation and frank fantasy. Hope's *Prisoner of Zenda* is a classic romance, a novel length fairy-tale. Henry James, on the other hand, who was often criticised for his allegedly passionless, over-refined and mannered prose, could legitimately claim to have observed and experienced every incident in his fiction. For Besant the unpardonable offence was to bore the reader by being either too clever or too dull. At all costs the writer must keep the reader's attention, and not just a reader but the vast majority of readers. The result was the fashioning, under the guidance of Besant and others, of the middle-brow novel. 'Ought we not to be full of hope for the future', concludes a sanguine Besant, 'when such women as Mrs Oliphant and Mrs Thackeray Ritchie write for us – when such men as Meredith, Blackmore, Payn, Wilkie Collins, and Hardy are still at their best, and such men as Louis Stevenson, Christie Murray, Clark Russell and Herman Merivale have just begun?' The lumping together of such varied talents shows how unsure – or diplomatic – Besant was in his literary judgments.

Henry James's response to Besant, also called *The Art of Fiction* (1884), was to suggest, kindly but firmly, that there was more to fiction than Besant somewhat arbitrarily allowed.[28] There was subtlety, psychology, imagination; there was Art where Besant preached Craft.

James went on to explore this theme in a group of short stories written at the end of the 1880s and in the 1890s.[29] In 'The Next Time' (1894) published in the *Yellow Book*, a serious, artistic novelist Ray Limbert, 'an exquisite failure', does his best to succeed in the market-place by attempting to imitate the style of his sister-in-law who is a 'prolific' popular novelist. Echoing Gissing's Jasper Milvain, Limbert vows to 'cultivate the market, it's a science like any other'. Inspite of all his efforts to write a best-selling bad book he succeeds in writing a non-selling good book. He fails to add to 'the age of trash triumphant' and retires with his family to an inexpensive country cottage the better to survive on a meagre literary income. James leaves us in no doubt that Limbert, far from being a victim of the market-place, remains true to his art and unbowed by his failure. True artists should not expect, let alone seek, financial rewards. Whenever an artist is captivated or captured by money and the prospect of glittering social success, as is Henry St George in 'The Lesson of the Master' (1888) and Neil Paraday in 'The Death of the Lion' (1894), the outcome is either a diminution of literary quality or the drying up of the muse altogether.

Even while James was formulating his philosophy of artistic reticence in his short stories he was trying to win a popular audience through writing for the theatre. But after the total failure of his play *Guy Domville* in 1895 he not only abandoned the theatre, but also all pretensions of sustaining a popular reputation. He wrote to W.D. Howells, 'I have fallen upon evil days – every sign or symbol of one's being in the least *wanted*, anywhere or by any one having so utterly failed. A new generation that I know not, and mainly prize not, has taken universal possession.'[30] Luckily for James he had private means and did not have to support a wife and family. He was able, therefore, to write against the public taste where Gissing and Conrad found themselves under a constant pressure, to which they both bowed, to write more popular and remunerative novels at some cost to their artistic integrity.

James's stories, like Gissing's novels, suggest that in an age of well-rewarded trash, art and profit are irreconcilable. This view leaves literature in the hands of a privileged, well-educated élite with private incomes – it leads, inevitably, to Bloomsbury. Middle-class middle-brow writers like Besant resented the charge that because they earned money instead of inheriting it, they somehow lacked integrity. Besant could see no conflict of interest between achieving social and financial rewards and aiming to be an artist. He devoted much of his *Art of Fiction* to a discussion of the status of writers. He wanted the 'Master of

Fiction', a Jamesian phrase, to be treated with the respect and devotion accorded to the 'world's greatest men'. This was a solidly bourgeois aspiration; it put the emphasis squarely on the creator rather than the creation. James satirises this emphasis in his story 'John Delavoy' (1898). The public interest in 'the wonderful writer, the immense novelist' John Delavoy does not extend to actually buying or reading his works. Instead it is confined to satisfying an insatiable curiosity about his very uneventful private life. The editor of the monthly journal *Cynosure*, ostensibly an intelligent magazine, rejects a sensitive critical study of Delavoy's writings in favour of a portrait of Delavoy framed in a light, chatty article about his life and personality. The biographical approach is 'something the public will stand', says the *Cynosure*'s editor, who claims that a critical study would lose the magazine between five thousand and ten thousand readers. In 'Death of the Lion' the great, though uncommercial novelist Neil Paraday is tracked down to his modest seaside villa by Mr Morrow, the representative of a syndicate of thirty-seven 'influential journals' and writer of 'the Tatler's celebrated column Smatter and Chatter'. What Morrow craves from Paraday is personal disclosure, 'there's a great interest always felt in the scene of an author's labours. Sometimes we're favoured with very delightful peeps.'

Such personality cults were hardly new, they went back at least as far as the Boswellising of Dr Johnson and were the result of an uncomplicated public interest in the lives of the famous. T.P. O'Connor, whose paper the *Star* was often attacked for its practise of the 'new journalism', vigorously defended the objectives of the gossip column: 'I hold that the desire for personal details with regard to public men is healthy, rational, and should be yielded to.'[31] What was undeniably new in the 1880s was the direct equation between publicity and sales. The whole tribe of middle-brow novelists scrambled and jostled for the privilege of a gossip column entry. Even George Gissing was not above permitting his photograph and (censored) biography to appear in the lighter journals: 'In the rush of authors nowadays, it is vastly important to keep one's name frequently before the public.'[32]

Books about the makers of books far outnumbered critical works. *My First Book* (1894), edited by Jerome K. Jerome, pretended to be a collection of autobiographical accounts of the apprentice years of such well-known writers as Besant, Payn, Caine, Christie Murray, Kipling, Braddon, Corelli, Rider Haggard, Morley Roberts, Grant Allen and John Strange Winter. In fact it was a lavishly illustrated tour around the homes of the famous. Each contribution was illustrated with 'delightful peeps' into the writer's working environment. Hall Caine, for example, had a bust of Shakespeare above his writing desk; Mary Braddon's wealth was on display – 'Miss Braddon's Favourite Mare', 'Miss Braddon's cottage at Lyndhurst' (the size of a country house), 'The Orangery', 'The Evening Room' and so on through an album of opulence. There was even a snapshot of the dwarfish Robert Buchanan standing outside his front door and flanked by his devoted wife and sister-in-law. The essays in *My First Book* had first appeared in the *Idler*, one of the better illustrated monthlies, edited by Jerome. But even the twopenny weeklies printed column upon column of gossip about literary men and women. Both Besant and James understood that the new journalism and the new fiction were interdependent. The mass readership could only be won for the novel if the novelist featured prominently in the popular press, while the popular press was able to sustain and increase its circulation with tit-bits about best-selling writers. The modern equivalent would be the preoccupation of the tabloid press with the lives and loves of soap-opera stars.

In his *Literary Manual*, Percy Russell praises the general competence of the new fiction, 'the public standard insensibly rises, and works which would in 1850 have earned a solid reputation, hardly obtain a place in the third class in 1880'.[33] Besant would have agreed and no doubt both he and Russell would have wished to claim some of the credit. For, allowing for a modicum of literary aptitude, the diligent student of Besant's lectures or Russell's manual could practise the craft and business of fiction with relative success.

The ultimate and ultimately confusing guide to the theory and practice of the new fiction was George Bainton's *The Art of Authorship* (1890), which offered the views of 187 authors on the art of good writing. The enterprising Bainton had told potential contributors that their views on authorship would help him prepare a series of lectures for 'the benefit of youth'. When their private letters to him were edited and published without permission there was a general outcry and the Society of Authors accused Bainton of piracy.[34] But however devious Bainton's motives may have been, the collection presents a fascinating group portrait of literary contemporaries and is a valuable source for glimpsing the literary credos of such writers as Hall Caine, Rider Haggard and Andrew Lang, as well as Hardy, Gissing and James. James's contribution was attractively hesitant: 'The question of literary form interests me indeed, but I am afraid I can give no more coherent or logical account of any little success I may have achieved in the cultivation of it than simply saying that I have always been *fond* of it.' The popular novelists were, as usual, more ready with advice. John Strange Winter's contribution demonstrates how seriously the popular writers viewed their craft, how indeed they viewed it as an art. The author of the best-selling *Bootle's Baby* (1885) told of the enormous effort that went into her resounding success: 'I have many a time written a story eight or nine times over before I have satisfied myself with it.'[35] The hacks of the 1850s would never have taken so much trouble, but then the rewards for hack writing in the 1850s were a great deal smaller. It was ironic that in the age of 'trash triumphant' so much expertise and skill went into the manufacture of the trash.

The novelty of the new fiction consisted of its preoccupations as well as its alleged proficiency. To some extent it grew naturally out of the sensation novels of the 1860s and 1870s but by the 1880s the previously blended ingredients of passion, crime and melodrama had begun to separate. The new genres were distinct: the detective novel, the adventure story, the sex novel, science fiction, even the spy novel; by the 1890s the grid of today's genre fiction had been firmly laid. The three most prominent and characteristic fin-de-siècle genres were realism (also called naturalism), sex, and adventure. Because realism was serious and high-brow it was the least successful commercially, though in 1886 Russell was predicting 'we have in this craving for something new the key to the extraordinary success of Zola in France, and it is probably in Realism only that great and fortune-making successes in the art of Fiction will be attained'.[36] In fact, although Zola's own novels sold well in England, buoyed up by scandal and the controversy surrounding the imprisonment of Vizetelly, his publisher and translator, the vogue for realism did not survive the channel crossing. The work of realists writing in English, such as Gissing and George Moore, met with mixed success and the younger realists, such as Edwin Pugh, failed almost completely. The problem for realism was that the faithful and exact representation of lower-class life was simply too monochromatic, too dull for the sensation-seeking public, unless it deliberately focused on sex and crime, a favourite combination of Zola's and the English sensation novelists', but not of writers like George Gissing.

The great fortunes were made in the field of adventure novels, usually novels of contemporary swashbuckling as distinct from the historical novels of Ainsworth, G.P.R. James and others. Writers like G.A. Henty and R.M. Ballantyne had been profiting from boys adventure stories for some years, and in the 1880s R.L. Stevenson brought both art and maturity to the juvenile adventure story. The well-crafted adult adventure story was to dominate the bestseller market from Rider Haggard's *King Solomon's Mines* (1885) and Anthony Hope's *Prisoner of Zenda* (1894) to John Buchan and beyond. The middle-brow novelist felt particularly comfortable with the adventure novel as it was perfectly suited to rulebook composition; pace, incident, location and character could be nicely mixed into the formula. And of course the age was uniquely favourable to plotting and scene-setting as the sun never set on Britain's still expanding Empire.

The most controversial development in fiction was the franker treatment of sexual relations. In Henry James's 'Death of the Lion' Mr Morrow calls it the fiction of 'the larger latitude', and its exponents, women writers like George Egerton, are satirised by James for coating the sexually sensational with a veneer of art. The same charge was made by the reviewer James Noble in a thoughtful essay 'The Fiction of Sexuality', published in the *Contemporary Review* in April 1895. His essay was a response to an attack on 'sexual sensualism' by 'a philistine' in the *Westminster Gazette*. While Noble defends the right of the novelist to treat 'sex questions squarely' and praises Hardy for so doing, he sees the bulk of sex novels as crudely opportunistic: 'the greater number of the books referred to are not the outcome of any spontaneous impulse whatsoever, either healthy or diseased, but of a deliberate intention to win notoriety and its cash accompaniment by an appeal to the sensual instincts of the baser or vulgar portion of the reading public'. He went on to challenge the notion that sexual passion is the mainspring of action, 'Is this persistent presentation of the most morbid symptoms of erotomania a seeing of life steadily and wholly?' In so far as many of the novels Noble attacked treated sex from a woman's point of view, he was simply a male critic made uncomfortable by the concerns of feminist writing. Nevertheless he was a shrewd judge of the dividing line between integrity and sham. He attacked George Egerton for her 'lack of artistic truth' and he found Sarah Grand's *The Heavenly Twins* (1893), regarded by her admirers as a work of genius, as 'ridiculously overpraised'. Overpraised perhaps, but its enormous sale, 20,000 copies in the first week, clearly demonstrated that in the 1890s those 'pruderies and reticences' which had been such a cherished part of Victorian civilisation had been squarely breached.

This rapid feedback of public opinion through a novel's sales was far more important for the commercial writer than the opinion of a reviewer like Noble. Above all else the success of the new fiction depended on its ability to respond and adapt to changing and sometimes whimsical public tastes. Gissing noted in 1895 that in spite of generally favourable reviews, 'my long novels simply *will not* sell; they disappoint everyone connected with them'.[37] His inability to cater for the fads of the day was most evident during the Boer War: 'Just as I was hoping to earn a little more money comes this scoundrelly war, and the ruin of the book trade.'[38] Rudyard Kipling, Rider Haggard, Conan Doyle and other popular writers made considerable profits by the war but Gissing's pacifist novel *The Crown of Life* sold exceptionally badly.

For Gissing, and James in his later stories, it was an article of faith that the 'real thing', the genuine work of art, would completely fail to 'take' with the public. But for all that they recognised the isolation of the artist, they were puzzled and hurt by public indifference. It took a tradesman like Percy Russell to state the obvious: 'There will be at all times a cultured public willing to read thoughtful philosophical Fiction, but the writers able to supply that demand must not look for sudden popularity nor great pecuniary returns. In this as in other matters of our higher and nobler life, the purer forms of art must be of themselves the writer's incorruptible and enduring reward.'[39] Scant comfort for the pure who are also poor. The publisher G.H. Putnam put the matter less gently, in his *Authors' Complaints and Publishers' Profits* (1891):

It must be borne in mind, however, that the compensation for literary production can never be made proportionate to the amount of labor, skilled or unskilled, that has been put into it, but depends entirely upon the amount that the community is willing to pay for the results of the work, that is, upon the estimate placed by the community upon the value to itself of the service rendered by the author [p. 74].

New Grub Street: case studies

W H E N *New Grub Street* was published reviewers seized the opportunity to air their prejudices and experiences. The novel was either praised, with some reservations about its seaminess, as a valuable antidote to glamorous success stories, or it was attacked for its distortion of a meritocratic literary world. The *Graphic*, a paper that regularly peeped into the lives of famous authors, accused Gissing of being 'grossly one-sided' by describing 'that minority of writers who inhabit the British Museum and work for second-class publishing houses' – as if the majority of writers were members of the Garrick and the London Library and wrote for first-class publishing houses. In the *Author* Besant praised *New Grub Street* for its 'fidelity', only to receive a dressing down from Andrew Lang in the next issue, 'I am also a dweller in Grub Street but am so fortunate not to know anybody who resembles these unhappy rates.'[40]

In fact *New Grub Street* contains several sketches of successful men of letters. There is Ralph Warbury, the 'all round man of letters', 'he began with money and friends; he came from Oxford into the thick of advertised people'; it is a career not unlike Andrew Lang's. There is Markland the best-selling novelist, 'a dwarfish fellow with only one eye'; Mrs Boston Wright, editor of *English Girl*; Miss Wilkes, the Miss Braddon of the novel, married to her publisher; and half a dozen others. What is distinctive about these characters is that they are all peripheral; none of them has a speaking rôle. Of the eleven characters with speaking rôles only two, Milvain and Whelpdale, find literature at all profitable. The reason for this identification of the major characters with failure, and the minor characters with success has much to do with Gissing's own life.

Until the publication of *New Grub Street* Gissing had led one of the more reclusive lives in the history of authorship. His entrance into literary society was auspicious enough. Frederic Harrison praised his first novel, employed him to tutor his sons and introduced him to Morley, who promptly offered him work on the *Pall Mall Gazette*. The career of Jasper Milvain beckoned, but Gissing's social awkwardness coupled with his contempt for journalism caused him to decline the offer. Over the next ten years he mixed with very few authors. The one writer with whom he had unbroken contact was his brother Algernon. His two close literary friends were Eduard Bertz, a political exile who returned to Germany for good in 1884, and Morley Roberts, a fellow student at Owen's College Manchester, who had a taste for Bohemian adventure and did not settle down to a writing career in London until 1887. Gissing made occasional contact with upper middle-class writers but appears to have felt acutely inadequate in their company. In 1887, for example, he met Edward Clodd, an agreeable and wealthy litterateur. It was to take the patient Clodd several years to establish a reciprocal friendship: 'He [Gissing] was shy; he had a hunted-hare look; he struck me as morbidly self-conscious.'[41] In 1888 Gissing confided to his sister Ellen, 'it seems so miserable that a man of my age should be so utterly companionless'.[42] Small wonder that the speaking parts in *New Grub Street* went to what the *Athenaeum* chose to call 'lower middle class writing folk'. Bertz, Algernon Gissing, Morley Roberts and his friend W.H. Hudson, were, if not strictly lower middle-class, all exiles of one sort or another and roughnecks by the standards of the educated upper middle-class literary world.

However, the publication of *New Grub Street* marked a turning point in Gissing's private and professional life. Its relatively warm reception at the hands of fellow authors, perhaps anxious to be seen on the side of the angels, led to Gissing's entrance into the world of Jasper Milvain and Ralph Warbury. He joined the convivial Omar Khayyám Club and the Society of Authors; he wrote short stories for sixpenny magazines; he sat for his photograph; he permitted interviews and profiles to appear in gossipy literary journals; he hired and fired literary agents; he began to enjoy the company of fellow writers – Grant Allen, H.G. Wells and W. Robertson Nicoll. He obviously felt that the companionable pleasures of literary life, so long delayed, were worth having and that he deserved them. But this change in his own circumstances did not change his perception of the conflicts of authorship. If anything, his broader experience of the literary world during the 1890s reinforced his critical view of his profession:

I surmise that the path of 'literature' is being made too easy. Doubtless it is a rare thing nowadays for a lad whose education ranks him with the upper middle class to find himself utterly without resources, should he wish to devote himself to the profession of letters. And there is the root of the matter; writing has come to be recognised as a profession, almost as cut-and-dried as church or law.[43]

Jasper Milvain

MORE THAN ANYTHING else it was 'the opening of the great doors of journalism' that led to increasing numbers of young men and women choosing the profession of literature. The central economic theme of *New Grub Street* is that books are all very well, some may even pay their way, but the most profitable area of authorship is journalism. The insidious consequence of this state of affairs, in Gissing's view, was that journalism, although it masqueraded as literature, was effectively replacing literature. Literature never had been and never could be a 'profession'; it had value but no price. Journalism on the other hand, with its hierarchy and its unwritten constitution, had some claim to be considered one of the professions. This distinction between literature and journalism was appreciated by Jasper Milvain – 'I have the special faculty of an extempore writer. Never in my life shall I do anything of solid literary value. . . . But my path will be that of success.'[44] The great George Augustus Sala, the epitome of the *Daily Telegraph* and bête noir of Matthew Arnold, cheerily made a similar confession. Recalling his decision to abandon literature for journalism in the 1850s Sala wrote in his autobiography: 'I knew perfectly well that I was altogether destitute of a particle of that genius without which I could never excel or become famous in pure letters; but, on the other hand, I was fully cognisant of the fact that I learned my trade as a journalist, and that I could earn a handsome income by it.'[45] Sala was one of the first writers to write exclusively for the press; apart from his autobiography all his published volumes were reprinted collections of his journalism. Although Sala disclaimed any ambition in 'pure letters', the publication and preservation of his ephemeral articles in volume form was the outstanding example of the blurring of the worlds of journalism and literature. In 1881, when Jasper Milvain embarked on his journalistic career, Sala was not only 'the king of journalists', but had won a place as an eminent man of letters.

A sure sign that journalism had become the primary route to literary success was the publication in 1880 of a little career guide, *Journals and Journalism: with a Guide for Literary Beginners*, by 'John Oldcastle'. Although there is no evidence that Gissing had read this manual he would have noted its existence as it was widely advertised in the same week as his first novel *Workers in the Dawn*. Oldcastle's book received kindly reviews and went into a second edition. As a sensible, practical and informative guide it was the best, if not the first of its kind. It was exactly the sort of book that the young Jasper Milvain would have studied with profit. Journalism, in Oldcastle's view, is the natural field of literary activity for a beginner. Milvainisms abound: 'Let it be always remembered that the tact which produces *marketable* work is sometimes more useful than the talent which produces *good* work. . . . A composition of real power and originality may in fact, and not merely in the terms of editorial courtesy, be unsaleable because it is unjournalistic in manner or inopportune to the time. . . . A journalist is bound to be a man of the world, as an author is bound to be a student. . . . He [the journalist] produces work which is eminently marketable; and the more of this quality appears in his writings, the more successful he will be.'[46]

Success is measured in pounds, shillings and pence. Oldcastle notes that the high-class quarterlies pay one pound a page; that the shilling monthlies pay on average 'rather under than over half that sum', and that the literary weeklies pay about ten shillings a column. He cites the experience of a 'young littérateur' of twenty-eight who had begun writing at the age of twenty-five:

I have kept a record of my third year's labour. I had about 200 paragraphs in *The World*; a still greater number, and ten articles besides in another society paper, thirty paragraphs in *Truth*; five articles in *The Queen*; three articles in *The Spectator*; a poem in *Good Words*; a poem in *The Quiver*; thirty-five articles in different monthly magazines; fifty-two columns of London correspondence in a provincial paper (at 12s. 6d. a column); twenty-six London letters in a colonial paper (at 10s. a letter); and a few odds and ends besides. These are the accepted contributions, but they represent little more than half that which I actually wrote – the balance having missed fire. My total proceeds were £247 13s. 2d. I often worked twelve hours a day, and I never had a week's holiday.[47]

Oldcastle comments that if this journalist had had a 'speciality', 'any subject to treat that was peculiarly his own', he could have earned a less arduous living. Nonetheless the account clearly shows that the freelance journalist had any number of paying outlets and could earn a fair living. The fictional Milvain writes for slightly more prestigious papers but displays the same versatility and earns the same income. Between 7.30 and 10.30 in the morning he reads and reviews a book for the *Evening Budget*; by lunchtime he has written his 'Saturday causerie for the *Will o' the Wisp*; in the afternoon he sketches a paper for the *West End*; in the early evening he continues work on an article for the monthly *Current*. Allowing for a holiday, weekends and days of idleness, he reckons to earn between £200 and £300 a year in his third year of authorship.

Milvain's work schedule is a parody of Andrew Lang's facile working habits, which were well known throughout literary London. H.G. Hutchinson in *Portraits of the Eighties* (1920) gave a typical specimen of Lang's bravura:

He was indeed the quickest writer that I have ever known. I have heard him say: 'Is it humanly speaking possible to write an article before dinner?' – taking out his watch – 'Twenty minutes before we need go and dress! Yes, I think it just is.' And off he would go – I think it was for the *Daily News* that he was writing at this time occasional articles about all things in general, and a few more.[48]

Freelance literary journalists were, as a rule, less well paid than their salaried Fleet Street counterparts. Percy Russell states that a middle-ranking journalist of 'model' ability would expect to earn £300 a year in the mid-1880s. By the 1890s Russell was writing that a journalist of 'fair' ability was earning £300 to £400 a year.[49] Lang, of course, was earning above £1,000 with little difficulty. But then he was one of those 'public school men, University men, club men, society men',[50] whom Gissing so envied and despised. The majority of literary journalists were lucky to earn £300 a year. They might dream of rich literary editorships but there were few enough of these and most of them went to men who belonged 'to certain social circles'. Editorial salaries depended on circulation and advertising revenue. Morley was paid a generous £2,000 as editor of the daily *Pall Mall Gazette*. Clement Shorter thought himself poorly paid as the £655 a year editor of the weekly *Illustrated London News*. However, few papers and magazines could afford such sums. Most of the specialised monthlies and trade journals paid their editors £100 or so a year. There was only a remote chance that the assiduous student of Oldcastle's guide would achieve the editorship of any of the 230 listed papers and periodicals and no chance at all of obtaining one of the handful of lucrative editorships so sought after by Jasper Milvain.

James Ashcroft Noble was a 'model' literary journalist, a Milvain who failed to marry a rich widow, an Alfred Yule of a sunnier disposition.[51] Born in 1844 he achieved a modest reputation as a reliable and decent man of letters whose criticism was 'both kindly and penetrative'.[52] His chief source of income was a regular literary column in the *Manchester Examiner* and he also wrote reviews and articles for nearly all the intellectual journals of the day, including the *Contemporary Review*, the *Athenaeum*, the *Yellow Book* and the *Spectator*. He was an example of a fastidious writer who managed to keep body and soul together without contributing to *Tit-Bits*. He wrote sensitively on such subjects as 'The Charm of Autobiography', 'Christina Rossetti', 'Oliver Wendell Holmes', 'The Sonnet in England'. These essays were distinguished enough to enjoy a small sale in volume form. Publishers in the 1890s, in Noble's case J.M. Dent, made something of a speciality of such slim, decorative collections of essays. None of this earned Noble much of an income. From November 1881 to November 1882, for example, Noble earned £212 from literary work after fifteen years as a critic and reviewer. Fortunately he had a small private income of £100. Lacking the social status as well as the managerial energy to become an editor, Noble was one – if one of the best – of perhaps a hundred or so reliable writers who were the backbone of the literary reviews. However, as he was neither precious nor self-advertising he failed to achieve the dignity of an index entry in the literary histories. If he is known at all today it is as the father-in-law of that pre-eminent literary drudge, the poet Edward Thomas.

'John Oldcastle' was rather more fortunate than Noble. 'Oldcastle' was the pseudonym of Wilfrid Meynell, whose Catholic (in both senses) literary career managed to reconcile the Besant-Milvain approach to literature, as exemplified by his *Journals and Journalism* and his founder membership of the Society of Authors, with marriage to the poet Alice

Meynell and patronage of the fin-de-siècle poet Francis Thompson. It was as the husband of Alice and the friend of Thompson that Meynell earned his index entry in Holbrook Jackson. In his own right he was a successful journalist and editor of the *Weekly Register* and *Merry England*. His first editorial venture was a short-lived literary periodical *The Pen*, the first number of which was published in the same week as his guide to journalism. *The Pen*, which ran to twelve numbers during 1880, might have been Gissing's model for Alfred Yule's stillborn *Letters*. It was one of the very few magazines to carry an advertisement for Remington's spring list, which included Gissing's *Workers in the Dawn*, perhaps because its advertising rates were necessarily cheap.

In *New Grub Street* Alfred Yule happily plans to spend his daughter's legacy on establishing *Letters*, a monthly literary review to be edited by himself: 'It would take a place between the literary weeklies and the quarterlies. The former are too academic, the latter too massive, for multitudes of people who yet have strong literary tastes.'[53] Yule convinces himself that such a magazine would be a sound investment, yielding an interest rate of at least 15 per cent. *The Pen*, which began life on May 22, 1880, was subtitled 'A Journal of Literature' and was published weekly at 2d. until, after eight issues, it became a 6d. monthly. Its prospectus, published in the *Athenaeum* as well as in its own columns, declared Yule-like:

The Pen will give an almost exclusive attention to Letters; and there will, therefore, be space in its pages for such full quotation of the representative passages of important works as will make *The Pen* a permanently interesting reflex of our Literature. . . . And if an effort is made to please the more fugitive fancy by paragraphs of literary table-talk, entire care will be taken that the reader is not amused at the expense of any private or professional interest whatever.

The principal item of gossip concerned the wedding and honeymoon of George Eliot. Apart from this concession to the new journalism *The Pen* was a serious-minded magazine that still managed to be entertaining. From a literary point of view it was an unqualified success. Each issue scrutinised the work of some major contemporary – Tennyson, Ruskin, Eliot, Browning, Newman, D.G. Rossetti and Samuel Smiles – most of these were written by Alice Meynell. There were reviews of new books by Trollope, Swinburne, Blackmore and Rhoda Broughton. Alfred Yule's *Letters*, with its articles by Hinks on historical drama and by Quarmby on the Spanish poets, would have found *The Pen* stiff competition. Yet *The Pen*, like almost every other similar venture, failed to make a profit. The Meynells abandoned it in June, after the eighth issue, and it turned into a 6d. monthly claiming, rather feebly, to have its readers' interests at heart: 'It has been thought that there are many in this age of hurry and bustle, who have but little time to devote to the pursuit of literature . . . systematically to read one more weekly journal might easily become a task. . . . But most people can afford the quiet hour which will enable them, once a month, to master the general details of what has been going on around them in the literary, artistic, and social world.' And so *The Pen*, deserted by the Milvains, passed into the control of a cantankerous Yule.

Alfred Yule

As a MONTHLY *The Pen* appears to have been conducted by Edward Walford, a fifty-seven year old quarrelsome Catholic bookman.[54] It survived for four issues. In the concluding number the bitterness which the monthly management felt for the weekly management erupted in a savage review of Meynell's pseudonymous *Journals and Journalism*, a work of 'unctuous gossip', 'evident toadyism', 'eminently calculated to lure unsuspecting youngsters into an already excessively overcrowded field of labour, in which the prizes are few and not astonishingly valuable. . . . a remarkable monument of snobbishness and puff'. Meynell's evident toadyism had included a kind mention of the monthly *Antiquary*, edited by Walford, 'in whose hands it has become one of the most successful of the periodicals having 1880 for the year of their birth'. In fact Walford was in the middle of an acrimonious dispute with the proprietor of the *Antiquary*, the publisher Elliot Stock, whom he publicly vilified, in pamphlets and in the press, for paying him a mere 5 guineas for editing each issue, including copy. There were no other paid staff and Walford was obliged to pay a sub-editor 2 guineas an issue from his own pocket. 1880 was not a good year for Walford.

Whether or not he wrote the Oldcastle review, and it has all the hallmarks of Walford vitriol, he had bitter first-hand experience of the 'excessively overcrowded' field of periodical writing. His first signed article in *The Pen* was an obituary notice of the magazine *Once a Week* set up by Bradbury and Evans in opposition to Dickens's *All the Year Round*. Walford had been appointed the editor of the magazine in 1865, a post he held for three years in conjunction with the editorship of another Bradbury and Evans journal, the *Gentleman's Magazine*. His relationship with his publishers was never happy: 'I do not feel myself free to act in my position as Editor. I constantly find myself controlled, and my judgment over-ruled in matters of detail, in a way which not only disheartens me, but which also makes it impossible for me to reply to letters which require an answer from the Editor.'[55] He resigned or was sacked from the editorship in 1868; his account of the affair in *The Pen* is predictably snide: 'I was superseded (as editor) by the late Mr Dallas, who was better calculated than I could hope to be, in attracting the audience of a magazine which was lowered from 3d. to 2d.'

Walford survived as an antiquary and biographer of passing repute but, by the 1880s, like so many worn-out men of letters, he felt himself to be under a constant, unequal pressure from thrusting young Meynells and Milvains. Walter Besant, in his review of *New Grub Street*, remarked that, 'the truest, saddest figure in the book is that of the old *littérateur*, a critic of the former school, who hangs on to letters getting more and more soured every day'. He may well have had Walford in mind. The two men had publicly quarrelled in the *Athenaeum* in 1890, over Besant's forthright assault on the SPCK. Besant wrote to the editor: 'It is a consolation to think that Mr Walford has quarrelled with others.' Walford's retort was characteristically abusive: 'In the "Dictionary of Heraldry" I find a "Besant" described as a Byzantine coin, usually of gold or silver. I fear that there are some of baser metal.'[56] This weak little antiquarian quip is pure Yule, impotently snarling at the successful and complacent Clement Fadge. Walford's feud with Besant lasted, on his side, until his death. Walford's bitterness, like Yule's, stemmed from his comparative failure. A scholar of Balliol College and contemporary of Lord Coleridge and Matthew Arnold, his descent into journeyman authorship must have been deeply humiliating. In 1892 Lord Sandford wrote to Balfour to recommend Walford for a Civil List pension. Of Walford's many dull but diligent works Sandford wrote, 'the drudgery of compiling them must have been terrible to one who was one of the most "elegant" scholars of his time at Oxford; and I have always felt very much for him.'[57]

A more obscure writer than Walford, and therefore even more like Alfred Yule, or at least Mr Hinks, was the biographer, essayist and hack, Henry Barton Baker (1835–1906), whose letters to the Royal Literary Fund read like a chapter in *New Grub Street*. In 1881 Baker's income had shrunk from its 1870s average of £300 a year to £50. Like Walford, he could not compete with the young, professional graduate of Oldcastle's academy:

an obscure periodical the Civil Service Review, for which I wrote reviews and leaders, worth about eight or nine pounds a month came to an end. For several years

I had been writing series of articles for Temple Bar, but during the past eighteen months the editor has used my articles less and less frequently and it has been the same with the 'Gentleman's' and 'Belgravia'. This is not, the editors assure me, because my papers are less acceptable, but on account of the ever increasing press of matter which accumulate upon their hands and the increasing numbers that thrust themselves into the literary profession [30 May 1881].

Baker specialised in articles on French lives and letters, and on neglected English poets and dramatists. His papers on Madame de Sévigné, Colley Cibber, Charles Churchill are exactly the sort of thing that Alfred Yule 'supplied on stipulated terms for anonymous publication'.[58] Yule's essays include 'French Authoresses of the Seventeenth Century', 'Lord Herbert of Cherbury' and a proposed paper on Thomas Shadwell. As well as anonymous periodical writing, Baker wrote an unsuccessful historical novel, *Strafford* (1878), published by Tinsley, and several works on the history of the theatre such as *Our Old Actors* (1878) and *The London Stage* (1888). In *New Grub Street*, Hinks, the author of an *Essay on the Historical Drama*, earns 'perhaps a hundred a year out of a kind of writing which only certain publishers can get rid of'.[59] By the end of the novel, Hinks is 'kept from the Workhouse only by Charity'. Perhaps this is an oblique reference to the Royal Literary Fund which gave Baker a total of £270 between 1881 and his death in 1906. William Senior, editor of the *Field*, summed up Baker's literary career in a sentence which applies to most of the denizens of Gissing's *New Grub Street*: 'Poor Barton Baker was a hard worker, a clean living man, a fighter against many difficulties, but he always fell short of the market that pays.'

Edwin Reardon

THE CENTRAL CHARACTER of *New Grub Street*, if it is not Jasper Milvain, is the novelist Edwin Reardon. Unlike Yule, who in his heyday earned £250 a year and throughout the novel is earning around £150, Reardon has never experienced a regular literary income. He uses a small legacy of £400 to launch himself as a writer. His third novel sells for £50 and he reaches his peak with £100 for his fourth novel *On Neutral Ground*, a modest critical success, and receives the same sum for his next book *The Optimist*, which is 'practically a failure'. At the start of *New Grub Street* Reardon is the author of five novels, only one of which has proved at all marketable. As the action of the novel progresses Reardon's work slips rapidly in value from £75 for the three-volume *Margaret Home* to an outright rejection of his attempt at a one-volume sensation story. This is only a little worse than Gissing's own experience. For *Demos* (1886), his first moderately successful novel, Smith, Elder and Co. paid £100 for the copyright. Eight months after publication they reissued it as a 6s. reprint at no benefit to Gissing. They then offered him £100 for the copyright of *Thyrza* (1887) or £50 in advance and 10 per cent royalties after the sale of the first edition of 500 copies. Having gained nothing from the reprint of *Demos*, Gissing opted for a royalty agreement. However by August 1890, Smith, Elder and Co. had only managed to sell 412 copies and Gissing accepted their offer of £10 for the copyright. He therefore received £40 less for *Thyrza* than for his previous novel. His publishers, however, having obtained the copyright, promptly found a market for no less than four cheap editions of *Thyrza* helped by the success of *New Grub Street*, which they had bought outright for £150. Up to and including *New Grub Street* Gissing never earned more than £150 a year from his fiction.

That Reardon's experience was typical can be seen from Besant's 1898 calculation of novelists' average earnings. Out of 1,300 living novelists the top 70 or so earned more than £1,000; 150 novelists earned over £400 (Gissing earned £525 in 1898 and £427 in 1899); 200 novelists earned between £100 and £400; and the rest, the vast majority, earned under £100 a year.[60] One need look no further for a representative low-income novelist of the rank of Edwin Reardon than Gissing's own brother Algernon.

Algernon's first novel, the two-volume *Joy Cometh in the Morning* (1888), set the tone for the rest of his writing career. It was an agreeable and tolerably written tale of country life which sold a respectable (for a first novel) 392 copies and earned £16 in royalties. His second novel *Both of this Parish* (1889) he sold outright to Hurst and Blackett for £25. Both novels were written under the tutelage of his elder brother whose letters of faint praise were meant to be encouraging – 'your Rustics, I am convinced, are as good as Hardy, in places'.[61] For his three-decker *A Village Hampden* (1890), Hurst and Blackett paid him £40. It was to be a slow climb to the £50 novel. Gissing thought that his brother's novels improved by degrees and in 1892, after the publication of Algernon's fifth novel, he wrote to Bertz: 'My brother's latest book has been respectfully treated. It is not strong, but there is some good writing in it . . . I think he may in time develop a style which will be a distinct improvement upon that of William Black.'[62] Black was famous for his purple prose which put him into the £1,000 a year bracket.

Although Algernon made repeated attempts to change publishers he was branded a Hurst and Blackett author. Like Reardon he was firmly locked into the three-decker system, publishing a novel a year and living on the slender proceeds. In 1894, when the major circulating libraries announced that they would refuse to pay more than 12s. for the three-volume novel, Gissing noted in his diary: 'The publishers seem disposed to give up the 3 vol. publication altogether . . . . How, by the bye, will it affect poor Alg?'[63] If Joseph Shaylor's figures for the production of three-volume novels are to be believed, then Algernon succeeded in writing one of the four last three-deckers in the nineteenth century, *The Scholar of Bygate*, published by Hutchinson in 1897.[64] Happily *The Scholar of Bygate*, his tenth novel, was one of his best received works and was the first to be issued as a 6s. reprint. The success of the novel enabled him to graduate to Chatto and Windus who published his next two novels, both of one-volume length. This was the high point of his unfortunate literary career. His income was about £130 a year, a sum which appears to have included his wife's small private income of £25. By January 1904 he had slipped back below the £100 level into literary pauperdom. W.H. Hudson sponsored his application to the Royal Literary Fund: 'I should say that his novels are considerably above the average as literature. Some of them – The Scholar of Bygate, & A Secret of the North Sea, may be instanced – are excellent works. Unfortunately they have had no great sale, owing, I believe, to the fact that he has to some extent been overshadowed by the greater reputation of his brother.' On Algernon's second application to the Fund, in February 1908, Hudson was more forthright:

His best work was in 1893 & the three or four years following; from that time onward his life has been one incessant struggle with misfortune. If his work declined in quality – it was not strange; the wonder is that with his children to keep & his wife, an excellent mother & careful housekeeper, an almost hopeless invalid, he was still able to produce his volume each year.

Algernon was an Edwin Reardon who did not die at the nadir of his career but who continued to churn out a volume a year as the drudge of the publisher F.V. White. By October 1911 he had slipped beyond the edge of failure: 'as the fifty guineas received for my last published novel is now reduced to twenty-five for one recently disposed of the battle is beyond me'. His assessment of his literary chances were accurate enough; he was to survive, more or less on the breadline, for another twenty-five years.

Harold Biffen

THE ONE CHARACTER in *New Grub Street* who possesses unshakeable literary integrity is Harold Biffen, whose novel *Mr Bailey, Grocer*, dealing with 'absolute realism in the sphere of the ignobly decent',[65] is the ultimate in unmarketable fiction. In the circumstances an advance of £15 on half-profits was a generous contract. Both Reardon, with his 'purely psychological' novels, and Biffen, with his passion for 'ordinary vulgar-life' and the 'unutterably tedious', thought that the novelty of dullness would make for original novels. In fact it made for avant-garde tedium. *Mr Bailey, Grocer* was condemned by the reviews for its failure to attempt to entertain: 'Let Mr Biffen bear in mind . . . that a novelist's first duty is to tell a story'; 'Mr Biffen . . . seems not to understand that a work of art must before everything else afford amusement.'[66] While Gissing intended to attack the philistinism of the reviewers, his own work was rarely criticised for lack of narrative power, but rather for its tragic or sordid themes. Even the tragic and sordid could entertain the quarter-educated public as long as it was not dull.

Biffen was of the realist school, and significantly he acknowledges a debt to Dickens, though he is careful to dissociate himself from the Dickensian vice of caricature. His real-life colleagues could not afford such scruples. Of the handful of novelists who were associated with realism at the turn of the century – Arthur Morrison, Edwin Pugh, W. Pett Ridge, Barry Pain and even Israel Zangwill – all found it necessary to incorporate large doses of Dickensian cockney humour in order to reach a paying audience.

Edwin Pugh was a quintessential realist, a blend of Biffen and Reardon in his literary life, though closer to their creator in his early achievement. He was born into the cockney lower middle class in 1874, his father was an advertising agent. With the benefit of a Board school education and first hand experience of poverty he soon displayed a precocious literary talent. In 1895, when he was just twenty-one, Heinemann published his collection of loosely connected short stories, with the Biffenesque title *A Street in Suburbia*. His first novel, *A Man of Straw*, was published a year later and won him unstinted critical praise. W.E. Henley, an early patron and editor of Pugh's work, wrote enthusiastically, 'lower-middle class London . . . has had, to my thinking, very few more faithful and, at the same time, more masterly and brilliant exponents than the author of *A Man of Straw*'.[67] Pugh's second novel, *Tony Drum: A Cockney Boy* (1898), consolidated his growing reputation as a leading novelist of 'mean streets'; he sent a complimentary copy to George Gissing as a tribute to Gissing's reputation and influence. With three well-noticed works of fiction published by the age of twenty-four, Pugh was understandably sanguine. Like Edwin Reardon, the author of *The Optimist*, 'because one book had a sort of success he imagined his struggles were over'.[68] As a result of his modest good fortune, in the words of Frank Swinnerton, 'Pugh was encouraged to throw up a job in order to become a professional novelist, and he had not quite the moral stamina to support what followed'.[69]

What followed was that the moment for the never very fashionable novel of 'vulgar-life' was very brief. The ground for its fair reception had to a large extent been prepared by Gissing, so that with the collapse of the three-decker in 1895, there was a sudden flurry of one-volume novels and short stories on working-class and lower middle-class themes. Rising out of and above this little movement were H.G. Wells, Arnold Bennett and Somerset Maugham. But by the reign of Edward VII the vogue for the 'purely mean' was over. In September 1902 the twenty-eight year old Pugh made his first application to the Royal Literary Fund, supported by Henley, Sarah Grand and Alice Meynell. Heinemann no longer wanted his work and so he had recourse to Hurst and Blackett. His books had never earned him large sums, probably no more than £50 or £60 apiece, and he came increasingly to rely upon hack journalism for his living. Among his more valuable non-fiction projects was a study of Dickens for A.R. Orage's New Age Press in 1908.

In December 1909 his annual income had sunk to £65. Clement Shorter wrote him a sympathetic note: 'I greatly regret that the public taste is incapable of appreciating books in which the melancholy side of life is brought uppermost . . . . I fully recognise that your talent does not lie in the direction of catering for a public which seems to demand less and less of the literary artist.' Orage warmly supported Pugh's second application to the Royal Literary Fund:

Since his first book that made such a great impression on me I have regarded Mr Pugh as one of the few writers of our day who may be said to have written no word except with his blood. Nothing of his that I have seen has been allowed to appear until it had been chiselled and smoothed and minutely and lovingly stamped with the hand of the conscientious craftsman. In his subjects he has been compared with Dickens; but I find in him a passion for perfection and truth that Dickens never had . . . a rare spirit that would never descend to the merely popular [20 December 1909].

But Pugh was desperately poor, and in his desperation he began to write comic works of cockney life such as *Harry the Cockney* (1911), *Punch and Judy* (1913), *The Proof of the Pudding* (1913), *The Cockney at Home* (1914). The last three were published by Chapman and Hall whose managing director, Arthur Waugh, praised Pugh's industry, 'He has not been one of those people who give themselves airs, and consider that some forms of hack-work are beneath their dignity.'[70] Pugh could hardly afford the luxury of dignity. From the outbreak of war until his death in 1930 he was only saved from the workhouse by the charity of friends and Royal Literary Fund grants. His letters to the Fund were always heart-rending: 'I am practically penniless, my clothes are mostly things of shreds and patches' (1922); 'Last Saturday we were literally destitute. Only the timely acceptance of a short story . . . saved my wife and me from the workhouse . . . . We have had to sell up our home, and are now living in a bed-sitting-room. Our few small personal belongings are all in pawn' (1927). Fortunately for Pugh, his wife, despite the fact that she had once been personal maid to the Duchess of Bedford, did not have the social ambition of Amy Reardon. Indeed, she seems to have been something of a saint as Pugh, by now an alcoholic, was frequently violent and ill-tempered. His pathetic career came to an end in 1930 when he cracked his head open on a London pavement. Swinnerton's obituary comment sums up the dilemma of the Edwin Reardons as well as the Edwin Pughs: 'and another poor author who might have done good work if only he had been able in some way to earn a living sank without visible trace from the book market'.[71] It may be that Pugh was one of those self-destructive writers who would fail in the most encouraging literary environment. But it is as likely that, like Reardon, he 'was the kind of man who cannot struggle against adverse conditions, but whom prosperity warms to the exercise of his powers'.[72]

Whelpdale

SWINNERTON'S REMARK about Pugh's failure to earn a living reveals the self-satisfaction of a lower middle-class writer who has managed to earn a living. Swinnerton was a good example of those young Edwardian writers who were able to take advantage of the huge increase in ancillary jobs in the book trade. At the age of fifteen he became office boy to the *Scottish Cyclist*, from where he moved to the *Estates Gazette*, and in 1902 he entered publishing as junior clerk to J.M. Dent. There followed an eighty year career as a writer and publisher. The young Swinnerton was very much a child of New Grub Street for by the end of the nineteenth century the professional man of letters had been transformed into a dealer in literature. One of the most engaging characters in *New Grub Street* is Whelpdale, the failed novelist turned literary entrepreneur; very much a character who earns his living in literature rather than at it.

Whelpdale is even more typical of the pervasive spirit of commercialism than Milvain – who persists in hankering after the social status of a 'higher' journalist. Whelpdale is solely concerned with turning literature into money. In the course of *New Grub Street* he takes a number of jobs connected with books that do not actually involve writing them. After failing to publish his own novels and stories he sets up as a freelance adviser 'to Young Authors and Literary Aspirants', and to consolidate his position he publishes an 'Authors' Manual', quickly selling 600 copies. Thus established he became a fully-fledged literary agent, working as a specialist in syndication with the newly founded Fleet & Co. Whelpdale's vision of establishing a paper that would appeal 'to the quarter-educated; that is to say, the great new generation that is being turned out by the Board schools, the young men and women who can just read, but are incapable of sustained attention',[73] leads to the founding of *Chit-Chat* on which he becomes sub-editor at £250 a year. Although *Chit-Chat* and its advocacy of the 'lightest and frothiest' journalism clearly refers to George Newnes's *Tit-Bits* (1881), Whelpdale is no energetic capitalist but rather a failed writer who cannot disengage himself from the literary world (he tries, and fails, to earn a living as a sewing-machine salesman).

In creating Whelpdale, Gissing may have had in mind Percy Russell, the fifth edition of whose *Authors' Manual* was announced in the same week as *New Grub Street*. Russell, rather like Frank Swinnerton, began his literary career in the humblest department of the book trade, as a printer's proofreader. In 1871 he became a reporter on the *Surrey Advertiser* from where he moved in 1875 to become assistant sub-editor of the *Miller*. He remained on this monthly trade journal for nearly twenty years, ending up as its editor from 1890 to 1894. Also in the 1890s he became the last editor of the children's monthly the *Welcome Hour*, published by Marshall Bros., an evangelical publishing house. Russell wrote the entire magazine himself – from a serial story of 'missionary enterprise in China', *The Bible and the Bullet*, to such regular features as 'Peeps at the Poets' and 'Battle Ballads'. Such monthly journalism left him time to write eighteen novels and occasional poetry including *King Alfred and other Poems*, which the *Surrey Advertiser* kindly compared to

Macaulay's 'Lays' and the *Clerkenwell Press* found 'marked by rare eloquence and beauty'. He was, in short, a writer of the humblest class and the final irony was that his *Authors' Manual*, which ran into eleven editions and gained him the devotion of many young writers and the opprobrium of Gissing, earned him just £25. He had written it on commission and received no royalties. His last composition was *Immortality: a Philosophical Essay* published in 1924. He died a year later, half-blind, a client of the Royal Literary Fund.

THERE IS ANOTHER WAY of looking at literary life – James Payn's way. Of all the figures in the book world of the 1880s and 1890s James Payn (1830–98) was the most infuriatingly smug, though apparently lovable. He came from a wealthy professional middle-class home, was educated at Eton and Cambridge, and, through his undergraduate contacts and his family friendship with Miss Mitford and Harriet Martineau, found his entry into the literary world exceptionally smooth. At the age of twenty-eight he became editor of *Chambers Journal* and in 1874 he became reader to Smith, Elder & Co., editing their magazine the *Cornhill* in conjunction with his other duties from 1883 to 1896. He was also a literary gossip columnist on the *Illustrated London News* and a novelist who, in Gissing's scornful phrase, quickly achieved 'commercial rank'. One of his novels, *Heir of Ages* (1886), gives an account of the literary world in marked contrast to Gissing's. A young governess escapes the drudgery of country house servitude to discover the streets of literary London are paved with laurels and gold; it is a world, as the *Athenaeum* wryly noted, 'where the first contributions of unknown authors are accepted and paid for well, and where an editor leaves no letters unanswered'.[74]

Like many men of letters who had got on in the world, Payn's sympathy for unsuccessful writers, especially those who fancied themselves neglected artists, was negligible. Having achieved an eminent position in the book trade, and a popular reputation as a novelist, his distance from the literary Pantheon did not unduly worry him. The problem for the more ambitious writer was that men like Payn were always held up, or held themselves up, as models of sensible literary endeavour. They were completely blind to the fact that there was no room at the top for a multitude of Payns. And Payn, a publisher's reader and acceptor or rejector, as the fancy took him, of Gissing's novels, would have been the first to object to a literary army consisting entirely of generals. As for his observations, in *Gleams of Memory* (1894), on his own literary rank, they are too wonderful to pass over. With their emphasis on status and cash they are the perfect expression of the gilded image of authorship which Gissing set out to destroy:

As to the calling of Literature, which has been so much abused of late by some of its own followers, if I were to live twenty lives I would choose no other profession. It is the brightest and most genial of all of them, and, so far at least as my experience goes, the most free from jealousies and acrimonies . . .

I suppose without vanity I may say that, as regards popularity, I have been in the first dozen or so of story-tellers; but my gains have been small indeed when compared with anyone in the same position in any other calling. A judge and a bishop get 5,000 l. a year and a retiring pension. I have been exceptionally fortunate in receiving such small prizes as literature has to offer in the way of editorships and readerships, but the total income I have made by my pen has been but an average of 1,500l. a year for thirty-five working years. As compared with the gains of Law and Physic, and, of course, of Commerce, this surely is a very modest sum, though it has been earned in a most pleasant manner.[75]

In 1892 Gissing wrote to Bertz 'we are always being told that the struggle against adverse circumstances is for the good of our art, and that with prosperity comes relaxation of effort. It is so, undoubtedly, with some men, but chiefly with those who have nothing very particular to say.'[76] There have been many gifted writers for whom adversity has been insurmountable. There are, unfortunately, no good grounds for supposing that a Dickens or a D.H. Lawrence will pull through regardless, that genius will rise above neglect. Both men were lucky as well as exceptional. The merely exceptional leave the merest traces. This is not to deny that lasting literary success requires intense dedication and conviction, as well as talent. But the fact remains that the bulk of what we call English Literature was written by people whose circumstances were both comfortable and conducive.

Among the swarms of common writers there must have been men and women with great, bottled-up talents that were never allowed to explode into life. Perhaps it doesn't matter, except that the more varied and energetic a literature is the better. In this the common writer still has a part to play, not only as an ephemeral entertainer or instructor, but also as the foundation of the publishing industry. The common writer labours to give the publisher enough units of production to make a profit. A profitable publishing industry can afford to take a risk with the uncommon writer, though it does not always do so.

NOTES

I have made extensive use of the Royal Literary Fund archive and, in most cases, have not thought it necessary to provide a separate footnote. Unless otherwise indicated quotations are from the RLF and can be located in the archive through the name of the correspondent and the year: see *The Archives of the Royal Literary Fund: 1790–1918* (World Microfilms, London, 1984) which contains the case files and catalogues, and my printed notes to the archive together with the index of applicants, *The Royal Literary Fund: 1790–1918*.

Quotations from works published in first editions only are given full references. Quotations from works which exist in many editions are given chapter references. References to articles and reviews give the date but not volume or page number – few articles are long enough to justify so much extra print. Place of publication is London, unless otherwise stated.

Bibliographical note

The field covered by this book is too wide to admit a useful bibliography. However, I have found the following secondary sources particularly valuable in helping me to acquire some perspective on various aspects of authorship.

For the general background see R.D. Altick, *The English Common Reader* (Chicago, 1957); Victor Bonham-Carter, *Authors By Profession* vol. 1 (1978); Royal A. Gettman, *A Victorian Publisher* (Cambridge, 1960); Guinevere L. Griest, *Mudie's Circulating Library* (Indiana, 1970); John Gross, *The Rise and Fall of the Man of Letters* (1969); James Hepburn, *The Author's Empty Purse* (Oxford, 1968); J.A. Sutherland, *Victorian Novelists and Publishers* (1976). For working-class authorship the two pioneering studies are: Louis James, *Fiction for the Working Man* (Oxford, 1963), and Martha Vicinus, *The Industrial Muse* (1974). Elaine Showalter's *A Literature of Their Own* (Princeton, 1977) is the best work on women's authorship I have read.

Introduction: the common writer

1. Robert Darnton, 'What is the History of Books', *Daedalus* III, 1982.
2. E.P. Thompson and Eileen Yeo, *The Unknown Mayhew* (1971), pp. 12, 47.
3. Figures for new titles are notoriously inaccurate. See Marjorie Plant, *The English Book Trade* (1965); also *Bent's Monthly Literary Advertiser*, and the *Publishers' Circular*. Figures for 1880–1900 from V.K. Daniels, *New Grub Street: 1890–1896* (Ph.D. Sussex, 1966).
4. Raymond Williams, *The Long Revolution* (1961). R.D. Altick, 'The Sociology of Authorship', *Bulletin of the New York Public Library*, 1962. See also D.F. Laurenson, 'A Sociological Study of Authorship', *British Journal of Sociology*, 1969.

1 Literature and charity: the Royal Literary Fund from David Williams to Charles Dickens

1. David Williams, *Incidents in My Life*, ed. P. France (Sussex, 1980), p. 16.
2. David Williams, *Claims of Literature* (1802), p. 9.
3. Williams, *Incidents*, p. 38.
4. Ibid. p. 43.
5. Ibid. p. 14.
6. *Annual Biography and Obituary*, 1818, p. 21.
7. Williams, *Incidents*, p. 21.
8. *Annual Biography*, 1818, p. 24.
9. D. Williams, 'The Missions of David Williams and James Tilly Matthews to England (1793)', *English Historical Review*, October 1938.
10. *Gentleman's Magazine*, July 1816.
11. Thomas Morris, *A General View of the Life and Writings of the Rev. David Williams* (1792), p. 16.
12. Ibid. p. 17.
13. See Williams, *Incidents*, p. 1.
14. Williams, *English Historical Review*, p. 660.
15. Williams, *Incidents*, pp. 43–6.
16. Williams, *Claims*, p. 103.
17. Thomas Dale to Samuel Stanton, 9 July 1791, RLF.
18. See E.V. Lucas, *David Williams* (1920), p. 12.
19. Sir Henry Ellis to Octavian Blewitt, 21 July 1842, RLF.
20. *Annual Biography*, 1818, p. 46.
21. Williams to the Earl of Chichester, May 1805, RLF.
22. Williams, *Incidents*, p. 55.
23. Ibid. pp. 51–3.
24. *Annual Report*, 1820, p. 6.
25. Reported by Charles Butler to Daniel Moore, 2 July 1808, RLF.
26. Samuel Smiles, *A Publisher and His Friends* (1891), i, 237.
27. Note to 'Loyal Effusion by W.T.F.' in Horace and James Smith, *Rejected Addresses* (18th edition, 1833).
28. *Morning Chronicle*, 3 May 1811.
29. See E.C. Gaskell, *The Life of Charlotte Brontë* (1857), ii, Chapter VI.
30. *Byron's Letters and Journals*, ed. Leslie A. Marchand (1974), ix, 206–7.
31. R.H. Horne, *Exposition of the False Medium and Barriers Excluding Men of Genius From the Public* (1833), p. 282. Among the grants awarded to subsidise a specific work were: 10 guineas to Thomas Maurice to help pay for 'the publication of his great work "Indian Antiquities"'; 10 guineas to Charles Macklin as a subscription 'to the publication of Mr C. Macklin's plays'; £50 to Leigh Hunt, acknowledged by him as a donation towards 'my volume of poems' (*Poetical Works*, 1832).
32. *The Times*, 18 June 1863.
33. Charles Dickens, *The Answer to the Committee's Summary of 'Facts'* (1858), p. 13.
34. Dickens to Forster, 13 May 1857, quoted by K.J. Fielding in 'Dickens and the Royal Literary Fund 1856', *Review of English Studies* 6, 1955, p. 382.
35. See Chapter 2, pp. 70–6.

36. Dickens to Collins, 19 March 1857, Pierpont Morgan Library.
37. H. Crabb Robinson, *Crabb Robinson on Books and their Writers*, ed. E.J. Morley (1938), ii, 758–9.
38. Dickens to Macready, 15 March 1857, Pierpont Morgan Library.
39. Robert Bell, *A Summary of Facts: Drawn from the Records of the Society* (1858), p. 1.
40. Ibid. p. 5.
41. John Britton, *Autobiography* (1850), i, 87.
42. Dickens, *Answer*, p. 16.
43. See for example: N. and J. Mackenzie, *Dickens: A Life* (Oxford, 1979); and J.A. Davies, *John Forster: A Literary Life* (Leicester, 1983).
44. Anthony Trollope, *An Autobiography*, ed. P.D. Edwards (Oxford, 1980), p. 212.

2   From prisons to pensions: Grub Street and its institutions

1. William Jerdan, *Autobiography* (1852–3), ii, pp. 37–8.
2. Fyodor Dostoyevsky, *The Gambler*, trans. J. Coulson (Harmondsworth, 1968), Chapter 2, p. 28.
3. Samuel Johnson, *Selected Writings*, ed. P. Crutwell (Harmondsworth, 1968), p. 124.
4. Tobias Smollett, *Peregrine Pickle*, Chapter XCIV.
5. Tobias Smollett, *Humphrey Clinker*, J. Melford to Sir Watkin Phillips, 10 June.
6. Sir Samuel Romilly, *Memoirs of the Life of Sir Samuel Romilly* (1840) ii, 453.
7. See R.P. Gillies, 'Law of Debtor and Creditor', *British and Foreign Review*, July–October 1837.
8. See also Angus Easson, 'Imprisonment for Debt in Pickwick Papers', *Dickensian*, May 1968.
9. *Hansard Parliamentary Debates*, 3rd series, xxxix, 551.
10. 'Dickens's Tales', *Edinburgh Review*, October 1838.
11. See William Maginn, *Miscellaneous Writings*, ed. R. Shelton Mackenzie (New York, 1857), v, p. xc.
12. Maginn, *Miscellaneous Writings*, v, p. xcv.
13. See RLF Case File 392.
14. J.G. Lockhart, 'Theodore Hook', *Quarterly Review*, May 1843.
15. Thomas Ashe, *Memoirs and Confessions* (1815), iii, 118.
16. Thomas Apperley to W.H. Landon, 6 May 1838, RLF.
17. *Fourteenth Report of the Inspectors of Prisons in Great Britain* (1849), p. 13.
18. R.P. Gillies, *Memoirs of a Literary Veteran* (1851), ii, 319–20.
19. *Morning Chronicle*, April 1854, RLF.
20. J.G. Raymond, *The Life of Thomas Dermody* (1802), i, 75.
21. Ibid. i, 92.
22. Ibid. i, 255.
23. Ibid. ii, 253.
24. Ibid. ii, 161.
25. Dermody's application to the Fund has not survived. The Fund's treasurer, Richard Yates, provided Raymond with the details. See Raymond, *Life of Dermody*, ii, 206–19.
26. Ibid. ii, 170.
27. David Williams, *Claims of Literature* (1802), pp. 85, 79.

28. George Crabbe, 'The Patron', *Tales in Verse* (1812).
29. S.T. Coleridge, *Biographia Literaria* (1817), Chapter XI.
30. T. De Quincey, *Recollections of the Lakes and the Lake Poets*, ed. D. Wright (Harmondsworth, 1970), p. 97.
31. *Collected Letters of Samuel Taylor Coleridge*, ed. E.L. Griggs (Oxford, 1956–68) i, 582.
32. *The Times*, 9 September 1850.
33. J.G. Lockhart, *Memoirs of the Life of Sir Walter Scott Bart* (1837–8), v, 58.
34. Jerdan, *Autobiography*, iii, 160.
35. T.B. Macaulay, 'On the Royal Society of Literature', *Knight's Quarterly Magazine*, June 1823.
36. For this and other quotations from Besant, see Walter Besant, 'The First Society of British Authors', *Contemporary Review*, July 1889.
37. Charles Mackay, *Forty Years' Recollections* (1877), i, 174.
38. See E. Evelyn Barron, *The National Benevolent Institution* (1936).
39. Mrs Newton Crosland, *Landmarks of a Literary Life* (1893), p. 167.
40. See John Pye, *The Patronage of British Art* (1845).
41. Anniversary dinner 1860, RLF.
42. *London Review*, 30 April 1864.
43. Four-page circular 'The Newspaper Press Benevolent Association', 31 December 1849, RLF.
44. This and other information from the minute books of the Newspaper Press Fund, Dorking.
45. Newspaper Press Fund, *Annual Report*, 1866, pp. 20–1.
46. See Mary Howitt, *An Autobiography*, ed. M. Howitt (1889), ii, 55.
47. Sir G.O. Trevelyan, *Life and Letters of Lord Macaulay* (popular edition 1899), p. 640.
48. George Hodder, *Memories of My Time* (1870), p. 245.
49. Francis Espinasse, *Literary Recollections and Sketches* (1893), p. 392.
50. Barron, *National Benevolent Institution*, p. 75.
51. *Speeches of Charles Dickens*, ed. K.J. Fielding (Oxford, 1960), p. 150.
52. See E.L. Bulwer, 'Proposals for a Literary Union' *New Monthly Magazine*, November 1832; and R.H. Horne, *Exposition of the False Medium and Barriers excluding Men of Genius from the Public* (1833).
53. *The Letters of Thomas Babington Macaulay*, ed. T. Pinney (Cambridge, 1981), v, 164, n.163.
54. This and subsequent quotations are from the Minute Book of the Guild, Parish Collection (AM 21673), Princeton University.
55. *The Times*, 31 July 1865.
56. *The Times*, 1 August 1865.
57. Bulwer Lytton to Dickens, 17 September 1865, Pierpont Morgan Library.
58. J.R. Robinson, 'Charles Dickens and the Guild of Literature and Art' *Cornhill*, June 1904.
59. F.G. Kitton, *Charles Dickens: His Life, Writings and Personality* (1902), p. 329.
60. See Edgar Johnson, *Charles Dickens: His Tragedy and Triumph* (1977), p. 381.
61. 'Guild of Literature and Art', *Household Words*, 10 May 1851.
62. Gordon N. Ray, *Thackeray: The Age of Wisdom* (Oxford, 1958), p. 475.
63. G.E. Anson to William Jones, 22 October 1843, RLF.

64. W. Wickenden, *Reasons for Resigning His Appointment as a Poor Brother of the Charterhouse* (n.d.), RLF.
65. G.S. Davies, *Charterhouse in London* (1922), p. 243.
66. G.M.L. Strauss, *Reminiscences of an Old Bohemian* (1882), ii, 232.
67. Davies, *Charterhouse in London*, p. 246.
68. Ibid. p. 244–5.
69. T.B. Macaulay, 'William Pitt', *Edinburgh Review*, January 1859.
70. Harriet Martineau to Shirley Brooks, 15 May 1861, quoted in G.S. Layard, *A Great 'Punch' Editor* (1907), p. 185.
71. This, and other figures, are from a confidential treasury report by F.S. Parry, 'Civil List Pensions', 4 May 1901 (ref. 4851), RLF.
72. Ibid. p. 13.
73. *Elizabeth Barrett to Miss Mitford*, ed. Betty Miller (1954), p. 30.
74. Layard, *A Great 'Punch' Editor*, p. 185.
75. Parry, 'Civil List Pensions', p. 9.
76. *Saturday Review*, 9 November 1895.
77. Octavian Blewitt, 'Civil List Pensions', *Quarterly Review*, April 1871.
78. Parry, 'Civil List Pensions', p. 14.
79. Balfour to Parry, 30 December 1897, Treasury Papers 98/7195, Public Record Office.
80. Parry, 'Civil List Pensions', p. 15.
81. Ibid. p. 8.
82. 7 January 1904, Treasury Papers, 1904/5641, Public Record Office.
83. Parry, 'Civil List Pensions', p. 21.
84. See Treasury Papers, 69/8711, Public Record Office.
85. William Rothenstein, *Men and Memories* (1934), ii, 61.
86. Layard, *A Great 'Punch' Editor*, p. 185.
87. On the operation of Civil List pensions in the twentieth century see Nigel Cross, 'Civil List Pensions', *Times Literary Supplement*, 19 December 1980.

3 Bohemia in Fleet Street

1. See Edith Heraud, *Memoirs of John A. Heraud* (1898), p. 19.
2. S.T. Coleridge, *Biographia Literaria* (1817), Chapter XI.
3. William Bates, *The Maclise Portrait Gallery* (1883), p. 231.
4. *Morning Chronicle*, 12 February 1847.
5. G.J. Worth, *James Hannay: His Life and Works* (Lawrence, Kansas, 1964), pp. 1, 2.
6. G.A. Sala, *Things I have Seen and People I have Known* (1894), i, 115.
7. G.A. Sala, *The Life and Adventures of George Augustus Sala* (1895), i, 314.
8. G.A. Sala, *Twice Round the Clock*, ed P. Collins (Leicester, 1971), p. 17.
9. M.H. Spielmann, *The History of 'Punch'* (1895), p. 285.
10. Sala, *Life and Adventures*, i, 329.
11. From Sala's memoir in R.B. Brough's *Marston Lynch* (1860), p. viii.
12. Edmund Yates, *Edmund Yates: His Recollections and Experiences* (1884), i, 314.
13. *Leader*, 11 July 1857.
14. Yates, *Recollections*, i, 313.

15. *The Wellesley Index to Victorian Periodicals* III, ed. Walter Houghton (Toronto, 1979), p. 387.
16. J. McCarthy, 'The Literature of Bohemia', *Westminster Review*, January–April 1863.
17. M. Collins, 'Bohemia', *Temple Bar*, July 1863.
18. Yates, *Recollections*, i, 299–300.
19. Ibid. ii, 90.
20. Edmund Downey, *Twenty Years Ago* (1905), p. 247.
21. H. Sutherland Edwards, *Personal Recollections* (1900), p. 180.
22. Spielmann, *History of 'Punch'*, p. 17.
23. Ibid. p. 200.
24. A.A. Adrian, *Mark Lemon: First Editor of Punch* (Oxford, 1966), p. 58.
25. 'Comic Journalism', *Saturday Review*, 1 March 1856.
26. Worth, *James Hannay*, p. 28.
27. F.C. Burnand, *Records and Reminiscences* (1904), ii, 42.
28. Henry Vizetelly, *Glances Back Through Seventy Years* (1893), ii, 45.
29. See Aaron Watson, *The Savage Club* (1907).
30. Thackeray, *The Adventures of Philip* (1861–2), Chapter v.
31. Yates, *Recollections*, ii, 11.
32. Ibid. i, 218.
33. See John Gross, *The Rise and Fall of the Man of Letters* (1969).
34. Yates, *Recollections*, i, 328.
35. Brough, *Marston Lynch*, p. 292.
36. Ibid. pp. 238–41.
37. Charles Mackay, *Forty Years' Recollections* (1877), i, 151.
38. Brough, *Marston Lynch*, p. 319.
39. Thackeray to Mrs Reach, 5 April 1857, RLF. Thackeray to Octavian Blewitt, 29 November 1857, RLF.
40. Brough, *Marston Lynch*, p. 318.
41. Ibid. p. 315.
42. Yates, *Recollections*, i, 315.
43. Burnand, *Records*, ii, 41.
44. Thackeray, *Philip*, Chapter v; Yates, *Recollections*, i, 301; Brough, *Marston Lynch*, p. 315; Sala, *Life and Adventures*, i, 332, 410.
45. Sala, *Life and Adventures*, ii, 309–10.
46. George Hodder, *Memories of My Time* (1870), p. 250.
47. Ibid. p. 148.
48. Sala, *Life and Adventures*, i, 400.
49. Anniversary dinner 1867, RLF.
50. Anthony Trollope, *An Autobiography*, ed. P.D. Edwards (Oxford, 1980), p. 151.
51. See A. Blainey, *The Farthing Poet: a Biography of Richard Hengist Horne* (1968), pp. 97–8.
52. W. Tolles, *Tom Taylor and the Victorian Drama* (New York, 1940), p. 63.
53. 3 July 1848, BM Additional 44615 f. 105, British Museum.
54. 22 September 1849, ibid. 197.
55. 10 November (probably 1849), ibid. 210.
56. *Spectator*, 2 November 1850.
57. *Athenaeum*, 4 January 1851.

58. James A. Davies, *John Forster: A Literary Life* (Leicester, 1983), pp. 222, 116.
59. 15 September 1853, Knebworth House Archives.
60. See *The Letters of Anthony Trollope*, ed. N. John Hall (Stanford, California, 1983), i, 382.

4   The labouring muse: working-class writers and middle-class culture

1. 'An Author in Difficulties', undated press-cutting, RLF.
2. Thomas Miller, *Godfrey Malvern* (1842), p. 59.
3. Charles Kingsley, *Alton Locke* (1850), Chapter 8.
4. For the history of working-class autobiographies see David Vincent, *Bread, Knowledge and Freedom* (1981).
5. Charles Kingsley, 'Burns and his School' *North British Review*, November 1851.
6. See Philip Collins, *Thomas Cooper, The Chartist: Byron and the Poets of the Poor* (Nottingham, 1969).
7. Thomas Cooper, *The Life of Thomas Cooper* (1872), p. 35.
8. James Dawson Burn, *Autobiography of a Beggar Boy*, ed. D. Vincent (1978), p. 193.
9. *Byron's Letters and Journals*, ed. Leslie A. Marchand (1973–8), ii, 132.
10. This, and other poems, from *The Remains of Joseph Blacket*, ed. S.J. Pratt (1811).
11. Ibid. p. 8.
12. Ibid. p. 97.
13. *Byron's Letters and Journals*, ii, 53, 76.
14. Cooper, *The Life of Thomas Cooper*, p. 13.
15. Spencer T. Hall, *Biographical Sketches* (1873), pp. 321–2.
16. Henry Vizetelly, *Glances Back through Seventy Years* (1893) i, 308.
17. Louis James, *Fiction for the Working Man* (Oxford, 1963), p. 103.
18. G.A. Sala, *The Life and Adventures of George Augustus Sala* (1895), i, 226.
19. Vizetelly, *Glances Back*, i, 308.
20. *Bookseller*, 6 November 1874.
21. Miller, *Godfrey Malvern*, p. 53.
22. Ibid. p. 93.
23. Ibid. p. 120.
24. Ibid. p. 106.
25. Ibid. pp. 196–207 (Lady Smileall's soirée).
26. Ibid. p. 398.
27. Sarah Nesbit, *The Times*, 16 October 1873.
28. James, *Fiction for the Working Man*, p. 173.
29. Martha Vicinus, *The Industrial Muse* (1974), p. 141.
30. J.G. Lockhart, 'Southey and John Jones, Butler and Verse Maker', *Quarterly Review*, January 1831.
31. Rev. J.W. Lester, n.d., RLF.
32. *Poetical Works of J.C. Prince*, ed. R.A. Lithgow (Manchester, 1880), i, 105.
33. R.A. Lithgow, *The Life of John Critchley Prince* (Manchester, 1880), p. 116.
34. Kingsley, *Alton Locke*, Chapter 41.
35. Lithgow, *Life of Prince*, p. 117.
36. Ibid. p. 118.
37. Ibid. p. 125.

38. Ibid. p. 243.
39. Ibid. p. 260.
40. See Thomas Carlyle, 'Corn Law Rhymes', *Edinburgh Review*, July 1832.
41. See R.G. Gammage, *A History of the Chartist Movement* (1894), p. 48.
42. Kingsley, *North British Review*, November 1851.
43. *Testaments of Radicalism*, ed. David Vincent (1977), p. 198.
44. Gammage, *History of the Chartist Movement*, p. 240.
45. Cooper, *The Life of Thomas Cooper*, p. 251.
46. Devlin to the Royal Literary Fund, 1 May 1844, RLF.
47. Carter to the Royal Literary Fund, 24 February 1836, 5 January 1838, RLF.
48. Knight to the Royal Literary Fund, 30 April 1844, RLF.
49. Charles Knight, *Passages of a Working Life* (1864–5), iii, 13–14.
50. *Charles Kingsley: His Letters and Memories of His Life*, edited by his wife (1879) i, 377.
51. Kingsley, *Alton Locke*, Chapter 2.
52. Ibid. Chapter 3.
53. Ibid. Chapter 27.
54. Ibid. Chapter 20.
55. Cooper, *The Life of Thomas Cooper*, pp. 266–7.
56. *Letters of Browning to Elizabeth Barrett Browning*, ed. R.B. Browning (1899), i, 238.
57. Cooper, *The Life of Thomas Cooper*, p. 279.
58. Ibid. pp. 387–8; 25 February 1867, RLF.
59. Samuel Smiles, *Self-Help* (1859), p. 346.
60. This and other opinions are taken from Massey's Civil List Memorial 1861, RLF.
61. John Murray to Octavian Blewitt, 29 January 1862, RLF.
62. James Milne, 'Gerald Massey: Poet and Thinker' *Book Monthly*, September 1907.
63. Cooper, *The Life of Thomas Cooper*, p. 55.
64. Francis Espinasse, *Literary Recollections and Sketches* (1893), p. 361.
65. Joseph Whitaker to Octavian Blewitt, 17 April 1882, RLF.
66. Espinasse, *Literary Recollections*, p. 362.
67. Ibid. p. 361.
68. This and other poems from Edwin Waugh, *Poems and Songs*, ed. G. Milner (1893).

5 The female drudge: women novelists and their publishers

1. Elizabeth Rigby, 'Jane Eyre and Vanity Fair', *Quarterly Review*, December 1848.
2. George Eliot, *Mill on the Floss*, Book Second, Chapter 11.
3. R.D. Altick, 'The Sociology of Authorship', *Bulletin of the New York Public Library*, 1962.
4. George Eliot, 'Silly Novels by Lady Novelists', *Westminster Review*, October 1856.
5. Mrs Newton Crosland, *Landmarks of a Literary Life* (1893), p. 64.
6. *Wellesley Index to Victorian Periodicals* III, ed. Walter Houghton (Toronto, 1979), p. xvi.
7. See introduction p. 3.

8. Mrs Newton Crosland, *Landmarks*, pp. 65–6.

9. Dorothy Blakey, *The Minerva Press* (1939), p. 114.

10. M. Sadleir, *Things Past* (1944), pp. 167, 179.

11. T.B. Macaulay, 'Madame D'Arblay', *Edinburgh Review*, January 1843.

12. See Blakey, *Minerva Press*, p. 60.

13. Sadleir, *Things Past*, p. 184.

14. Ellen Moers, *Literary Women* (New York, 1976), p. 119.

15. R.A. Davenport to John Britton, 6 June 1850, RLF.

16. Gaskell to James Crossley, February 1854, in *The Letters of Mrs Gaskell*, eds. J.A.V. Chapple and Arthur Pollard (Manchester, 1966), p. 265.

17. Ibid. p. 208.

18. Louis James, *Print and the People, 1819–1851* (1976), p. 42.

19. Montague Summers, *A Gothic Bibliography* (1942), p. 81.

20. *Athenaeum*, 5 August 1829.

21. Jones to Octavian Blewitt, 12 March 1839; Jones to the Royal Literary Fund, 6 July 1831, RLF.

22. Jones to the Royal Literary Fund, 10 March 1839, RLF.

23. W.M. Thackeray, 'The Fashionable Authoress' in Kenny Meadows, *Heads of the People* (1840).

24. M.W. Rosa, *The Silver Fork School* (New York, 1936), p. 178.

25. Theodore Besterman, *The Publishing Firm of Cadell and Davies* (Oxford, 1938) p. 77.

26. Newton Crosland, *Rambles Round My Life* (1898), p. 216.

27. Rosa, *Silver Fork School*, pp. 157–8.

28. See M. Sadleir, *Blessington-D'Orsay: A Masquerade* (1933), p. 231.

29. Mrs Newton Crosland, *Landmarks*, p. 116.

30. E.C. Gaskell, *The Life of Charlotte Brontë* (1857), i, Chapter 14.

31. Anthony Trollope, *The Way We Live Now* (1875), Chapter 2.

32. Anthony Trollope, *An Editor's Tales* (1870), p. 107.

33. Henry James, 'Greville Fane', *The Real Thing and Other Stories* (1893), pp. 255–7.

34. *The Notebooks of Henry James*, ed. F.O. Matthiessen and K.B. Murdock (Oxford, 1947), p. 94.

35. Vineta Colby, *Yesterday's Women* (Princeton, 1974), p. 4.

36. James, 'Greville Fane' *The Real Thing*, p. 256.

37. Anthony Trollope, *An Autobiography*, ed. P.D. Edwards (Oxford, 1980), p. 331.

38. M. Sadleir, *XIX Century Fiction* (1951), ii, p. 146.

39. See M. Dalziel, *Popular Fiction 100 Years Ago* (1957), p. 80.

40. Bulwer Lytton to Octavian Blewitt, 2 September 1850, RLF.

41. *The Jilt* (1844) pp. 53–4.

42. Sophia Oakes to the Royal Literary Fund, 4 February 1873, RLF.

43. Smythies to the Royal Literary Fund, 5 May 1862, RLF.

44. *Athenaeum* 16 October 1847; *Spectator*, 8 May 1844; *Quarterly Review* April 1863.

45. Bulwer Lytton to Octavian Blewitt, 19 December 1864; 16 June 1860, RLF.

46. Mrs Milner Gibson to the Royal Literary Fund, 29 April 1862, RLF.

47. Thomas Frost, *Reminiscences of a Country Journalist* (1886), p. 179.

48. Patricia Thomson, *The Victorian Heroine* (Oxford, 1956), p. 54.

49. E.L. Burney, *Mrs G. Linnaeus Banks* (Manchester, 1969), p. 82.

50. James Hurnand to Octavian Blewitt, 26 February 1880, RLF.

51. Burney, *Mrs G. Linnaeus Banks*, p. 151.
52. Mrs Riddell, *A Struggle For Fame* (1883), ii, 262.
53. Ibid. i, 118.
54. Ibid. ii, 133–4.
55. *Autobiography and Letters of Mrs Margaret Oliphant*, ed. Mrs H. Coghill (1899).
56. Riddell, *A Struggle For Fame*, iii, 45.
57. Ibid. iii, 65.
58. Ibid. iii, 55.
59. Ibid. iii, 252.
60. Ibid. iii, 329.
61. Ibid. iii, 331.
62. *Athenaeum*, 18 August 1883.
63. Oliphant, *Autobiography and Letters*, p. 130.
64. Mrs Desmond Humphreys to A.L. Roberts, 6 July 1916, RLF.
65. Quoted by Elizabeth Lee in the *Dictionary of National Biography*.
66. William Sinclair to A.L. Roberts, 21 March 1908, RLF.
67. Oliver Bainbridge, *John Strange Winter* (1916), pp. 159–60.
68. Percy Muir, *English Children's Books 1600–1900* (1954), p. 116.
69. Mary Howitt to Octavian Blewitt, 3 June 1851, RLF.
70. George Gissing, *New Grub Street*, Chapter 1.
71. See Victor Bonham-Carter, *Authors by Profession* 1 (1978), p. 149.
72. Mary Howitt, *An Autobiography* (1859), pp. 197–8.
73. Beatrice Marshall, *Emma Marshall: A Biographical Sketch* (1900), pp. 277–8.
74. Ibid. p. 98.
75. Ibid. pp. 305–6.
76. Ibid. p. 281.
77. Ibid. pp. 328–9.
78. Ibid. p. 296.

6 Gissing's New Grub Street, 1880–1900

1. Walter Besant, *The Pen and the Book* (1899), p. 55.
2. Frederic Harrison, *The Choice of Books* (1886), p. 1.
3. See R.D. Altick, *The English Common Reader* (Chicago, 1957), pp. 171, 306.
4. See Simon Eliot, 'Three-decker Novel and its First Reprint', *The Library*, March 1985.
5. See V.K. Daniels, *New Grub Street: 1890–1896* (Ph.D. Sussex, 1966) p. 243.
6. For Mudie see: Guinevere L. Griest, *Mudie's Circulating Library* (Newton Abbott, 1970); and George Moore, *Literature at Nurse*, ed. P. Coustillas (Sussex, 1976).
7. *George Gissing on Fiction*, eds. J. and C. Korg (1978), p. 67.
8. See Frank Singleton, *Tillotsons 1850–1950* (1950).
9. 21 October 1889, *The Letters of George Gissing to Edward Bertz, 1887–1903*, ed. A.C. Young (1961), pp. 75–7.
10. *C.K.S. An Autobiography*, ed. J.M. Bulloch (1927), p. 84.
11. Quoted by J.W. Robertson Scott, *The Life and Death of a Newspaper* (1952), p. 156.

12. 24 August 1893, *Letters to Bertz*, p. 174.
13. *My First Book*, ed. J.K. Jerome (1894), p. 8.
14. See Alan J. Lee, *The Origins of the Popular Press in England 1855–1914* (1976).
15. See James Hepburn, *The Author's Empty Purse and the Rise of the Literary Agent* (Oxford, 1968).
16. Besant, *Pen and Book*, p. 215.
17. See F. Whyte, *William Heinemann: A Memoir* (1928) p. 124.
18. See Victor Bonham-Carter, *Authors By Profession* I (1978).
19. W. Robertson Nicoll, *A Bookman's Letters* (1913), p. 148.
20. 27 August 1895, *Letters to Bertz*, p. 203.
21. H.G. Wells, *Experiment in Autobiography* (1934), ii, 506.
22. 27 April 1893, F.E. Hardy, *The Later Years of Thomas Hardy* (1930).
23. Holbrook Jackson, *The Eighteen Nineties* (Harmondsworth, 1939), p. 51.
24. Anniversary dinner 1897, RLF.
25. 16 February 1892, *Letters to Bertz*, p. 145.
26. 16 November 1902, ibid. p. 313.
27. R.W. Buchanan, *A Look Round Literature* (1887), pp. 359–60.
28. See Henry James, *The House of Fiction*, ed. Leon Edel (1957).
29. Collected in *The Complete Tales of Henry James: 1893–1898* vol. 9, ed. Leon Edel (1964); also 'The Lesson of The Master', vol. 8.
30. James, *Complete Tales*, vol. 9, p. 8.
31. T.P. O'Connor, 'The New Journalism', *New Review*, October 1889.
32. 3 November 1892, *Letters to Bertz*, p. 161.
33. P. Russell, *The Literary Manual: A Complete Guide to Authorship* (1886), p. 40.
34. See Bonham-Carter, *Authors By Profession* I, pp. 160–1.
35. G. Bainton, *The Art of Authorship* (1890), p. 208 (James), p. 25 (Winter).
36. Russell, *Literary Manual*, p. 41.
37. 23 June 1895, *Letters to Bertz*, p. 203.
38. 2 January 1900, *The Letters of George Gissing to Members of His Family*, eds. A. and E. Gissing (1927), p. 368.
39. Russell, *Literary Manual*, p. 41.
40. For this and other reviews see *Gissing: The Critical Heritage*, eds. P. Coustillas and C. Partridge (1972).
41. Edward Clodd, *Memories* (1916), p. 165.
42. 14 March 1888, *Letters of George Gissing to His Family*, p. 211.
43. George Gissing, 'Autumn xxi' *The Private Papers of Henry Ryecroft* (1902).
44. George Gissing, *New Grub Street*, Chapter 6.
45. G.A. Sala, *The Life and Adventures of George Augustus Sala* (1895), i, 435.
46. John Oldcastle, *Journals and Journalism* (1880), pp. 33–40.
47. Ibid. p. 49.
48. H.G. Hutchinson, *Portraits of the Eighties* (1920), p. 210.
49. Russell, *Literary Manual* (1886), p. 211; *Authors' Manual* (1894), p. 128.
50. See Besant's review of *New Grub Street* in *Critical Heritage*, p. 182.
51. See Helen Thomas, *Time and Again*, ed. M. Thomas (Manchester, 1978).
52. Edmund Dowden to the Royal Literary Fund, 19 October 1883, RLF.
53. Gissing, *New Grub Street*, Chapter 23.
54. See Library of Congress Catalogue for identification of Walford's editorship of *The Pen*.

55. 4 December 1867, quoted by W.E. Buckler in 'Edward Walford: A Distressed Editor', *Notes and Queries*, December 1953.
56. *Athenaeum*, 2 August 1890; 9 August 1890.
57. Sandford to A.J. Balfour, 12 January 1892, Treasury Papers 92/10305, Public Record Office.
58. Gissing, *New Grub Street*, Chapter 7.
59. Ibid. Chapter 8; Chapter 37.
60. Besant, *Pen and Book*, p. 143.
61. *George Gissing on Fiction*, p. 41.
62. 1 May 1892, *Letters to Bertz*, p. 152.
63. 9 August 1894, *London and the Life of Literature in Late Victorian England: The Diary of George Gissing: Novelist*, ed. P. Coustillas (Sussex, 1978) p. 343.
64. See Griest, *Mudie's Circulating Library*, p. 208.
65. Gissing, *New Grub Street*, Chapter 10.
66. Ibid. Chapter 35.
67. W.E. Henley to Sydney Pawling, 26 September 1902, RLF.
68. Gissing, *New Grub Street*, Chapter 1.
69. Frank Swinnerton, *Swinnerton: An Autobiography* (1937), p. 241.
70. Arthur Waugh to A.L. Roberts, 12 October 1914, RLF.
71. Swinnerton, *An Autobiography*, p. 241.
72. Gissing, *New Grub Street*, Chapter 5.
73. Ibid. Chapter 33.
74. *Athenaeum*, 12 June 1886.
75. James Payn, *Gleams of Memory* (1894), pp. 185–6.
76. 19 June 1892, *Letters to Bertz*, p. 156.

INDEX

Index

Index

Index